Emeril's TV Dinners

Also by Emeril Lagasse

Emeril's New New Orleans Cooking, with Jessie Tirsch (1993)

Louisiana Real & Rustic, with Marcelle Bienvenu (1996)

Emeril's Creole Christmas, with Marcelle Bienvenu (1997)

Emeril's TV Dinners

Emeril Lagasse

with Marcelle Bienvenu and Felicia Willett

Photography by Brian Smale

WILLIAM MORROW
An Imprint of HarperCollins*Publishers*

A hardcover edition of this book was published in 1998 by William Morrow.

EMERIL'S TV DINNERS. Copyright © 1998 by Emeril Lagasse. Photography © 1998 by Brian Smale. All rights reserved. Printed in the United States of America. No part of this book may be used or reproduced in any manner whatsoever without written permission except in the case of brief quotations embodied in critical articles and reviews. For information address HarperCollins Publishers, 10 East 53rd Street, New York, NY 10022.

HarperCollins books may be purchased for educational, business, or sales promotional use. For information please write: Special Markets Department, HarperCollins Publishers, 10 East 53rd Street, New York, NY 10022.

First William Morrow paperback edition published 2009.

Book design by Richard Oriolo

The Library of Congress has cataloged the hardcover edition as follows:

Lagasse, Emeril.
    Emeril's TV dinners / Emeril Lagasse with Marcelle Bienvenu and Felicia
    Willett; photography by Brian Smale—1st ed.
        p.   cm.
      Includes index.
      ISBN 0-688-16378-5
      1. Cookery. I. Bienvenu, Marcelle. II. Willett, Felicia.

TX714 .l335 1999
641.5—dc21   98-25857
                                                  CIP

ISBN 978-0-06-187169-6 (pbk.)

09 10 11 12 13 QW 10 9 8 7 6 5 4 3 2 1

Here's to all the people at the Food Network who had the dream and the belief to make it what it is, a channel devoted to the education and inspiration of food and all its components.

This, too, is for the people—viewers, fans, supporters, friends—who believe that a life surrounded by good food is a life to be enjoyed.

MOTTO: ALWAYS FOOD OF LOVE

Contents

Preface

Emeril Lagasse worked long and hard for many years to become an overnight sensation.

In fact, Emeril has probably starred in more TV shows than any other chef in history: 832 episodes for Food Network alone, including the network's original *How to Boil Water* series, going back to Emeril's debut on our air in November 1993.

From the beginning, Emeril was a true television original. Intimate and passionate, he shot energy straight through the camera and out the other side. People were fascinated by his exquisite food and impeccable technique, wrapped in a package of high-voltage intensity. The man just packed a wallop, TV-wise.

Two years later, when I joined Food Network, we decided to send that wallop into orbit—or, as Emeril would say, to kick it up a few notches. We let the creative juices really fly, and were rewarded when *Time* named *Essence of Emeril* one of the Top Ten Best Television Shows of 1996, followed by *TV Guide*'s selection of *Emeril Live* as the Best Cooking Show of 1997. These accolades helped catapult Emeril—and our network—to fame.

Our audiences and our affiliates love Emeril. His shows are consistently among our highest rated and his recipes among our most requested. We are proud to be part of bringing them to his fans here in his first book based on Emeril's Food Network shows.

I want to add my thanks to the cast and crew and everyone else at Food Network who is part of the success of *Emeril's TV Dinners*. Thanks, too, to our loyal viewers and fans. And, most of all, thanks to Emeril: You teach us and you inspire us and we love you, babe!

—Erica Gruen
President and Chief Executive Officer
Food Network

Acknowledgments

Many thanks to:

My daughters, Jessica and Jillian Lagasse.

My parents, John and Hilda Lagasse.

My brother and sister, Mark Lagasse and Delores Cotter.

Marcelle Bienvenu, a dear friend, buddy, and exceptional writer, who always believes and always captures the essence! And to Rock Daddy!

Felicia Willett, for her constant support and love of food. For her continued focus and attention to detail. Many thanks for her tireless efforts and delicious treats!

Marti Dalton, special thanks for always guiding us and keeping us on course from the beginning, and for her constant dedication, creativity, and support.

Brian Smale, a great friend and a fantastic photographer who somehow always captures the moment, and to Shelly, his wife.

To Reese Schonfeld, for the vision in the beginning, Joe Langhan, for his constant dedication, Erica Gruen, a president with a smile, and Eileen Opatut.

To Michael Murphy, my publisher; Pam Hoenig, my patient editor; Richard Oriolo, my book designer; and Rich Aquan, who designed the great jacket; Ann Cahn and Karen Lumley, who worked hard to bring the book out on time.

To Carrie Weinberg, a dynamo in a small package who has helped bring the vision on the road.

To Paul Fedorko, my good friend.

To my right hands and my *consiglieri* in all matters, Eric Linquest, Tony Cruz, and Mauricio Andrade.

At Homebase, Beth Lott, Mara Warner, Dana Martinson, Huck Kakish, Carol Ripley, and Michelle Lefort.

To my managers and staffs at Emeril's, NOLA, and Delmonico Restaurant and Bar in New Orleans, and Emeril's New Orleans Fish House in Las Vegas.

To Chefs de Cuisine Bernard Carmouche, David McCelvey, Dwight Sherman, and Sean Roe, and to Pastry Chefs Lou Lynch and Joe Trull.

To Dr. James Goad, who took his work in the test kitchen very seriously.

Emeril Live Production Staff

EXECUTIVE PRODUCER: Karen Katz

DIRECTOR: Michael Schear

PRODUCERS: Emily Schwartz and Rochelle Brown

EXECUTIVE CHEF/FOOD PRODUCER: Susan Stockton

PRODUCTION MANAGER: Sean T. Dowd

ASSOCIATE PRODUCERS: Melissa Roberts, Leigh Ann Ambrosi, Todd Warner, Michael Newborn, and Hope Allen

ASSISTANT DIRECTOR: Keith Kielty

STAGE MANAGER: Rhoda Gilmore

SET DESIGN: Wendy Waxman and Rebecca Flaste

AUDIENCE COORDINATORS: Kathryn Kurtz and Mathew Stillman

PRODUCTION ASSISTANTS: Patricia LaMortie, Jimmy Johnson, Danny Zanoni, Cindy Bruno, Tony Travis, Adina Epstein, Jordan Flaste, and Fred Heath

MAKEUP ARTIST: Janet Arena

LIGHTING DIRECTOR: Cheryl Thacker

TECHNICAL DIRECTOR: Rob Child

AUDIO: Steve Watson, Brian McNamee, and Jeff Lieb

CAMERA: Eric "Buck" Buchanan, Hugh "Houston" Walsh, Jay Eidt, Jon Graboff, Eddie Lenzo, Al Ligouri, Tore Livia, Phil Salanto, and Jim Ryan

EDITOR: Jason Watkins

TAPE OPERATOR: Ellie Rhitt

ELECTRONIC GRAPHICS: Layne Dornstein

DESIGN DIRECTOR: Leon Tinker

UTILITY: Stewart Foreman and Jeremy Duffy

GRIPS: Tom Cestare and Kevin Mair

Emeril Live Musicians

Leonard "Doc" Gibbs

Will Brock

Robert Landum

Mindy Jostyn (Jammin Queen)

Marc Muller

David Hamburger (C. F. Steaks)

Matt Weiner (Bouillabaisse)

Emeril Live Kitchen Staff

SOUS-CHEFS: Leslie Orlandini and Emily Rieger

CHEFS: Amy Stevenson, Marie Ostrosky, Robert Bleifer, Mariam Garron, Lisa Sigelman, and Kristine Delatour

FOOD AND BEVERAGE MANAGERS: Derek Flynn and Marisa Palmisano

INTERNS: Scott Wyatt, Sal Passalacqua, Ellen Lucas, Patty Collins, John Sowienski, and Nigel Spence

Essence of Emeril Production Staff

PRODUCERS: Ricki Stofsky, Julia Harrison, and Emily Schwartz

DIRECTORS: Dini Diskin-Zimmerman and Leigh Lofgren

ASSISTANT DIRECTORS: Alcira Boxill, Mason Pettit, and Elizabeth Porter

STAGE MANAGERS: Cindy Cammon, Rhoda Gilmore, and Emily Rubin

PRODUCTION ASSISTANTS: Jean Marie Lally and Karen Porter

SET DESIGNER: Wendy Waxman

MAKEUP-ARTISTS: Janet Arena, Pam Arnone, and Keira Schlessinger

CAMERA: Humberto "Burt" Del Carpio, Eric "Buck" Buchanan, Jay Eidt, Bridgette Long, Victor Longtin, Keith Porter, and Hugh "Houston" Walsh

AUDIO: Brian McNamee, Michael Messologitis, and Al Thuerer

VIDEO ENGINEERS: Brooke Haznedar and Miles Taylor

TECHNICAL DIRECTOR: Eli Lazar

ELECTRONIC GRAPHICS: Stephanie Butler and Alicia Sells

TELEPROMPTER: Stephanie Butler

LIGHTING/GRIPS: Dan Blank, Jeff Dorr, and Kelvin Green

Essence of Emeril Kitchen Staff

DIRECTOR OF CULINARY: Georgia Downard

EXECUTIVE CHEF: Susan Stockton

SOUS-CHEFS: Leslie Orlandini and Emily Rieger

CHEFS: Robert Bleifer, Lauren Dean, Rebecca Flaste, Miriam Garron, Cathy Lowe, Melissa Lynch, Joanne McDermott, Moise Alvarez, Elizabeth Jackson, Lynne Kearney, and Maureen Luchenko

FOOD AND BEVERAGE MANAGERS: Derek Flynn and Marisa Palmisano

KITCHEN SERVICES: Juan Galderon and Athen Fleming

And to the entire Marketing Department

Introduction

It was the spring of 1993 and life was good for Emeril Lagasse.

Ten years before, the Massachusetts native had come south to New Orleans to take the prestigious

position as Executive Chef at Commander's Palace, owned and operated by the Brennans, a family of celebrated restaurateurs. After several months of being interviewed by Ella Brennan, the matriarch of the clan, he had somehow convinced her that he was capable, at the tender age of twenty-six, to

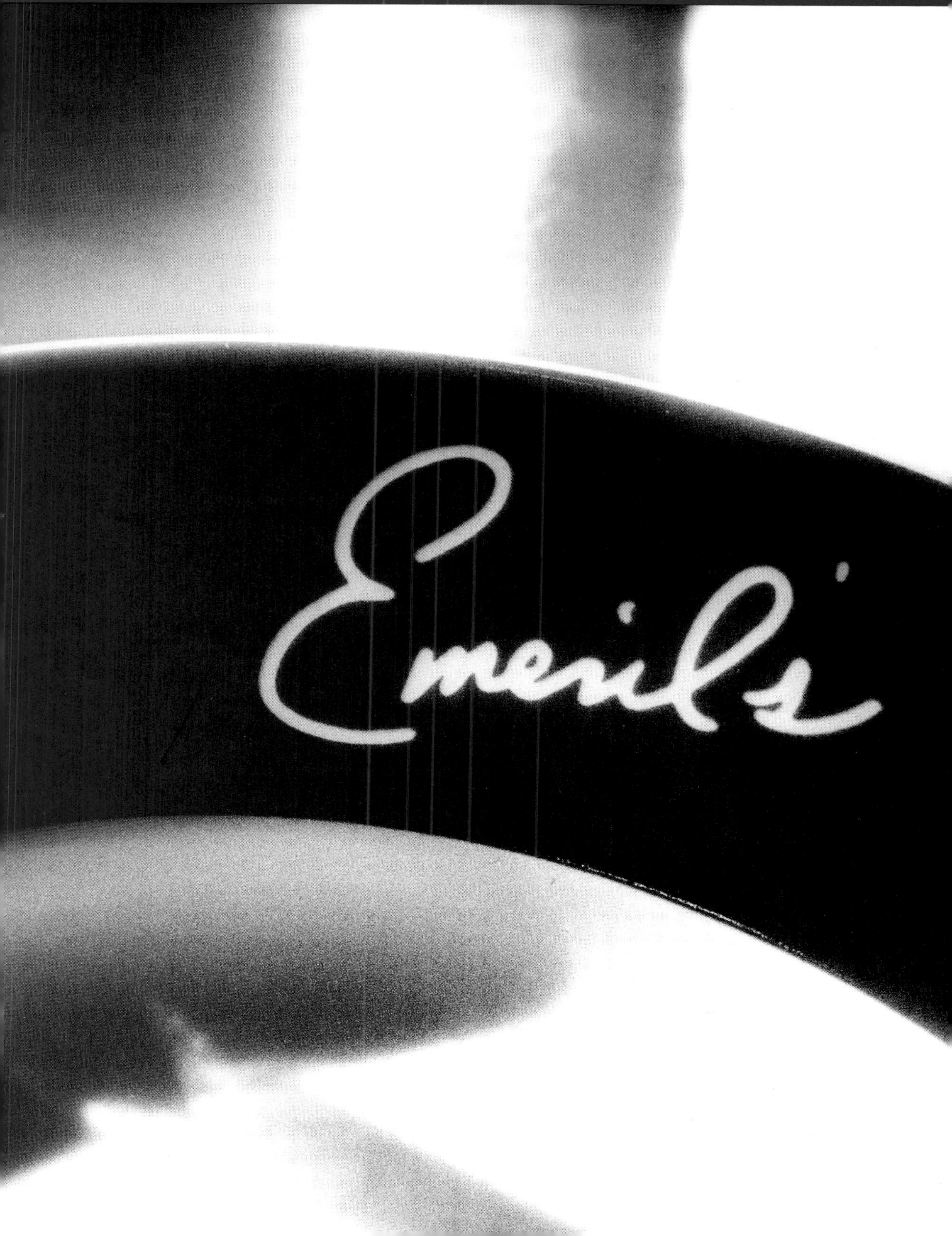
Emeril's

succeed the legendary Paul Prudhomme. After all, he had graduated from Johnson and Wales University in Providence, Rhode Island, having studied the culinary arts, then had gone to work and study in Paris and Lyon before returning to the United States and jobs in New York, Philadelphia, and Boston.

It wasn't easy being a Yankee, a young one at that, in the Deep South, working at a restaurant that served Creole fare, but gradually Emeril proved himself not only to the Brennan family but to the demanding clientele as well, and the restaurant became ranked as one of the top ten restaurants in America by food critics.

But after about seven years, Emeril felt that it was time for him to strike out on his own and he bid adieu to his friends and mentors to open Emeril's in the Warehouse District of his adopted city. Everyone told him he was nuts; the area was in a run-down section of the city with virtually no streetlights, but he had a vision. (It's now one of the most fashionable neighborhoods in downtown New Orleans, with Emeril's as its epicenter.) He opened in March 1990 and it quickly became the "in" place to dine in the city. In 1991, it was named Restaurant of the Year by *Esquire* magazine.

Not long after, Emeril realized that there was another audience he wanted to entertain, one that was more casual. Thus was born a second restaurant, NOLA (acronym for New Orleans, LA), in the French Quarter, where T-shirts and shorts are *de rigueur*. It was a smash hit and was named the Best New Restaurant of 1993 by *Esquire* magazine.

To top it all, Emeril Lagasse won the title of "Best Southeast Regional Chef" in 1991, given by the James Beard Foundation, and Emeril's had earned the prestigious Ivy Award, given by *Restaurant & Institution Magazine*.

But overseeing two restaurants and cooking until the wee hours of the morning weren't enough to keep the energetic fellow busy, and his first cookbook, *Emeril's New New Orleans Cooking*, was released in 1993. He was going to spend the better part of three months on a whirlwind book tour that would take him across the United States.

He was on the proverbial roll!

By the time he finished the book tour, Emeril needed a break. But in August, on one of those hot, dog days of summer, a telephone call came from Nashville. Alan Reid, a television producer with Reid/Land Productions Inc., had gotten wind of this new kid on the block and wanted to talk television.

He didn't know it yet, but Emeril's life was getting ready to be kicked up to notches unknown to mankind!

Reid had an idea for a cooking show. Cooking shows were not a new idea; after all, Julia Child, Graham Kerr, and Merle Ellis had proven that television viewers liked to watch someone fooling around in the kitchen. And Reid figured it was time to have a new face and a new talent out there. Would Emeril consider doing a pilot?

"When I got the call, I really didn't give it much thought. I was busy with the restaurants, and I had no idea of when I would have the time to go to Nashville where Mr. Reid was headquartered," Emeril recalls.

"I mentioned it to Marti, my right hand, and to some of the people on my management team, and they all told me to go for it."

What "it" exactly was, was still a little vague. The first series was entitled *How to Boil Water*, for which Emeril was a tad overqualified.

"But," laughs Emeril, looking back, "I figured what the heck. Here was something that I had never done before and I was willing to give it a try. I thought it would be fun trying to teach the rudiments of cooking. It was tough because we didn't really know what we were doing. Marti and I were writing scripts and recipes on legal pads in our already-overcrowded restaurant office we shared with managers and chefs. Looking back, it was pretty crazy!"

After that series they went on to do a new show called *Emeril and Friends*, which was not the most widely acclaimed series either.

"Hey, I wasn't used to scripts and I told them to go get an actor to do these shows. I wasn't comfortable and I felt like Dracula with all that makeup!"

Then the Television Food Network was formed in 1993 and soon thereafter Emeril was invited to be featured as the first restaurant chef on the network, where the series *Essence of Emeril* was born.

That was a move in the right direction, but Emeril had his fingers in a lot more pots by then. He was working on a second cookbook and both New Orleans restaurants were doing blockbuster business, but the Energizer Bunny kept going, going, going.

For a time, Emeril (in a T-shirt and jeans) would spend a few hours a day in the test kitchen with Anne Kearney (a chef from Emeril's who ran the test kitchen), then he would don his chef's uniform and dart over to the restaurant for the evening service, while Anne cleaned up and banged out scripts and recipes.

"It was pretty basic and primitive in the beginning. There were times I boarded a plane in the dead of night, carrying an ice chest loaded with crawfish, some local fish, a jar of Creole seasoning, and a couple of bottles of Steen's syrup, which we needed for the show," he laughs. "Man, I guarded that ice chest like it contained gold!"

The first day of taping for *Essence of Emeril* was August 15, 1994, and the staff was comprised of two, sometimes three, people, who assisted Emeril, as well as a culinary staff, who prepped food for the cooking shows.

To help as a food producer and ease the load, Felicia Willett joined Emeril in writing recipes and scripting the shows. In the beginning, they taped six shows during a four-day period. By the end of the run they had taped 456 *Essence* shows and by that time Emeril was "making friends with the camera" and enjoying it more. During the taping of the last two series of *Essence,* Emeril was often in the studio in the wee hours of the morning with only a couple of cameramen, a kitchen worker, and a floor director. To keep their spirits up, Emeril entertained them and himself with interjections like "Hey, wake up out there," "Bam," and "Kick it up a notch." So it was that the so-called "Emerilisms" were born.

When the *Louisiana Real & Rustic* book was launched in the summer of 1996, the network had rented a studio to begin taping a cooking game show called *Ready, Set, Cook* and someone had the idea of taping two one-hour shows dedicated to the new book when the studio wasn't in use.

The production staff was given two weeks to pull it together. It was decided that the shows would be taped before a live studio audience, so a set had to be built, menus had to be planned, and a kitchen had to be organized, but it was an amazing experience and *Emeril Live* as we know it today was born.

"Now we were having fun!"

Emeril had found his niche. He likened it to cooking in front of people at the food bar at Emeril's.

"This is what cooking is all about, at least for me," he says. "You get to see people's reaction to the food—they can smell it, see it, taste it. Plus I didn't need a script. Here was something that I could do off the top of my head."

By November a production crew had been hired, and the first *Emeril Live* show was taped on Wednesday, January 15, 1997. They were taping three shows in four days and people were jamming up the phone lines to get tickets to be in the audience. It was wild. The first season was eighty-four shows and ratings for his one-hour prime time show skyrocketed.

Young kids, manly men like firemen and cabdrivers, as well as doctors, lawyers, and businessmen, became devotees along with ladies of all ages. Emeril has made cooking cool to everyone from all walks of life.

"Hey, even young children now know what *foie gras* is," he beams proudly.

He became a celebrity overnight everywhere but in his hometown of New Orleans. The cable company there didn't carry the Food Network.

But if they picked up any one of several national news magazines, they would have seen him featured in *Time* (which named *Emeril Live* in its list of "best television of 1996" along with sitcom *Seinfeld* and the lush production of *Pride and Prejudice*), *People* magazine, and just about every food-oriented magazine, and all the major, and not-so-major, newspapers across America.

By this time, too, Emeril had been approached about opening a restaurant in Las Vegas and so it was that Emeril's New Orleans Fish House opened at the MGM Grand. Who ever heard of a seafood restaurant in the middle of a desert? Only someone like Emeril could get away with it! It opened in 1995 to raves and has been named Best Restaurant in Las Vegas by the *Zagat Guide*.

A third cookbook, *Emeril's Creole Christmas,* was in the works and, by the fall of 1997, two specials dedicated to it were taped. One show was "kid friendly" and the other was a "rockin'" Creole Christmas.

The show always rocks, no matter what the subject. There's live music, real food, and an audience that gets to taste as Emeril cooks—it's indeed a show like no other. And all the effort has paid off. *Emeril Live* won a Cable Ace Award for the best informational program. That says a lot for a guy who just likes to cook and believes that cooking can and should be fun!

And that's why there's this book, *Emeril's TV Dinners*, devoted to some of his personal favorite shows and dedicated to everyone—the staff at the Food Network and all you fans out there who made it all happen.

Not a man to rest on his laurels, Emeril's newest New Orleans restaurant, Delmonico Restaurant and Bar, featuring old New Orleans favorites with a new twist opened this past summer.

What next? Who knows!

Emeril's
TV Dinners

Back to the Basics

Hey, all of you out there in TV land, and to those who

 haven't tuned in yet, listen up, there's

some things I want to talk about before

we get in the kitchen and rattle some pots

and pans.

This is only a cookbook. It's not the bible of

cooking according to Emeril, it's only a compilation of

some of the dishes I've demonstrated on television and

in particular those I've had fun doing.

I want to share them with you and perhaps you will

learn a few little tricks here and there that will make cooking

and entertaining as much fun for you as it is for me.

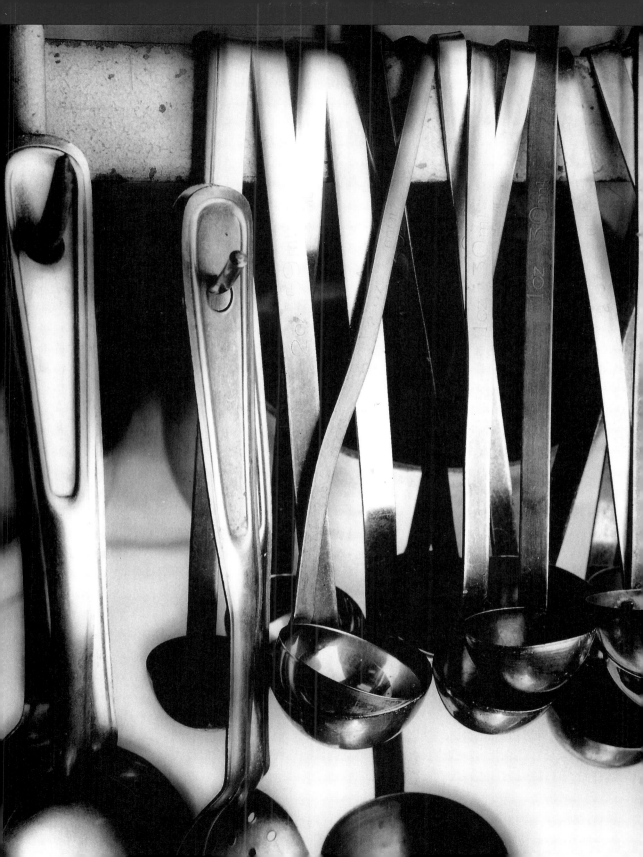

I've said it many times before and I'll say it again—we're not building any rocket ships, we're cooking—plain and simple. Sure, some dishes are a little more complicated than others, but that doesn't mean you can't do them. And don't go thinking that we're using exotic or weird ingredients. Look, if you don't have crawfish, use shrimp or scallops, or chicken. If you can't get a certain item, or maybe you don't like some of these things, there's no rule that says you can't substitute something else. Just use some common sense. Remember, the only thing that's important is that the food taste good. It doesn't have to be pretty, although that sometimes helps, but it should give you a thrill when you put it in your mouth.

Now, before you begin cooking anything, just be sure you have everything that you need. Read and study the recipe you plan to make. Make a grocery list. Get organized. There's nothing more frustrating than to begin preparing a dish and having fun, then have to drop everything because you're missing an ingredient.

Make a quick check of the kitchen. Do you have the right pots, pans, baking equipment, utensils, good, sharp knives, measuring spoons and cups, clean dishcloths? Man, you can't whip up something without the proper equipment. You don't have to go and spend a trillion dollars, but you will need some basic stuff.

Be sure you have salt, fresh peppercorns, cayenne, and a few dried herbs in that old spice cabinet. Don't go buying that stuff in those big containers unless you're opening a restaurant or cooking for an army. Buy small containers so the herbs and spices will be fresh.

This is as good a time as any to tell you about my philosophy on seasoning. Do as I do: put your seasonings in small saucers or bowls rather than using the box or jar, and keep them handy near the stove and work area. Season as you cook and don't overseason. Just add a pinch here and a pinch there. Taste as you cook, so you'll keep on top of it. If you add everything at the end, the seasoning will not have balanced out during the cooking time.

Usually I use regular old table salt, unless otherwise specified in a recipe, and freshly ground black pepper or freshly ground white pepper. Then again, I think there are certain dishes that need a little jazzing up with a bit of cayenne as well. And there are times when you need not only salt and some kind of pepper but maybe a hit or two of "bam," which is simply my own personal blend of seasonings which we all know as "Essence." But look, you can make up your own blend. Check out some of the blends on the market. In Louisiana, just about every cook worth his or her salt (ha, sorry about that) has a preferred combination of spices and herbs. Experiment—that's the fun of it.

The same goes for hot sauces. I personally like Tabasco sauce, my assistant, Felicia, has the hots for Crystal Hot Sauce, and Marcelle, my co-writer, says that Tabasco is great to use as a condiment to season things at the table, but she also likes a green hot sauce put out by Cajun Chef, a company in her hometown, which she uses both as a condiment and a marinade for meats, poultry, and fish. So you see, to each his own. After you've tasted a few, you'll figure out which one feels good on your palate.

Do you know what the "trinity" is? If you've watched my show, you know—it's onions, bell peppers, and celery—and it's very important to many of my dishes. Most of the time I use all three, sometimes I might use one or two together. If you add carrots to the trinity and take out the bell peppers, you then have what's called in French a mirepoix. I like to use green onions, which are called scallions everywhere else. I am also a great fan of garlic. Fresh parsley, chives, and other herbs are very aromatic and flavorful, and are often used for garnishes as well.

When you're getting ready to cook, it's best to have your *mise en place*, which is a French culinary term referring to having all the ingredients necessary for a dish prepared and ready to combine up to the point of cooking. All that really means is to have your onions, bell peppers, or whatever else needs chopping done and measured, liquids measured, butter measured, spices and herbs ready—get the idea?

I also believe in having homemade stock, if at all possible, prepared and stored in the refrigerator or freezer. I don't know why, but many people are intimidated by the word *stock*, which is really nothing more than a strained liquid made by cooking vegetables, meat, or fish and other seasoning ingredients in water. Sure, you can buy stocks, broths, and consommés in cans, or you can make some by adding water to granules or cubes that you can get at your neighborhood grocery store. But, ah, they are full of salt and the ones you can make at home are so much better. I've said it many times, we're not building a rocket ship; we're only really boiling water with bones and seasonings, then straining it. Once you've mastered making stocks, you'll never go back to that commercial stuff again. You don't need all kinds of special equipment and gadgets to make stock, just a stockpot (an 8- or 12-quart size), a strainer or a colander lined with cheesecloth, and, if you wish to store the stock in the freezer, some pint- and quart-size containers.

The ingredients are simple enough. First you'll need some bones—chicken, beef, veal, pork, or fish—or shrimp and lobster or crab shells and/or fish frames (bones). Now don't be getting crazy about this. You can usually get bones from your butcher or, in the case of fish, shrimp, or crabs, your seafood supplier. Hey, you can begin collecting stock ingredients yourself. Whenever you buy something with bones, if you don't need them, store them in an airtight container in the freezer. Same goes for fish bones, crab shells, or shrimp shells. Store them in the freezer until you have time to make your stock. Then you'll need some carrots, onions, garlic, and, of course, salt, pepper, and what is called in culinary terms a *bouquet garni (boo-KAY gahr-NEE)*, which is simply a bunch of herbs (the basic trio being parsley, thyme, and bay leaf, but sometimes I add my own stuff) that are either tied together or placed in a cheesecloth bag and used to flavor the stock. Hey, you don't have to call it a bouquet garni, you can call it a flavor bag or pouch of herbs, whatever makes you happy. You can wrap the herbs in your sock if you want—just make sure you wash it first. Oh, and you might need a roasting pan and maybe some tomato paste if you're going to make a brown stock.

See, very simple!

You should also know about roux. The term *roux* (pronounced *roo*) as used in Louisiana cooking is equal parts flour and oil slowly cooked and constantly stirred until the mixture is brown and has a nutlike aroma and taste. It serves as a base and thickening agent for bisques, gumbos, stews, and gravies. I use three different colors of roux. Blond roux, the color of sandpaper, is used in delicate soups. A medium brown roux, the color of peanut butter, is preferable for gravies and dishes made with fish and some fowl. A dark brown roux, the color of chocolate, which has an intense flavor, is used in gumbos and stews.

I've also included in this chapter some basic sauces that I use from time to time in other recipes, like mayonnaise and tartar sauce. Check them out and just keep in mind that you can make them your own by adding your personal favorite spice or herb. Use them as a guidepost.

Now, let's go in the kitchen and have fun!

Essence

Makes about 1½ cups

Combine all the ingredients in a small mixing bowl and blend well. Store in an airtight container in your spice cabinet for up to 3 months.

5 tablespoons sweet paprika

¼ cup salt

¼ cup garlic powder

2 tablespoons freshly ground black pepper

2 tablespoons onion powder

2 tablespoons cayenne

2 tablespoons dried oregano

2 tablespoons dried thyme

Bouquet Garni

Place all the ingredients in the center of a 6-inch square of cheesecloth. Bring the ends together and tie securely with kitchen twine.

5 sprigs of fresh thyme

2 bay leaves

10 black peppercorns

3 sprigs of fresh parsley

Emeril tasting some Mardi Gras food with *Emeril Live* food producer Felicia Willett

Chicken Stock

Makes about 5 quarts

4 pounds raw chicken bones, including the
   carcass and necks, rinsed in cool water

8 quarts water

2 cups coarsely chopped carrots

1½ cups coarsely chopped celery

2 cups coarsely chopped yellow onions

6 cloves garlic, peeled

2 teaspoons salt

1 recipe Bouquet Garni (page 7)

Put the chicken bones in a large stockpot and cover with the water. Add the remaining ingredients and bring to a rolling boil over high heat. Skim off any cloudy scum that rises to the surface, then after the scum stops rising to the top reduce the heat to medium and simmer, uncovered, for 2 hours.

Strain the stock through a fine-mesh sieve and let cool. Refrigerate for 8 hours or overnight, then remove any congealed fat from the surface. It will keep in the refrigerator for 3 days, or can be stored in 2- to 4-cup containers in the freezer for up to 1 month.

Dark Chicken Stock

Makes 4 cups

Break and crack the bones of the carcasses.

Heat the vegetable oil in a 6-quart stockpot over medium-high heat. Season the bones with 1 teaspoon of the salt and the pepper. Add the bones to the pot and brown for about 10 minutes, stirring often.

Add the carrots, celery, onions, garlic, and the remaining teaspoon salt. Cook, stirring often, until the vegetables are soft, about 5 minutes.

Add the wine and tomato paste and stir to mix. Cook for 5 minutes, stirring occasionally. Add the water and the bouquet garni, and bring the mixture to a boil. Skim off any cloudy scum that rises to the surface, then reduce the heat to medium and simmer, uncovered, for 3 hours.

4 pounds raw chicken bones, including the carcass and necks, rinsed in cool water
1 tablespoon vegetable oil
2 teaspoons salt
⅛ teaspoon freshly ground black pepper
1 cup coarsely chopped carrots
1 cup coarsely chopped celery
3 cups coarsely chopped yellow onions
1 head garlic, split in half
1 cup dry red wine
¼ cup tomato paste
3 quarts water
1 recipe Bouquet Garni (page 7)

Strain the stock through a fine-mesh strainer and let cool. Refrigerate for 8 hours or overnight, then remove any congealed fat from the surface. The stock will keep in the refrigerator for 3 days or in 1- to 2-cup containers in the freezer for up to 1 month.

Duck Stock

Makes about 4 cups

Follow the recipe for Dark Chicken Stock, substituting duck carcasses for the chicken carcasses.

Veal Stock

Makes about 2 quarts

7 pounds veal marrow bones, sawed into
   2-inch pieces (ask your butcher)
One 6-ounce can tomato paste
2 cups coarsely chopped onions
1 cup coarsely chopped celery
1 cup coarsely chopped carrots
2 cups dry red wine
1 teaspoon salt
5 cloves garlic, peeled
1 recipe Bouquet Garni (page 7)
6 quarts water

Preheat the oven to 450°F.

Put the bones in a shallow roasting pan and roast for 1 hour. Remove from the oven and spread evenly with the tomato paste. Combine the onions, celery, and carrots and lay on top of the bones. Return to the oven and roast for another 30 minutes. Remove from the oven and drain off any fat.

Place the roasting pan over medium heat on the stove and pour the wine over the bones and vegetables. Using a wooden spoon, deglaze, scraping the bottom of the pan for browned particles. Put everything into a large stockpot. Add the salt, garlic, bouquet garni, and water. Bring to a boil over high heat. Skim off any cloudy scum that rises to the surface, then reduce the heat to medium and simmer, uncovered, for 4 hours.

Strain the stock through a fine-mesh strainer and let cool. Refrigerate for 8 hours or overnight, then remove any congealed fat from the surface.

The stock will keep in the refrigerator for 3 days or in the freezer in 1- to 2-cup containers for up to 1 month.

Veal Reduction

Makes 1 cup

1 quart Veal Stock (above)
¼ teaspoon salt

Bring the stock seasoned with the salt to a boil in a medium-size saucepan over high heat. Reduce the heat to medium and simmer until it reduces by three-fourths, about 1 hour.

Fish Stock

Makes 3 quarts

When selecting bones for this stock, make certain that the heads and carcasses are very fresh. Do not use oily fish like pompano, redfish, or mackerel. Make friends with your local fishmonger so that he'll know to keep some good bones for you.

Place the fish bones with water (*not* the 4 quarts) to cover in a large stockpot over high heat and bring to a boil. Remove from the heat and drain off the water in a colander. Rinse the bones well under cold running water, then put them back in the pot with the 4 quarts cold water and the remaining ingredients. Bring to a boil over high heat, then reduce the heat to low and simmer for 10 minutes. Turn the heat up to medium and simmer, uncovered, for 30 minutes. Let cool completely and strain through a fine-mesh strainer. It will keep in the refrigerator for 3 days or in the freezer in 2- to 4-cup containers for up to 1 month.

8 cups very fresh raw fish bones (heads and carcasses) from fish such as cod, grouper, snapper, or flounder

4 quarts cold water

2 medium-size yellow onions, sliced

2 medium-size carrots, coarsely chopped

2 stalks celery, coarsely chopped

2 medium-size lemons, halved

1 recipe Bouquet Garni (page 7)

2 teaspoons salt

Producer Emily Schwartz and executive producer Karen Katz in the *Emeril Live* control room

Shrimp Stock

Makes about 5 quarts

Just so you'll know—shrimp stock can be a bit pungent, so don't use it in delicate dishes.

8 cups uncooked shrimp shells (from about
    1 pound large shrimp)

2 medium-size yellow onions, sliced

2 stalks celery, coarsely chopped

2 medium-size lemons, halved

1 recipe Bouquet Garni (page 7)

2 teaspoons salt

4 quarts cold water

Rinse the shrimp heads and shells under cool water and place them in a stockpot with the remaining ingredients. Bring to a boil over high heat, then reduce the heat to low and simmer for 10 minutes. Turn the heat to medium and cook, uncovered, for 30 minutes. Cool thoroughly, then strain through a fine-mesh sieve. Store in the refrigerator for 3 days or in 2- to 4-cup containers in the freezer for up to 1 month.

Mornay Sauce

Makes about 2½ cups

4 tablespoons (½ stick) unsalted butter

¼ cup bleached all-purpose flour

Salt and freshly ground white pepper to
    taste

Pinch of freshly grated nutmeg

2½ cups milk

½ cup freshly grated Parmigiano-Reggiano
    cheese

Heat the butter in a medium-size saucepan over medium heat until melted. Add the flour and whisk to blend. Season with salt and pepper, and add the nutmeg. Cook, stirring, for 2 minutes, then slowly add the milk and whisk to blend. Bring the mixture to a boil, then reduce the heat to medium-low and, with a wooden spoon, stir constantly until it thickens enough to coat the back of the spoon, about 4 minutes. Add the cheese and whisk until it melts completely. Remove from the heat and use warm. Can be refrigerated for up to 2 days, then reheated on low heat, with a little liquid added if necessary.

Tartar Sauce

Makes about 1⅓ cups

There isn't much that's not made better with tartar sauce, especially seafood, and especially fried seafood!

Put the egg, garlic, lemon juice, parsley, and onion in a blender or food processor and process until smooth, about 15 seconds. With the processor running, pour the oil through the feed tube in a steady stream. Add the mustard and Worcestershire, season with salt, pepper, and hot sauce, and pulse once or twice to blend.

Cover and let sit for 1 hour in the refrigerator before serving. Best if used within 24 hours.

1 large egg

1 tablespoon minced garlic

2 tablespoons fresh lemon juice

1 tablespoon chopped fresh parsley leaves

2 tablespoons minced yellow onion

1 cup olive oil

1 tablespoon Dijon mustard

1 teaspoon Worcestershire sauce

Salt, freshly ground black pepper, and hot
   sauce to taste

Emeril with Chef Norman van Aken of Normanís, Coral Gables, Florida, and _Emeril Live_ executive chef Susan Stockton

Salmonella warning: Let's talk about egg safety because I don't want any of you out there to get sick. I personally love homemade mayonnaise and I make it with fresh—and I mean FRESH—raw eggs. I've never had any trouble, but I want you to take some precautions. Always purchase your eggs from a reputable source, a place you can trust with your life. Don't use eggs after the expiration date on the cartons. Don't you go leaving your eggs in the back seat of your car while you're out and about, and once you get home, keep the eggs in the refrigerator. I use eggs pretty quick, so I don't have to worry about keeping them too long at home. But, I suppose there's a tiny risk some nasty old salmonella could sneak in to some eggs, so just be cautious about serving things containing raw eggs to very young kids or the elderly or to people who have health problems. OK? Got it?

Emeril's Mayonnaise

Makes about 2¼ cups

1 large egg

1 tablespoon Dijon mustard

2 tablespoons fresh lemon juice

2 cups olive oil

Salt and freshly ground black pepper to taste

In a food processor or blender, blend the egg, mustard, and lemon juice together for 20 seconds. With the machine running, slowly pour in the oil through the feed tube. The mixture will thicken. Season with salt and pepper and pulse once or twice to blend.

Store in an airtight container in the refrigerator. Best if used within 24 hours.

Variations

Aioli is a garlic-flavored mayonnaise that is very popular to serve with fish, meats, and vegetables. To make it, combine 2 teaspoons chopped garlic with the egg, mustard, and lemon juice, and proceed as directed.

Saffron Aioli is made simply by combining ¼ teaspoon saffron threads with 2 tablespoons hot water, then letting the mixture stand for 8 hours. When ready to use, whisk the saffron mixture to blend. The saffron mixture is added with the egg, mustard, and lemon juice; then proceed with the recipe as directed.

Roasted Garlic Mayonnaise can be made by adding 2 tablespoons Roasted Garlic (page 15) with the egg, mustard, and lemon juice, then proceeding as directed.

See salmonella warning on page 13 regarding raw eggs.

Cameraman Hugh "Houston" Walsh on *Emeril Live*

Roasted Garlic

Makes about 2 tablespoons

Preheat the oven to 400°F.

Cut a small square of aluminum foil. Cut the garlic head in half crosswise and place the halves on the foil. Drizzle both halves with the oil and season with salt and pepper. Bring the ends of the foil together to make a small pouch. Bake until the garlic is tender, about 45 minutes.

1 large head garlic

½ teaspoon olive oil

Salt and freshly ground black pepper to taste

Remove the foil bag from the oven and carefully open it up a bit. Return to the oven for about 10 minutes more. Remove from the oven and let cool. Remove the flesh by squeezing each clove between your thumb and index finger. Use immediately or refrigerate in a little olive oil in an airtight container for 2 to 3 days.

Skillet Corn Bread

Makes 6 to 8 servings

Preheat the oven to 400°F.

Combine the cornmeal, flour, salt, sugar, and baking powder in a large mixing bowl. Add the egg and milk and mix well but do not beat. Heat the shortening in a 10-inch cast-iron or other ovenproof skillet over medium-high heat until almost smoking. Pour in the batter and cook until the edges begin to turn golden, 3 to 4 minutes. Transfer the skillet to the oven and bake until golden brown, about 45 minutes. Remove from the oven and let cool about 5 minutes before using.

2 cups yellow cornmeal

1 cup bleached all-purpose flour

1 teaspoon salt

1 tablespoon sugar

1 teaspoon baking powder

1 large egg, beaten

1½ cups milk

3 tablespoons solid vegetable shortening

Fall River Memories

I grew up in Fall River, Massachusetts, where, I must say,

I had a great childhood. My father is French-Canadian and my mother is Portuguese– what a great combo–and my siblings and I were surrounded with lots of family

and good food. What more could you ask for, right?

There's a large Portuguese population in and around Fall River, so naturally we enjoyed the cuisine and traditions that were and still are maintained. Mom,

whom you know as Hilda, was always cooking up a storm and I was always close by her side. To me, kitchenwork wasn't work at all, it was fun! Chopping, stirring, and tasting were exciting, and, man, the aromas that permeated the kitchen were incredible.

We had linguiça and chorizo, fabulous sausages that made just about anything cooked with them delicious. *Malassadas*, plump fried doughnuts dusted with sugar, and hearty kale soup were staples in our home.

Then, to top it all off, we enjoyed local dishes like codfish cakes, clam chowder, and salmon pie, so revered by New Englanders.

When I went off to Boston as a young chef, I had the opportunity of working at the famed Parker House, where roasted scrod and that great dessert, Boston cream pie, were on the menu daily.

Was I happy? You betcha!

This chapter is one that is dear to my heart and I believe that every one of the recipes will tell you why.

St. John's Club Kale Soup

Makes 8 servings

St. John's Club was a favorite hangout of Hilda and John (my parents), and the cook, Inez, made a mean kale soup unlike any other. This signature dish of hers featured red beans and navy beans, which made an already hearty soup even more so. She knew what it meant to kick it up a notch.

Heat the olive oil in a heavy 8-quart stockpot over high heat. Add the sausage and onion, season with salt and pepper, and cook, stirring, for 2 minutes. Add the garlic, parsley, and beans and cook, stirring, for 2 minutes. Add the chicken stock and bring to a boil. Add the bay leaves, thyme, and the crushed red pepper. Season again with salt and black pepper. Reduce the heat to medium and simmer, uncovered, until the beans are tender, about 1½ hours. Add the potatoes and kale, season with salt and pepper, and continue to simmer until the potatoes are tender, about another 30 minutes. Skim off any fat that rises to the surface. Remove the bay leaves.

To serve, pour the soup into individual soup bowls and garnish each with a tablespoon of the mint. Allow the mint to steep for about 1 minute before serving with the bread.

2 tablespoons olive oil

1 pound chorizo sausage, cut into ½-inch-thick slices

1 large yellow onion, chopped

Salt and freshly ground black pepper to taste

6 to 8 cloves garlic, to your taste, minced

¼ cup chopped fresh parsley leaves

¼ pound dried navy white beans, rinsed, sorted over, soaked overnight in water to cover, and drained

¼ pound dried red beans, rinsed, sorted over, soaked overnight in water to cover, and drained

4 quarts Chicken Stock (page 8) or canned chicken broth

2 bay leaves

¼ teaspoon dried thyme

¼ teaspoon crushed red pepper

2 large Idaho potatoes, peeled and diced

1 bunch kale, well washed, stemmed, and torn into bite-size pieces

½ cup chopped fresh mint leaves

1 loaf crusty Portuguese bread

Codfish Cakes

Makes 4 appetizer servings

Off the New England coast cod is so abundant that there are many dishes in which it is featured, but perhaps the most popular and best loved is the codfish cake. In Louisiana everyone has his or her own recipe for crab cakes. New Englanders have the same penchant for these cakes. As far as I'm concerned, Hilda made the best and taught me well.

Salt cod is cod that has been salted and dried, and is an important ingredient in Mediterranean and Caribbean cooking. It is also used in many Portuguese-American dishes.

12 ounces salt cod

2 quarts plus 2 tablespoons milk

½ cup chopped yellow onions

¼ cup chopped celery

½ pound Idaho potatoes, peeled and diced

1 tablespoon plus 2 teaspoons chopped garlic

3 cups water

Salt and freshly ground white pepper to taste

3 tablespoons finely chopped fresh parsley leaves

1 tablespoon olive oil

3 large eggs

½ cup heavy cream

1 cup bleached all-purpose flour

Essence to taste (page 7)

2 cups fine dried bread crumbs

Vegetable oil for deep frying

1 recipe Tartar Sauce (page 13)

Two days before serving, soak the cod in 1 quart of the milk in a covered bowl in the refrigerator for 24 hours. The next day, discard the milk and rinse the cod well with cold water. Put the cod in a fresh quart of milk and refrigerate for another 24 hours. Discard the milk and rinse well with cold water. Pat dry and flake into small pieces.

In a large saucepan, combine the onions, celery, potatoes, 2 teaspoons of the garlic, and the water. Season with salt and pepper. Bring to a boil, then reduce the heat to medium and cook until the potatoes are fork tender. Drain and put the mixture into a large mixing bowl. Add the cod, 1 tablespoon of the parsley, the remaining tablespoon garlic, the olive oil, 1 of the eggs, and the heavy cream. With a potato masher, mash and mix until thoroughly blended. Season with salt and pepper. Let cool completely.

Divide the mixture into 2 equal portions. Place each portion in the center of 2 large pieces of plastic wrap. Wrap the mixture in the plastic wrap and form into logs, each about 1 inch in diameter and 12 inches long. Unwrap, then cut the log crosswise into 2-inch lengths. Put the flour in a small mixing bowl and season with Essence. In another small mixing bowl, whisk the remaining 2 eggs and 2 tablespoons milk together. Season with salt and pepper. In a third small mixing bowl, put the bread crumbs and season with Essence.

Heat 4 inches of oil in a large, heavy pot or electric fryer to 360°F. Dredge each cake in the seasoned flour, coating completely and tapping off any excess. Dip the cake in the egg wash, letting the excess drip off, then dredge in the seasoned bread crumbs, coating each side completely.

Fry the cakes several at a time without crowding in the hot oil until golden brown, 3 to 4 minutes, turning them around to brown evenly. Drain on paper towels. Season with Essence.

Serve warm with the tartar sauce and garnish with the remaining 2 tablespoons parsley.

During service at Emeril's Restaurant in New Orleans

Fall River Clam Chowder

Makes 10 servings

In New England clam chowder is like gumbo in Louisiana. There're any number of ways to prepare it, but I personally like the one we made in Fall River, which had bacon and leeks, chunks of potatoes, and littleneck clams. By the way, there is always discussion among New Englanders about whether to add milk or cream, carrots or not, bacon or salt pork. In Boston, the chowder has no milk or cream and is more brothy.

To prepare the littlenecks, scrub the shells under cold, running water, detaching any weeds and scraping off barnacles. Discard any broken shells and any that do not close when tapped.

¾ **pound sliced bacon, chopped**

2 **cups chopped leeks (white part only, well washed)**

1 **cup chopped celery**

1 **cup chopped carrots**

Salt and freshly ground black pepper to taste

6 **bay leaves**

¾ **cup bleached all-purpose flour**

8 **cups clam juice**

1½ **pounds Idaho potatoes, peeled and quartered**

1 **cup fresh sweet corn kernels (from 1 medium-size ear)**

1 **cup heavy cream**

½ **cup finely chopped fresh parsley leaves**

4 **pounds littleneck clams, shucked with liquor reserved**

Oyster crackers

In a large stockpot over medium heat, fry the bacon until crisp. Stir in the leeks, celery, and carrots, season with salt and pepper, and add the bay leaves. Cook, stirring, until the vegetables are soft and tender, about 10 minutes. Stir in the flour and cook for 10 minutes, stirring occasionally. Add the clam juice, potatoes, and corn, season with salt and pepper, reduce the heat to medium-low, and simmer until the potatoes are fork tender, about 15 minutes. Add the cream, parsley, and clams and their liquor and simmer for 5 minutes. Remove the bay leaves. Ladle into soup bowls and serve hot with oyster crackers.

Hilda's "Stuffies"

Makes 4 appetizer servings

During the season of Lent in Fall River, Hilda made these "stuffies" every Friday night. The Portuguese-American community in our area must have invented this unique dish because I've never found it anywhere else. Quahogs are large hard-shell clams that are best eaten young. You might want to have a partner with you in the kitchen when you fix these, because you'll need an extra pair of hands to help tie up the clams after they're stuffed. Man-oh-man, are these great, or what? Talk about happy!

The quahogs can be cleaned by scrubbing the shells under cold, running water. Detach any weeds and scrape off any barnacles. Discard broken shells and any that do not close when tapped.

Preheat the oven to 400°F.

In a large pot, bring about a gallon of salted water to a boil. Add the clams and cover. Cook until the shells open, about 6 to 8 minutes. Discard any shells that do not open. Drain.

Hold the clams with a clean cloth, then, with a sharp knife, sever the hinge muscle and loosen the muscle in the lower shell. Chop the clams and set aside. Place the shells on aluminum foil or a parchment-lined baking sheet.

Combine the butter and 1 tablespoon of the garlic in a mixing bowl. Season with salt and pepper. Spoon the mixture onto a large piece of plastic wrap. Form into a log 1 inch in diameter and roll tightly in the wrap. Refrigerate until firm, about 1 hour.

4 quarts plus ¼ cup water

Salt

1 dozen quahogs

¼ pound (1 stick) unsalted butter, softened

2 tablespoons minced garlic

Freshly ground black pepper to taste

½ pound chorizo sausage, chopped

½ cup minced yellow onions

¼ cup minced celery

¼ cup minced green bell pepper

Essence to taste (page 7)

1 cup fine dried bread crumbs

3 tablespoons chopped fresh parsley leaves

¼ cup freshly grated Parmigiano-Reggiano cheese

Butcher's twine

continued

In a medium-size sauté pan over high heat, fry the chorizo for 2 minutes. Add the onions, celery, and bell pepper and season with Essence. Cook for another 2 minutes, stirring. Stir in the remaining 1 tablespoon garlic and the bread crumbs and remove from the heat. Stir in the remaining ¼ cup water and 2 tablespoons of the parsley and season with Essence. Season the clams with Essence and stir into the sausage mixture.

Place about 3 tablespoons of the chorizo mixture into the bottom half of each clamshell and pat firmly. Remove the butter log from the refrigerator and cut crosswise into 12 equal slices. Place a slice of the butter on top of the stuffing and sprinkle with cheese.

Tie the shells together tightly with butcher's twine. Bake for 8 to 10 minutes. Remove from the oven and snip off the twine.

To serve, arrange the clams on a platter and garnish with the remaining 1 tablespoon parsley and some Essence.

**Shelly Smale
on the set of
*Emeril Live***

Salmon Pie

Makes 8 servings

This is one of my brother Mark's favorite dishes. Hey, one of mine, too! There was this neighborhood place back in Fall River that served this pie, made with mashed salmon (what else, right?) in a buttery piecrust that was, what's the word now, awesome? Hey, it was better than awesome!

I think this pie was influenced by the French-Canadians from Nova Scotia and I'm sure glad we had it as part of our repertoire at home.

Preheat the oven to 350°F.

Season the salmon with salt and pepper. Combine the fish stock, wine, quartered onion, and bouquet garni in a medium-size sauté pan over medium heat and bring to a gentle boil. Add the salmon and poach until it flakes, 6 to 8 minutes. Remove it from the cooking liquid and let cool to room temperature. Discard the poaching liquid. Flake the salmon into a large mixing bowl.

Heat the olive oil in another sauté pan over medium heat. Add the chopped onions, season with salt and pepper, and cook, stirring, for 2 minutes. Remove from the heat and add the garlic and parsley. Add to the salmon and mix well. Add the potatoes, egg, and heavy cream and mix again. Season with salt and pepper and set aside.

Divide the pie dough into equal portions. Lightly dust a work surface with flour. Roll out each piece into a circle 12 inches in diameter, about ⅛ inch thick. Fold each into fourths so that you can lift it without tearing and use one to line a 10-inch deep-dish pie pan. Spoon the salmon mixture into the pie shell. Place the second crust over the top of the mixture. With a sharp knife, cut away the excess dough. Using your fingers, crimp the edges of the pie firmly to seal completely. With a sharp knife, make several random slashes on the top crust. Bake until golden brown, 25 to 30 minutes. Cool for a few minutes before slicing to serve.

2 salmon fillets (about 8 ounces each)

Salt and freshly ground white pepper to taste

2 cups Fish Stock (page 11)

1 cup dry white wine

1 small yellow onion, peeled and quartered, plus 1 cup finely chopped yellow onions

1 recipe Bouquet Garni (page 7)

1 tablespoon olive oil

1 tablespoon chopped garlic

1 tablespoon finely chopped fresh parsley leaves

3 medium-size Idaho potatoes, peeled, diced, boiled in water to cover until tender, drained, and mashed

1 large egg

½ cup heavy cream

1 recipe Basic Savory Piecrust (page 168)

Bleached all-purpose flour for dusting

Roasted Scrod with Parsley Potatoes

Makes 6 servings

First, let me clear up some confusion about the word scrod. No, it's not the pluperfect of screwed. Scrod isn't a distinct fish, but was a term used in the 1800s at the Parker House restaurant in Boston, where, by the way, I worked a very long time ago with my good friend Joe Ribas. The word refers to young cod (and haddock), weighing under 2½ pounds, which are split, boned, dredged in bread crumbs, and broiled.

Scrod can be prepared any number of ways and is favored by New Englanders because of its delicate flavor. Back when I worked at the Parker House, the catch of the day featured on the menu was cod or haddock sometimes cooked like this–very simple, but very good.

1½ pounds new or small red potatoes,
quartered

Salt and freshly ground black pepper to
taste

4 young cod or haddock fillets
(6 to 8 ounces each)

24 Ritz crackers

1 stick (¼ pound) unsalted butter, melted

2 tablespoons finely chopped fresh parsley
leaves

Preheat the oven to 400°F. Line a baking sheet with parchment or waxed paper.

Put the potatoes in a large saucepan and cover with water. Season with salt and pepper and bring to a boil over high heat. Reduce the heat to medium and simmer until fork tender, about 12 minutes. Drain and set aside.

Season the fillets with salt and pepper. In a medium-size mixing bowl, crush the crackers with your hands into fine crumbs. Stir in 4 tablespoons of the butter and 1 tablespoon of the parsley and mix well. Place the fillets on the prepared pan and spread the cracker crumbs evenly over the top of each fillet. Bake until they flake easily with a fork, about 12 minutes.

In a medium-size sauté pan, heat the remaining 4 tablespoons of butter over medium heat, add the potatoes, and season with salt and pepper. Cook, stirring, for about 5 minutes. Remove from the heat and add the remaining tablespoon parsley.

To serve, spoon the potatoes in the center of 4 serving plates and lay a fillet on top of the potatoes.

Stage manager Rhoda Gilmore wrangling up the audience at *Emeril Live*

Fish 'n' Chips

Makes 4 servings

On some Friday nights when Hilda wanted a night off from the kitchen, she would send me to Sharpel's, another one of those great neighborhood spots in Fall River, to pick up fish 'n' chips. There was always a line, because there were only about 8 tables in the place, so 90 percent of their business was "take-out."

The menu featured fish 'n' chips, chowder, fried scallops, and fried clams. That was it, but they were done to perfection. I can still remember the sounds and smells of that place. Whenever I get nostalgic for it I make a batch of this stuff, my way, bammed with some Essence and served with tartar sauce.

2 pounds Idaho potatoes, peeled and cut crosswise into ¾-inch-thick chips

4 cod or haddock fillets (about 6 ounces each), cut in half lengthwise

Essence to taste (page 7)

1½ cups bleached all-purpose flour, sifted

1 tablespoon sugar

¼ cup dark beer

2 large egg yolks, beaten

½ cup milk

⅔ cup water

Salt and freshly ground black pepper to taste

2 large egg whites, beaten to stiff peaks

Vegetable oil for deep frying

Malt vinegar

6 tablespoons fresh lemon juice

1 recipe Tartar Sauce (page 13)

Soak the potatoes in cold water to cover for 30 minutes before frying. Season the fish on both sides with Essence.

In a mixing bowl, combine the flour and sugar. Add the beer, egg yolks, milk, and water and whisk until smooth. Season with salt and pepper. Cover and let rest for 30 minutes. Fold in the egg whites.

Heat 6 inches of oil in a deep, heavy pot or an electric fryer to 360°F. Dip the fillets in the batter, letting the excess drip off. Add the fish, several pieces at a time, and fry until golden brown, 4 to 6 minutes. Drain on paper towels. Season with Essence and keep warm.

Drain the potatoes and pat dry. Place them in a fry basket and fry in the hot oil for 3 minutes. Lift the basket out of the oil and drain over the fryer. Return the basket to the oil and fry until golden brown, another 3 to 5 minutes. Drain on paper towels. Season with salt and pepper.

Serve the fish 'n' chips on newspaper and drizzle with the vinegar and fresh lemon juice. Pass the tartar sauce.

Chorizo Stuffed Roasted Chicken

Makes 4 to 6 servings

The Portuguese like to use chorizo, a highly seasoned, coarsely ground pork sausage flavored with garlic, in just about anything, and you'll find out why when you taste this roasted chicken. I've seen guests at Hilda's fight over the stuffing. In fact, there will probably be some of the stuffing that won't fit into the cavity of the chicken—not to worry, spoon any extra right into the baking dish and bake during the last 30 minutes or so of cooking time so there isn't any waste. Just stand back so you won't get run over when you bring this dish to the table.

1 tablespoon olive oil

¼ pound ground pork

¼ pound fresh chorizo sausage, removed from the casing and crumbled

1 cup chopped yellow onions

½ cup chopped celery

¼ cup chopped green bell pepper

Salt and freshly ground black pepper to taste

1 tablespoon chopped garlic

12 slices white sandwich bread

2 cups Chicken Stock (page 8) or canned chicken broth

Pinch of crushed red pepper

¼ cup chopped fresh parsley leaves

1 large egg

1 roasting chicken (4 to 5 pounds), rinsed with cool water and patted dry

Butcher's twine

¼ cup water

Preheat the oven to 400°F.

Heat the oil in a large sauté pan over medium heat. Add the pork and chorizo and cook until completely browned, about 3 minutes. Add the onions, celery, and bell pepper, season with salt and black pepper, and cook, stirring until the vegetables are soft, about 5 minutes. Add the garlic and cook for 1 minute. Remove from the heat.

Put the bread in a large rectangular glass baking dish and pour in the chicken stock. Soak for 10 to 15 minutes. Remove and squeeze each slice, reserving the stock. In a large mixing bowl, combine the bread and stock with the pork-and-vegetable mixture. Mix well. Season with salt, black pepper, and crushed red pepper. Stir in the parsley. Let cool completely and season again with salt and black pepper. Add the egg and mix thoroughly.

Season the chicken generously with salt and black pepper. Stuff the cavity with the sausage mixture. Close the cavity and cross the legs, securing them with butcher's twine. Put the water in the bottom of a roasting pan and place the chicken in the center of the pan. Bake until the chicken browns evenly, about 1 hour. Reduce the heat to 375°F and continue to bake until it becomes very tender and the juices run clear, about another hour. Let the chicken rest for a few minutes before carving into serving pieces.

Serve with the stuffing.

Malassadas

Makes about 54 doughnuts

Malassadas are sugar-dusted dough fritters. Sounds kinda simple, huh? Well, don't underestimate these little doughnut-like pastries. As a kid I picked these up, 6 or 12 in a paper bag, for a snack when I needed a jolt. Then when I had children, I enjoyed making them a batch on cold mornings. Jessie, my older daughter, would help me pat them out before they were fried. We sure had fun.

Oh, and like New Orleans beignets, they are best enjoyed with a cup of good coffee.

1 envelope (¼ ounce) active dry yeast

¾ cup plus 1 teaspoon sugar

¼ cup warm water (110°F)

6 large eggs, at room temperature

4 tablespoons (½ stick) unsalted butter, melted

1½ cups milk, at room temperature

½ cup half-and-half, at room temperature

¼ teaspoon salt

8½ cups bleached all-purpose flour

Vegetable oil for deep frying

Sugar for sprinkling

In a small mixing bowl, combine the yeast, 1 teaspoon of the sugar, and the water. Stir to dissolve the sugar and set aside. If the yeast doesn't foam after a few minutes, you need to buy new yeast and start again.

In an electric mixer, beat the eggs and the remaining ¾ cup sugar until thick and pale yellow in color, about 6 minutes. Change the mixer attachment to a dough hook. With the machine on low speed, slowly add the yeast mixture, melted butter, milk, half-and-half, and salt. Add the flour, 1 cup at a time, and mix until a soft ball forms that leaves the sides of the bowl and climbs up the dough hook. Remove the dough and turn into a lightly oiled bowl, turning it to oil all sides. Cover the bowl with plastic wrap and set the bowl in a warm, draft-free place until it doubles in size, about 1½ hours.

Turn the dough out onto a floured work surface and dust it with flour. Roll out the dough into a rectangle about 12 × 17 inches and ½ inch thick. Cover the dough with a lightly oiled piece of plastic wrap. Put the dough in a warm, draft-free place and let rise until doubled in size, about 1 hour.

Heat 6 inches of oil in a deep, heavy pot or an electric fryer to 360°F.

With a sharp knife, cut the dough into 2-inch squares. Flour your hands, then pat the squares down a little to lightly flatten them. Fry the squares, 2 to 3 at a time, until golden brown, 3 to 4 minutes, turning them to brown evenly. Drain on paper towels. Sprinkle the doughnuts with sugar and serve warm.

Chef de cuisine Bernard Carmouche (far left) at Emeril's Restaurant and some of the kitchen brigade

Boston Cream Pie

Makes 1 cake; 16 servings

Boston's Parker House Hotel has been around since the mid-1800s and it was there that Boston cream pie was created. It's called a pie, but it's really a cake layered with a custard and topped with chocolate icing. There's a lot of recipes for this great concoction floating around, but this is my take on it. The cake is spongelike and the rich icing really gives it some kick—at least that's how I feel about it. Ask Hilda and John. They claim this really satisfies a sweet tooth.

¼ cup milk

2 tablespoons plus 2 teaspoons unsalted butter

8 large eggs, at room temperature

1 cup plus 2 tablespoons sugar

1 cup bleached all-purpose flour

1 teaspoon baking powder

⅛ teaspoon salt

1 teaspoon pure vanilla extract

1 recipe Pastry Cream (page 35)

1 recipe Chocolate Icing (page 35)

Preheat the oven to 350°F.

In a small saucepan, heat the milk and 2 teaspoons butter over medium heat. With an electric mixer fitted with a wire whip, beat the eggs and 1 cup of the sugar in a large mixing bowl on medium-high speed until the mixture is pale yellow and thick, and has tripled in volume, about 8 minutes. With the mixer running, slowly add the warm milk mixture, blending thoroughly.

In a small mixing bowl, sift together the flour, baking powder, and salt. Fold the flour mixture into the egg mixture and blend thoroughly until all lumps have disappeared and it is smooth. Add the vanilla and mix gently.

Grease two 9-inch round cake pans with 2 tablespoons butter. Sprinkle each with a tablespoon of sugar. Pour the cake batter evenly into the pans and bake until the cake springs back when touched, 20 to 25 minutes. Cool for about 2 minutes. With a thin knife, loosen the edges of the cakes, then flip onto wire racks. Let cool completely.

When the cakes are completely cool, slice each in half horizontally. Place a bottom layer on a 9-inch round cardboard and set it on a wire rack. Divide the pastry cream into 3 equal portions. Spread one third of the pastry cream evenly over one cake layer. Top with a second layer of cake. Spread another third of the pastry cream over it. Repeat the same process with the third layer. Top with the fourth layer. If necessary, shave off any uneven pieces of cake with a serrated knife so that it is smooth and even on all sides. Chill for 2 hours.

Put the cake on a wire rack. Spoon the slightly cool chocolate icing onto the top of the chilled cake, allowing the overflow to drip down the sides. Place in the refrigerator and chill for about 4 hours.

To serve, slice the cake into 16 pieces.

Pastry Cream

Makes about 4 cups

Combine ½ cup of the heavy cream with the cornstarch in a small mixing bowl and stir to make a paste. Combine the paste with the remaining 3½ cups cream, the sugar, and the vanilla in a large nonstick saucepan. Using a wire whisk, stir the mixture until it is well blended. Put the saucepan over medium-low heat and whisk constantly until it thickens like pudding, about 25 minutes. Pour the mixture into a bowl and cover with plastic wrap, pressing the wrap down on the surface of the pudding to keep a skin from forming. Let cool to room temperature. When ready to use, whisk it a couple of times before spreading it on the cake.

4 cups heavy cream

½ cup cornstarch

1 cup sugar

2 teaspoons pure vanilla extract

Chocolate Icing

Makes about 2½ cups

Combine the heavy cream and chopped chocolate in a medium-size nonstick saucepan over medium heat. Stir until the chocolate is completely melted and the mixture is smooth. Remove from the heat and stir to cool, lifting the mixture out of the pot several times with a rubber spatula or wooden spoon until it cools slightly. It should be glossy and slightly thick. Use as directed.

2 cups heavy cream

½ pound semisweet chocolate, chopped

Individual Custard and Macaroon Tartlets

Makes 12 servings

In Portuguese-American communities, you're likely to find these tartlets in neighborhood bakeries. There was such a place in Fall River called Lucky Loaf, where we would often stop to pick up pastries and sweets for snacks, and these were one of my favorites. They were baked right in little foil disposable cups, which was great for carting around to family gatherings or for after-school treats.

1 vanilla bean, split in half

2 cups heavy cream

1 cup granulated sugar

4 large egg yolks

1 recipe Basic Savory Piecrust (page 168)

Twelve 4-ounce disposable baking cups or custard cups

12 small coconut macaroons

2 cups Sweetened Whipped Cream (page 37)

Sprigs of fresh mint for garnish

Confectioners' sugar

Preheat the oven to 300°F.

With a sharp knife, scrape the pulp from the vanilla bean. In a medium-size saucepan, combine the heavy cream, granulated sugar, and vanilla pulp and bean over medium heat. Bring to a gentle boil and stir to dissolve the sugar. Simmer over medium heat for 3 minutes. Remove from the heat, strain through a fine-mesh sieve, and discard the vanilla bean.

In a medium-size mixing bowl, whisk the egg yolks until frothy. Add the cream mixture a little at a time, whisking until the mixture is slightly thick.

Divide the dough into 2 equal portions. Roll each out into a round 12 inches in diameter and ⅛ inch thick. Cut 6 rounds, 4 inches in diameter, out of each 12-inch round. Line each of the disposable foil cups or custard cups with a round of dough, pressing it on the bottom and sides with your fingers. Place the cups in a large shallow baking pan. Place a macaroon in the bottom of each cup. Pour about ¼ cup of the custard over the macaroons in each cup. Add enough water to the baking pan to come halfway up the sides of the cups. Bake until the custard sets and the tops are golden, about 45 minutes.

Remove from the oven. Let cool, then refrigerate for at least 4 hours before serving. Garnish with the whipped cream, mint, and confectioners' sugar.

Sweetened Whipped Cream

Makes about 3 cups

Combine the heavy cream, vanilla, and sugar in a medium-size mixing bowl and, using an electric mixer, whip until soft peaks form.

2 cups heavy cream

½ teaspoon pure vanilla extract

2 teaspoons sugar

Emeril Live **food producer Felicia Willett serving up soup for the audience**

Emeril's **TV** Dinners

Louisiana Specialties

I've called Louisiana my home now for about 15 years
and I've come to love the food, the people, the music,
and all that makes up the culture of
this very diverse state.

I've learned that just about
everyone in Louisiana has a great
respect and an even greater passion
for the cuisine, which is always
evolving. Yesterday, I might have enjoyed a fantastic
gumbo, then today someone might give me a taste of
something he or she just threw together with whatever

fresh ingredients were at hand from the garden or the nearest bayou, and tomorrow, *cher,* who knows what I'll find at a small café or neighborhood hangout. That's what's so intriguing about the place.

I remember one occasion when my friend Felicia and I went down to spend a weekend cooking for a group at Avery Island (where they make Tabasco sauce), but before we put a pot on the stove, Rock and Marcelle, along with our good friends Cary and Henry, and some other folks insisted on taking us out to dinner in Breaux Bridge at Café des Amis. What a meal we had! Hey, they taught me a couple of things about cooking and I've included some of those here.

No one is afraid of food in Louisiana—everyone gets in the kitchen and rustles up a thing or two. Cooking and eating are Louisiana's favorite pastimes!

In this chapter I'll offer you a collection of some old favorites with new twists.

Boiled crabs are enjoyed all over the state, but especially along the coast where they're caught in the bays fed by the Gulf of Mexico. The sweet crabmeat is a delicacy that needs little enhancement, but I think a spicy green onion dipping sauce adds just a bit of dazzle.

The pompano "cooked in a bag" is a new take on a favorite New Orleans dish that is served in several local restaurants, and I hope you like the Chicken Delmonico, which is a dish that is being served at my newest New Orleans restaurant called, what else, Delmonico Restaurant and Bar, which was a long-standing local favorite on St. Charles Avenue. The former owners have retired and it's my hope to bring back this famed dining place to those who loved it. The snapper served with coush-coush is a grassroots kind of dish—use simple ingredients to make an outstanding meal. Baked Alaska is a classic and now you can make it right in your own kitchen.

Come on, take a taste, relax, and enjoy these Louisiana specialties.

**Coauthor Marcelle
Bienvenu**

Stuffed Artichokes

Makes 4 servings

Franky and Johnny's, a neighborhood hangout in New Orleans, has some of the best stuffed artichokes—at least I think so. But there are a lot of other good ones around the city. The trick is not to overstuff the leaves so that you get the true taste of both the filling and the leaves.

To remove the choke, grasp the central core of leaves and, with a quick twist, lift it out. Carefully scoop out the choke with a teaspoon or melon baller and discard it.

Preheat the oven to 375°F.

In a medium-size mixing bowl, combine the bread crumbs, cheese, olive oil, and herbs and mix well. Season with Essence. Carefully stuff the mixture inside all the leaves of each artichoke.

Put the artichokes on a baking sheet, standing them up straight (you may have to trim the stems flat) and place in the oven. Bake until the stuffing is golden brown, about 25 minutes.

To serve, drizzle each artichoke with equal amounts of the aioli and a squeeze of lemon juice.

2 cups fine dried bread crumbs

1 cup freshly grated Parmigiano-Reggiano cheese

¼ cup olive oil

¼ cup chopped fresh herbs such as basil, parsley, and/or oregano

Essence to taste (page 7)

4 large artichokes, trimmed, boiled in water to cover until tender, and choke removed

1 cup Aioli mayonnaise (page 14)

2 medium-size lemons, cut in half

Creole Spiced Blue Crabs with Green Onion Dipping Sauce

Makes 4 appetizer servings

If and when you can get your hands on live blue crabs, give this a shot. Boil 'em up in seasoned water, crack 'em open, and serve with the dipping sauce. Zatarain's Concentrated Liquid Crab & Shrimp Boil, a New Orleans product, gives a real zip to crabs, but is not absolutely necessary. It's available in some supermarkets or seafood shops, or check our Source Guide in the back of the book.

You can use this same concept with live crawfish, fresh shrimp, or lobster. You can add new potatoes (called creamers in Louisiana), onions, and corn on the cob to the boiling water to make it a really grand meal. If you do, though, add more salt and cayenne to the water, as the vegetables absorb lots of seasoning. Serve the seafood and vegetables on newspapers spread on a picnic table in the backyard, on the patio, or even on a small balcony. I am of the opinion that food always tastes better when eaten outdoors.

Or, if you're ever in Las Vegas, visit Emeril's New Orleans Fish House where we offer this on the menu.

Combine the water, onion, celery, lemons, jalapeño, garlic, thyme, bay leaves, and crab boil in a large, heavy pot over high heat. Season the water with salt and cayenne and bring to a boil. Add the crabs and cook, covered, for 15 minutes. Drain and transfer the crabs to a large bowl or bowls of ice water. Cool for about 5 minutes, then drain. Set aside.

Combine the green onions, chopped garlic, and chicken stock in a large saucepan over medium heat. Season with salt and cayenne. Bring to a gentle boil and simmer for 10 minutes. Remove from the heat. In a blender or using a handheld blender, process the sauce until smooth. Strain through a fine-mesh strainer. Taste for seasoning, adding more salt and cayenne if necessary.

To serve, pile the crabs on a platter and serve with the dipping sauce on the side.

4 quarts water

1 medium-size yellow onion, chopped

2 stalks celery, chopped

2 medium-size lemons, halved

1 fresh jalapeño, cut in half lengthwise

1 head garlic, halved

3 sprigs fresh thyme

2 bay leaves

2 tablespoons Zatarain's Concentrated Liquid Crab & Shrimp Boil (optional)

Salt and cayenne to taste

2 dozen live blue crabs

3 bunches green onions, trimmed and chopped

2 tablespoons chopped garlic

2 cups Chicken Stock (page 8) or canned chicken broth

Marti Dalton, left, and Felicia Willett checking over photos for this book at Homebase in New Orleans

43

Fried Eggplant with Shrimp Stew-Fay

Makes 4 to 6 servings

Breaux Bridge, Louisiana, located in what is known locally as Acadiana, touts itself as the Crawfish Capital of the World, which is just fine with me. You can get some of the best crawfish dishes in that small town, and especially at a place that was once a mercantile store but now has taken on a new life as Café des Amis, run by Dickie and Cynthia Breaux. One of the best items on the menu is something called eggplant pinwheels topped with crawfish. Man, are they good! I enjoyed them so much, I came up with my version—but with shrimp instead of crawfish.

12 tablespoons (1½ sticks) unsalted butter

4 cups chopped yellow onions

2 cups chopped green bell peppers

2 cups chopped celery

Salt and freshly ground black pepper to
   taste

2 teaspoons chopped garlic

2 pounds medium-size shrimp, peeled and
   deveined

½ teaspoon cayenne

1 cup plus 2 tablespoons bleached
   all-purpose flour

2 cups water

6 tablespoons chopped fresh parsley leaves

½ cup chopped green onions (green part
   only)

Vegetable oil for frying

1 eggplant (about 1 pound), cut crosswise
   into ¼-inch-thick slices

Essence to taste (page 7)

Melt the butter in a large skillet over medium heat. Add the onions, bell peppers, and celery, season with salt and pepper, and cook, stirring, until soft and golden, about 10 minutes. Add the garlic and cook, stirring, for 2 minutes. Add the shrimp, 2 teaspoons salt, and cayenne and cook until the shrimp turn pink, about 4 minutes. Dissolve 2 tablespoons of the flour in the water, then add it to the shrimp mixture and stir until the mixture thickens slightly. Reduce the heat to medium-low and simmer for 6 to 8 minutes, stirring occasionally. Add the parsley and ¼ cup of the green onions, stir, and cook for another 2 minutes. Remove from the heat and keep warm.

Heat 4 inches of oil in a large, heavy deep pot or an electric fryer to 360°F. Season the eggplant slices on both sides with Essence. Put the remaining 1 cup flour in a shallow bowl and season with Essence. In another bowl, season the beaten eggs with salt and pepper. In a third shallow bowl, season the bread crumbs with Essence. Dredge each slice of eggplant in the flour, tapping off the excess, then dip in the egg wash, letting the excess drip off. Next, dredge in the bread crumbs, coating each side completely.

2 large eggs, beaten

2 cups fine dried bread crumbs

½ cup freshly grated Parmigiano-Reggiano cheese

Carefully lay several eggplant slices at a time in the hot oil and fry until golden brown, turning them over once. Drain on paper towels. Repeat until all the slices are fried. Season with Essence.

To serve, place 2 to 3 fried eggplant slices in the center of each serving plate. Spoon the shrimp mixture over the eggplant and garnish with the cheese and the remaining ¼ cup green onions.

Chef de cuisine of NOLA Restaurant, David McCelvey, getting ready for service with the kitchen brigade

Pompano en Papillote

Makes 2 servings

Pompano, with its firm, white flesh and smooth, silvery skin, is ideal for many different preparations. Since it is fished off the coast of Louisiana in the Gulf of Mexico (as well as off the coasts of Florida and the Carolinas), it's long been a local favorite. Perhaps one of the best-known old New Orleans dishes is pompano en papillote, or pompano steamed in a paper bag, which was derived from a classic French recipe in which the fish is heavily sauced. The "bag" is made with parchment paper, and when the paper is rolled back after the cooking process, it makes for a really kicked-up presentation.

2 pompano fillets (8 ounces each)

2 teaspoons olive oil

Salt and freshly ground black pepper to taste

½ pound lump crabmeat, picked over for shells and cartilage

1 tablespoon chopped garlic

Parchment paper

½ cup fresh lemon juice

¼ cup chopped shallots

½ pound (2 sticks) cold unsalted butter, cubed

2 tablespoons chopped fresh parsley leaves

5 sprigs of fresh parsley

Preheat the oven to 400°F. Lightly oil a baking sheet.

Rub the fillets with the olive oil and season with salt and pepper.

In a small mixing bowl, toss the crabmeat and garlic together. Season with salt and pepper.

Cut a piece of parchment paper about 2 inches longer than the fish. Fold the paper in half lengthwise, then open it flat. Place the fish on one half of the paper. Spread the crabmeat mixture evenly over the fish. Fold the other parchment half over the fish and roll the edges to seal the fish tightly in the bag. The bag should be formed in the shape of the fish. Place the bag on the baking sheet and bake for 10 to 12 minutes.

In a small nonreactive saucepan, combine the lemon juice and shallots. Bring to a gentle boil and cook until the liquid reduces by half, about 3 minutes. Add the cold butter cubes, 2 to 3 at a time, and whisk until completely melted. Season with salt and pepper. Stir in the chopped parsley.

To serve, cut off the top of the bag and roll it back with a fork to expose the fish. Spoon the sauce over the fish and garnish with the parsley sprigs.

Seared Snapper with Crawfish Coush-Coush

Makes 4 servings

Another dish inspired by the good people at Café des Amis is this superb snapper made with what is commonly known as coush-coush in south Louisiana. Coush-coush, not to be confused with couscous, is usually prepared by adding boiling water to a mixture of yellow cornmeal, baking powder, salt, and pepper, then turning the mixture into a skillet containing hot lard or bacon fat. When a toasty brown crust forms, it's broken up and stirred, making something like a crumbled corn bread. In my rendition, I use some milk and chicken stock in place of the boiling water to kick it up a notch.

5 tablespoons plus ¼ cup vegetable oil

1 cup chopped yellow onions

Essence to taste (page 7)

1 cup fresh sweet corn kernels
   (from 1 medium-size ear)

2 teaspoons chopped garlic

1 pound peeled crawfish tails

2 cups yellow cornmeal

1 cup bleached all-purpose flour

1 teaspoon salt

1 tablespoon sugar

1 teaspoon baking powder

¼ teaspoon cayenne

1 large egg, beaten

1 cup milk

½ cup Chicken Stock (page 8) or canned
   chicken broth

4 red snapper fillets (6 to 8 ounces each),
   skinned if possible

1 recipe Tasso Maque Choux (page 49)

Preheat the oven to 400°F.

Heat 2 tablespoons of the vegetable oil in a medium-size sauté pan over medium heat. Add the onions and cook, stirring, for 2 minutes. Season with Essence. Add the corn and cook for 1 minute. Add the garlic and crawfish and cook for 1 minute. Season with Essence, remove from the heat, and let cool.

Combine the cornmeal, flour, salt, sugar, baking powder, and cayenne in a large mixing bowl. Add the egg, milk, and chicken stock and mix well, but do not beat. Fold in the crawfish mixture.

Heat 3 tablespoons of the vegetable oil in a large ovenproof sauté pan over medium heat.

Pour in the batter and cook until the edges begin to turn golden, 3 to 4 minutes. Place the skillet in the oven and bake until golden brown, about 40 minutes. Remove from the oven and let cool. Break the coush-coush into small pieces. Set aside.

Season the snapper fillets with Essence. Heat the remaining ¼ cup vegetable oil in another large sauté pan over medium heat. Add the snapper and sear until it flakes easily with a fork, 3 to 4 minutes on each side. Remove and drain on paper towels.

To serve, put equal amounts of the coush-coush in the center of 4 serving plates. Lay a fillet on top of each and spoon over the tasso maque choux.

Tasso Maque Choux

Makes 4 servings

Melt the butter in a large sauté pan over medium heat. Add the tasso and cook, stirring, for 1 minute. Add the onion and bell pepper, season with salt and cayenne, and cook, stirring, until the vegetables are soft, about 2 minutes. Add the corn, season with salt and cayenne, and cook, stirring occasionally, for about 6 minutes. Add the garlic and tomatoes, season with salt and cayenne, and cook, stirring occasionally, until the corn is tender, 8 to 10 minutes. Add the milk, stir, and remove from the heat. Serve warm.

2 tablespoons unsalted butter

4 ounces tasso or smoked ham, chopped

½ cup chopped yellow onion

¼ cup chopped green bell pepper

Salt and cayenne to taste

**2 cups fresh sweet corn kernels
(from 2 medium-size ears)**

2 teaspoons chopped garlic

**½ cup peeled, seeded, and chopped fresh or
canned tomatoes**

¼ cup milk

Chicken Delmonico

Makes 4 servings

At my new restaurant, Delmonico Restaurant and Bar, in New Orleans, we offer this chicken dish that features some of my favorite ingredients. Pan-fried chicken strips are served with a sauce of exotic mushrooms, artichoke bottoms, and cream. Beautiful!

For the artichoke bottoms, simply boil four fresh artichokes until tender in salted boiling water to cover, cool, then remove the leaves and chokes and, voilà, you have artichoke bottoms. Easy enough!

4 skinless boneless chicken breast halves (about 6 ounces each)

Essence to taste (page 7)

1 cup plus 2 tablespoons bleached all-purpose flour

2 cups fine dried bread crumbs

2 large eggs beaten with 2 tablespoons milk

¼ pound (1 stick) unsalted butter

½ cup minced yellow onions

Salt and freshly ground black pepper to taste

¾ pound assorted exotic mushrooms, such as shiitakes, chanterelles, and black trumpets, wiped clean and sliced (about 4 cups)

4 cooked artichoke bottoms (see headnote)

¼ cup plus 2 tablespoons fresh lemon juice

2 tablespoons chopped garlic

1½ cups heavy cream

2 tablespoons finely chopped fresh parsley leaves

1 cup vegetable oil

Cut each breast half lengthwise into 4 equal strips. Season with Essence. Put 1 cup of the flour in a shallow bowl and season with Essence. In another shallow bowl, put the bread crumbs and season with Essence. Put the egg wash in another bowl. Dredge the chicken strips first in the flour, tapping off any excess, then in the egg wash, letting any excess drip off, then in the bread crumbs.

Melt 2 tablespoons of the butter in a large sauté pan over medium heat. Add several chicken strips at a time and cook until golden brown, 2 to 3 minutes on each side. Drain on paper towels. Repeat the process with the remaining chicken and a total of 6 tablespoons of the butter until all the chicken is cooked. Season the chicken with Essence and keep warm. Using a paper towel, wipe the pan clean.

Heat the remaining 2 tablespoons butter in the sauté pan over medium heat. Add the remaining 2 tablespoons flour and, stirring constantly, cook for 1 minute to make a blond roux. Add the onions and cook, stirring, for 2 minutes. Season with salt and pepper. Add the mushrooms and cook, stirring, for 2 minutes. Season with salt and pepper. Add the artichokes, lemon juice, and garlic and cook, stirring, for 2 minutes. Season with salt and pepper. Add the cream and bring to a gentle boil. Cook until the mixture thickens enough to coat the back of a spoon, 3 to 5 minutes. Remove from the heat and stir in the parsley. Season again to taste with salt and pepper.

16 large leaves fresh spinach, well washed, well dried, and tough stems removed

1 recipe Cheesy Bacon Grits (below)

Heat the oil in a large skillet over high heat, then fry the spinach leaves for about 30 seconds. Remove and drain on paper towels. Season with salt and pepper.

To serve, spoon the grits in the center of each serving plate. Lay 4 strips of chicken on top of the grits. Spoon the mushroom-and-artichoke sauce over the chicken, garnish with the spinach leaves, and serve.

Cheesy Bacon Grits

Makes 4 servings

Fry the bacon in a medium-size sauté pan over medium-high heat until just crispy and drain on paper towels. In a medium size saucepan combine the milk, salt, cayenne, and butter and bring to a boil. Add the grits and reduce the heat to medium. Stir for 30 seconds, then add the cheese and stir until the cheese melts. Stir in the bacon. Cook, uncovered, until the grits are tender and creamy, 4 to 5 minutes. Serve hot.

½ pound sliced bacon, chopped

4½ cups milk

1½ teaspoons salt

¼ teaspoon cayenne

1 tablespoon unsalted butter

2 cups quick-cooking white grits

1 cup grated white Cheddar cheese

Baked Alaska

Makes 1 cake; about 8 servings

At some of the old-line New Orleans restaurants, this dessert was, and still is, regarded as the quintessential part of any festive occasion, from birthdays to baptisms, engagements to anniversaries. At Commander's Palace, the lights were dimmed whenever a waiter brought the flaming cake to the table to make it all quite dramatic.

Now don't be intimidated by this dessert, which simply consists of sponge cake, topped with a thick layer of ice cream or, in this case, several layers of the cold stuff, then covered with a blanket of meringue. In the old days, it was put into a hot oven to allow the meringue to brown evenly, then flamed with brandy. Today, there's a little fancy gadget that's really a small blowtorch (you can get it at some kitchen shops), which you can use to brown the meringue without putting it in the oven. And hey, if you want, you can fill half a clean eggshell with brandy, cut out a little hole on top of the finished cake to settle it in, light the brandy (carefully!), and really impress your friends.

And it was Mr. Lou, the pastry chef at Emeril's, who perfected this sponge cake recipe. Thanks, buddy.

Preheat the oven to 350°F.

In a small saucepan, warm the milk and 2 teaspoons butter together over medium-low heat. With an electric mixer fitted with a wire whip, beat the eggs and 1 cup of the sugar on medium-high speed until the mixture is pale yellow, thick, and has tripled in volume, about 8 minutes. With the mixer on low, beat in the warm milk mixture.

Sift the flour, baking powder, and salt into a medium-size mixing bowl. Fold the flour mixture into the egg mixture and blend thoroughly until smooth. Add the vanilla and mix gently.

Grease a 17 × 12-inch baking pan or jelly-roll pan with 2 tablespoons butter. Sprinkle evenly with the remaining 2 tablespoons sugar. Pour the cake batter into the pan, spreading it evenly. Bake until the cake springs back when touched, about 15 minutes. Cool for about 2 minutes, then gently flip it out onto a large wire rack or a large sheet of parchment paper. Let cool completely.

Cut the sponge cake into 4 equal pieces (cut in half vertically, then cut each half in two). Spread the softened chocolate ice cream on one layer. Top with a second piece of sponge cake. If the ice cream begins to melt, put the cake in the freezer for about 30 minutes. Spread the softened chicory ice cream over the second cake layer. Lay the third piece of cake on top and spread with the praline ice cream. Again, if the ice cream begins to melt, return the cake to the freezer to let it firm up. Top with the last piece of cake. Wrap the cake tightly with plastic wrap and freeze until firm, about 2 hours.

Beat the egg whites with an electric mixer until soft peaks form. Add the sugar and beat until stiff peaks form. Remove the cake from the freezer and, with a rubber spatula, carefully spread the meringue evenly over the tops and sides of the cake. With a small blowtorch, brown the meringue. To brown it in the oven, preheat the oven to 400°F. Put the baked alaska in the hot oven until the meringue is tinged golden brown, 2 to 4 minutes.

Cut the cake crosswise into 1¼-inch-thick slices and drizzle with the chocolate sauce to serve.

Note: See salmonella warning on page 13 regarding raw eggs.

FOR THE SPONGE CAKE

¼ cup milk

2 tablespoons plus 2 teaspoons unsalted butter

8 large eggs

1 cup plus 2 tablespoons sugar

1 cup bleached all-purpose flour

1 teaspoon baking powder

⅛ teaspoon salt

1 teaspoon pure vanilla extract

FOR THE ICE CREAM

1 pint Chocolate Ice Cream (page 241), softened

1 pint Chicory Coffee Ice Cream (page 239), softened

1 pint Creole Cream Cheese and Praline Ice Cream (page 240), softened

FOR THE MERINGUE

4 large egg whites

2 tablespoons sugar

TO SERVE

1 recipe Chocolate Sauce (page 73)

Coconut Pots de Crème

Makes 8 servings

Pots de crème has long been a favorite recipe in New Orleans. We make all kinds at Emeril's and this one made with coconut is probably the most popular. Coco Lopez is the brand name for coconut cream. It's used in making piña coladas and other bar drinks and can be found in many supermarkets and most places that sell liquor and mixers. But hey, if you want to get a fresh coconut and cut it open, you can use the coconut milk, straight from the coconut. Whatever makes you happy!

1 vanilla bean, split in half

1 quart heavy cream

1 cup Coco Lopez coconut cream

10 large egg yolks

2 cups frozen unsweetened flaked coconut, defrosted

Sweetened Whipped Cream (page 37)

Chocolate shavings

Espresso powder

Preheat the oven to 300°F.

With a sharp knife, scrape the vanilla bean and combine the pulp, the bean, the heavy cream, and the Coco Lopez in a large, heavy saucepan over medium heat. Bring to a boil, then reduce heat to medium-low and simmer for 5 minutes. Remove from the heat and strain through a fine-mesh sieve. Discard the bean.

Beat the egg yolks with an electric mixer until fluffy and pale yellow. Gradually pour the hot cream into the eggs, mixing until completely incorporated. Strain the mixture into a medium-size mixing bowl. Fold in the flaked coconut.

Evenly divide the mixture among eight 6-ounce custard cups. Place the cups in a baking pan large enough to hold them comfortably. Fill the pan with enough water to reach three quarters of the way up the side of the cups. Cover the pan loosely with a sheet of aluminum foil and bake until the centers set, about 1½ hours. Remove from the oven and cool completely. Cover and refrigerate for at least 1 hour before serving.

To serve, garnish with sweetened whipped cream, chocolate shavings, and espresso powder.

Emeril signing a Christmas
toque for stage manager
Rhoda Gilmore while taping
his Creole Christmas special

Southern Favorites

Felicia Willett, my good friend who helps me with all

kinds of projects, is from Jonesboro,

Arkansas, where southern food rules.

On several visits there I really

learned about that southern

hospitality you hear so much about.

There is a certain graciousness that

exudes from these people. Wherever we went, there was

always a table full of food, most of which came from

their gardens and fields or from their well-stocked

pantries filled with canned and pickled goods. There's

lots of visiting back and forth with families and neighbors, and good food is the integral element in this tradition.

That's when I was introduced to all kinds of good things that true Southerners just can't live without, like fried green tomatoes, fried catfish, hush puppies, fried chicken, biscuits, dumplings, and heavenly desserts. No wonder Southerners are generally happy. Wouldn't you be blissful and contented if you had all that good food? Fortunately for us, they're willing to share their recipes.

What I want ya'll to do is try some of these recipes on your not-so-happy friends and see if you can get them to lighten up. Hey, if they don't like the coconut cream cake, something's wrong.

**Emeril and co-anchor Lisa
McRee on the set of ABC's
*Good Morning America***

Pan-Fried Catfish with Andouille Smothered White Beans

Makes 4 servings

A lot of people turn their noses up at catfish, but the South is dotted with an incredible number of ponds where the fish are farm-raised in clean water. They have a great texture and flavor, and are becoming more and more popular throughout the country. Southerners have always enjoyed fish-fries and I witnessed one firsthand when Felicia's grandfathers, Foster and Aaron, cooked us up a mess of fish one summer afternoon. Served with white beans cooked with sausage, you'll be happy, happy too.

Heat the oil in a large, heavy skillet, preferably cast-iron, over medium heat. Season the catfish fillets on both sides with Essence. Put the flour in a shallow bowl and season with Essence. Dredge the fillets in the flour, tapping off any excess. Pan-fry the fillets until golden brown, 3 to 4 minutes on each side. Drain on paper towels, then sprinkle with Essence.

Serve the catfish with the beans and pass the tartar sauce.

1 cup vegetable oil

4 catfish fillets (about 6 ounces each)

Essence to taste (page 7)

1 cup bleached all-purpose flour

1 recipe Andouille Smothered White Beans
   (page 60)

1 recipe Tartar Sauce (page 13)

continued

Andouille Smothered White Beans

Makes 8 servings

2 tablespoons vegetable oil

½ pound andouille or kielbasa sausage, finely chopped

2 cups chopped yellow onions

½ cup chopped celery

Salt and cayenne to taste

2 tablespoons chopped garlic

1 pound dried navy beans, rinsed, picked over, soaked in water to cover overnight, and drained

2 bay leaves

8 to 10 cups water, as needed

¼ cup chopped green onions (green part only)

Heat the oil in a large saucepan over medium heat. Add the andouille and cook, stirring, for 3 to 4 minutes. Add the onions and celery, season with salt and cayenne, and cook until the vegetables are slightly wilted, 2 to 3 minutes. Add the garlic, beans, and bay leaves, and enough of the water to cover, season with salt and cayenne, and bring to a boil. Reduce the heat to medium-low and simmer, uncovered, until the beans are soft and creamy, about 3 hours. Stir occasionally. Season with salt and cayenne. Remove the bay leaves, stir in the green onions, and serve hot.

Fried Green Tomatoes with Lump Crabmeat and Dave's Ravigote

Makes 6 servings

When the summer gardens are at their peak, Chef David McCelvey at NOLA, my French Quarter restaurant, likes to offer this fantastic dish. We use our local Creole tomatoes, but you can use whatever tomatoes are available in your area. Just be sure they're on the green side and not very ripe.

Creamy dressing on crunchy-fried green tomatoes—now that's a great southern treat! But you don't have to be from the South to enjoy this. Go ahead, share it and make some friends.

Combine the mayonnaise, mustard, lemon juice, onion, shallots, garlic, capers, 2 tablespoons of the parsley, chervil, and tarragon in a medium-size mixing bowl. Mix well. Add the crabmeat, then season with salt and pepper, and toss gently to mix. Cover and refrigerate for at least 1 hour.

Season the tomato slices with Essence. Heat ½ cup of the vegetable oil in a large sauté pan over medium heat. Put the flour in a shallow bowl and season with Essence. In another shallow bowl, whisk together the buttermilk and eggs. Put the cornmeal in another shallow bowl and season with Essence. Dredge the tomatoes first in the flour, coating evenly on both sides and tapping off any excess. Dip them in the egg wash and let the excess drip off. Then dredge in the cornmeal, tapping off any excess. Pan-fry several at a time in the hot oil until golden brown, about 2 minutes on each side. Add more oil to the pan as necessary to fry the remaining tomato slices. Drain on paper towels. Season with Essence.

Put the greens in a salad bowl and toss with the olive oil to coat evenly.

To serve, arrange equal amounts of the greens in the center of each serving plate. Top with fried tomato slices and the crabmeat mixture. Garnish with the remaining tablespoon parsley.

1½ cups Emeril's Mayonnaise (page 14)

2 teaspoons Dijon mustard

3 tablespoons fresh lemon juice

½ cup minced yellow onion

1 tablespoon minced shallots

1 teaspoon minced garlic

¼ cup drained capers, crushed

3 tablespoons chopped fresh parsley leaves

1 tablespoon chopped fresh chervil leaves

1 tablespoon chopped fresh tarragon leaves

1 pound lump crabmeat, picked over for shells and cartilage

Salt and freshly ground black pepper to taste

2 pounds (about 6 medium-size) Creole or other tomatoes, not very ripe and on the green side, cut crosswise into ½-inch-thick slices

Essence to taste (page 7)

½ to 1 cup vegetable oil, as needed

1 cup bleached all-purpose flour

½ cup buttermilk

2 large eggs, lightly beaten

1 cup yellow cornmeal

4 cups thinly sliced mesclun or other baby greens

3 tablespoons extra virgin olive oil

Southern Fried Chicken with Mashed Potatoes

Makes 4 servings

Lovis Downing, Felicia's grandmother, attests to the fact that she's never, I repeat never, fried chicken in anything other than the old black cast-iron skillet that's been passed down from one generation to the next in her family. The skillet is never washed. It's simply wiped clean, then lightly oiled all over before being stored until the next use.

This is their family's recipe, except that I sneaked some Essence into Arkansas and they allowed me to bam the chicken up a notch.

1½ cups vegetable oil

1 large frying chicken (about 3½ pounds), cut into 8 pieces

Salt and freshly ground black pepper to taste

2 large eggs, beaten

3 cups plus 2 tablespoons milk

Essence to taste (page 7)

3½ cups bleached all-purpose flour

1 recipe Mashed Potatoes (page 63)

Heat the oil in a heavy 9-inch skillet, preferably cast-iron, to 360°F.

Season the chicken well with salt and pepper. Combine the eggs with 2 tablespoons of the milk in a shallow bowl. Season with Essence. Put 3 cups of the flour in a large shallow bowl and season with Essence. Dredge the chicken pieces in the flour, coating each piece evenly and tapping off any excess. Dip the chicken in the egg wash, coating it completely and letting the excess drip off. Dredge again in the flour, shaking off any excess.

Fry several pieces of chicken at a time in the hot oil until golden brown, about 6 minutes on each side. Drain on paper towels, then season with Essence. When you're all done, carefully pour off the oil, leaving behind about ¼ cup of the oil along with the brown bits.

Over medium heat, add the remaining ½ cup flour and cook for 3 to 4 minutes, whisking constantly. Add the remaining 3 cups milk, ½ cup at a time, whisking constantly. Bring to a boil, then reduce the heat to medium-low. Season with salt and plenty of pepper. Cook for 8 to 10 minutes, whisking constantly. The gravy should be thick enough to coat the back of a spoon. If it is too thick, add a little water to thin it.

Serve the chicken and gravy with mashed potatoes.

Mashed Potatoes

Makes about 4 servings

Put the potatoes in a large saucepan and cover with salted water. Bring to a boil, then reduce heat to medium and cook, covered, until tender, 15 to 20 minutes. Drain, then return the potatoes to the pot. Add the butter and stir and mash until it melts completely. Add the milk and stir to mix. Season with salt and pepper and serve hot.

4 large Idaho potatoes, peeled and cubed

Salt

4 tablespoons (½ stick) unsalted butter

1 cup milk

Freshly ground white pepper to taste

Variation: *Roasted Garlic Mashed Potatoes* can be made by adding 2 tablespoons roasted garlic (page 15).

Spicy Chicken and Dumplings

Makes 6 to 8 servings

In Jonesboro, Arkansas, where Felicia's from, this dish was a staple for Sunday dinner, and I've been told that a true southern cook is judged on how good his or her dumplings are. These are from a family friend of theirs who taught them how to make these really kicked-up ones—they're outstanding!

1 hen (about 5 pounds)

Salt and freshly ground black pepper to taste

3 cups chopped yellow onions

1½ cups chopped carrots

1½ cups chopped celery

2 fresh jalapeños, seeded and chopped

6 cloves garlic, peeled

3 bay leaves

4 sprigs fresh thyme

2 cups bleached all-purpose flour

1 tablespoon plus 1 teaspoon baking powder

1 teaspoon salt

¼ cup vegetable shortening

1 cup milk

¼ cup heavy cream

¼ cup chopped green onions (green part only)

2 tablespoons chopped fresh parsley leaves

Rinse the chicken under cool water and pat dry with paper towels. Season with salt and pepper. Place the chicken in a large stockpot over medium-high heat. Add the onions, carrots, celery, jalapeños, garlic, bay leaves, thyme, and enough water to cover the hen. Season again with salt and plenty of pepper. Bring to a boil, then reduce the heat to medium-low and simmer, uncovered, until the meat begins to fall off the bones, about 2 hours. Skim off any foam that rises to the surface while cooking. Remove from the heat and cool for about 20 minutes.

Strain the stock through a fine-mesh strainer, reserving the stock, chicken, and ½ cup of the cooked vegetables. Put the stock in a smaller stockpot over medium heat and bring to a gentle boil.

Remove the meat from the chicken, discarding the skin and bones. Tear the meat into smaller pieces and add to the stockpot.

Combine the flour, baking powder, salt, and shortening in a medium-size mixing bowl. With your hands, work the shortening into the mixture until it resembles coarse crumbs. With a fork, mash the reserved cooked vegetables. Fold them and the milk, ¼ cup at a time, into the flour mixture, being careful not to overwork the dough.

Lightly dust a work surface and your hands with flour. Turn the dough out onto the floured surface. Dust the top of the dough with flour. With your fingers, lightly press the dough out very thin, about ⅛ inch thick, dusting as you work. With a sharp knife, cut the dough into strips about 4 inches long and ½ inch wide. Set aside.

Add the heavy cream to the chicken stock and stir to mix. Gently drop the dumplings into the mixture and cook, stirring occasionally, until the dumplings are cooked through, about 30 minutes. Remove the bay leaves, stir in the green onions and parsley, and serve hot.

In the weeds at Emeril's Restaurant in New Orleans

Southern Cooked Greens

Makes 8 servings

Cooked greens are another of those traditional southern dishes that I have come to love. All kinds of greens are grown in home gardens, so there's never a lack of one kind or another to throw in the pot to make a mess of greens cooked in the "pot likker," the rich, nourishing liquid that remains after the greens have been cooked. It takes a little time to wash and clean the greens, but once that's done, it's clear sailing. Oh, most southern cooks use regular white distilled vinegar, but I prefer rice wine vinegar. Whatever!

Bernard, one of my chefs at Emeril's, is the master of cooking greens and I can attest to the fact that he's probably cooked thousands of pounds of the stuff over a five-year period. They are a great side dish with fried chicken or any kind of pork.

½ pound sliced bacon, chopped

3 cups chopped yellow onions

Salt and freshly ground black pepper to taste

Pinch of cayenne

½ cup firmly packed light brown sugar

2 tablespoons minced shallots

1 tablespoon minced garlic

6 cups water

¼ cup rice wine vinegar

6 pounds assorted greens, such as mustard greens, collard greens, turnip greens, kale, and spinach, well washed and tough stems removed

Fry the bacon in a large, heavy pot over medium heat until slightly crisp. Add the onions and season with salt, black pepper, and cayenne. Cook, stirring, until the onions are wilted and golden, 6 to 7 minutes. Add the brown sugar and stir to dissolve. Add the shallots and garlic and cook, stirring, for 2 minutes. Add the water and vinegar and mix well. Begin adding the greens, about a third at a time, pressing the greens down as they begin to wilt. Season with salt and pepper. Reduce the heat to medium-low and cook, uncovered, until the greens are soft, about 1 hour and 15 minutes. Serve hot.

Jalapeño Hush Puppies

Makes about 18 hush puppies

In the South, where hush puppies are said to have originated, the story is told that these crisp, crunchy balls of corn bread, fried in deep fat, were thrown to howling puppies to make them hush, but nowadays they're a staple in southern cuisine. You'll find them served with fried seafood, fried chicken, and just about anything else that comes along.

My only complaint about some that I've tasted is that they lack a little punch, so what have I done to fix that? You got it, babe. I kicked them up with some jalapeño peppers and Essence. You're gonna like 'em.

Combine the cornmeal, flour, baking powder, salt, hot sauce, onion, and jalapeños in a medium-size mixing bowl and mix well. Add the eggs and milk and mix again.

Heat 4 inches of oil in a large, heavy, deep pot or electric fryer to 360°F. Drop in the batter a heaping tablespoon at a time, frying 6 at a time. When the hush puppies pop to the surface, roll them around in the oil with a slotted spoon to brown them evenly. Remove and drain on paper towels. Season with Essence and serve.

1½ cups yellow cornmeal

½ cup bleached all-purpose flour

1 teaspoon baking powder

1 teaspoon salt

1 teaspoon Crystal Hot Sauce or the hot sauce of your choice

¼ cup minced yellow onion

2 fresh jalapeños, seeded and minced

2 large eggs, beaten

½ cup milk

Vegetable oil for deep frying

Essence to taste (page 7)

Felicia's Biscuits

Makes 16 biscuits

What can I say, except that these are Felicia's pride and joy, and I know why—they're grrrrreat! The secret is that you have to learn the knack of not overworking the dough. Felicia calls them the true food of love because she was taught this technique by her grandmother, who patiently showed her how to work the dough gently and how to learn the feel and texture of it when you dusted them with flour and patted them out.

Felicia learned well. Have them for breakfast, or you might want to use them to sop up the white gravy served with the Southern Fried Chicken with Mashed Potatoes (page 62).

4 cups plus 2 tablespoons bleached all-
purpose flour (about 1 pound)

1½ tablespoons baking powder

1 teaspoon salt

1 cup plus 1 teaspoon vegetable shortening

1½ cups half-and-half

Preheat the oven to 375°F. Lightly grease a baking sheet with a teaspoon of shortening.

Combine 4 cups of the flour, the baking powder, and salt in a large mixing bowl and mix well. Add the shortening and work it into the dry ingredients, using your hands, until the mixture resembles coarse crumbs. Add the half-and-half and gently mix to incorporate. The dough will be sticky.

Dust your work surface with 1 tablespoon of the flour. Turn the dough onto the floured surface. Gently fold each side toward the center. Pick up the dough and dust the work surface with the remaining tablespoon flour. Return the dough to the surface and fold each side toward the center again. Turn the dough over and lightly press it out to a 1-inch thickness. Cut the biscuits using a 2¼-inch round cookie cutter. Place them on the baking sheet and bake until golden, about 30 minutes. Serve immediately.

Coconut Cream Cake

Makes one 3-layer 8-inch cake; 16 servings

Suzanne, Felicia's mama, makes this cake every Christmas. I think she should make it more often, but, then again, if she did, the family wouldn't have it to look forward to.

It's a wonderfully rich cake that is ideal for the holidays or any special event like a birthday or anniversary.

I don't know why, but the locals here have almost a fetish for coconut—it shows up in cakes, pies, puddings, pound cakes, cookies, and ice cream. I didn't see any coconut trees around, but somehow it got introduced to the state somewhere along the way and it's hung on.

Preheat the oven to 350°F. Lightly grease and flour three 8-inch round cake pans.

In a large mixing bowl with an electric mixer, cream the granulated sugar with ¼ pound (1 stick) of the butter. With the mixer running, add the oil in a steady stream. Add the egg yolks, one at a time, beating well after each addition.

Sift the flour and baking soda together into a medium-size mixing bowl. Add the ground pecans and mix. Alternately add the flour mixture and the buttermilk to the batter, mixing well. Fold in 1 cup of the coconut.

With the electric mixer, in another large mixing bowl (wash and dry the beaters well first), beat the egg whites until stiff peaks form, then fold them into the cake batter. Pour the batter evenly into the prepared pans. Bake until the

2 cups granulated sugar

½ pound (2 sticks) unsalted butter, softened

½ cup vegetable oil

5 large eggs, separated

2 cups bleached all-purpose flour

1 teaspoon baking soda

½ cup ground pecans

1 cup buttermilk

2 cups frozen unsweetened flaked coconut, defrosted

One 8-ounce package cream cheese, softened

1½ pounds confectioners' sugar (about 6 cups), sifted

1 teaspoon pure vanilla extract

2 tablespoons milk

1 cup pecan pieces

center springs back when touched, 25 to 30 minutes. Remove from the oven and cool on wire racks. After the cakes have cooled, invert them onto sheets of parchment paper. Set aside.

With an electric mixer, in another large mixing bowl (wash and dry those beaters), cream the remaining ¼ pound (1 stick) butter with the cream cheese. Add the sifted confectioners' sugar, about ½ cup at a time, mixing after each addition. Add the vanilla and milk and mix well. Fold in the pecans. Spread a thin layer of the frosting on top of each cake layer. Place the layers of cake on top of each other and ice the sides of the cake with the remaining frosting. Sprinkle the top of the cake with the remaining 1 cup coconut.

Janet Arena, makeup artist for *Emeril Live*, getting Emeril ready for the show

Fried Sweet Potato Pies

Makes 1 dozen

If you happen to pass through Jonesboro, Arkansas, be sure to make a pit stop at Couch's Barbecue, known not only for its barbecue but for its chocolate fried pies. I was so impressed, I was inspired to make these fried pies using sweet potatoes, which we have in abundance in Louisiana.

Preheat the oven to 375°F.

In a large mixing bowl, toss the sweet potatoes with the oil, salt, and pepper. Put them on a baking sheet and roast until tender, about 1½ hours. Remove from the oven and let cool completely.

In a large mixing bowl, combine the flour, salt, and 2 teaspoons of the granulated sugar. Add the shortening and work it in with your hands until the mixture resembles coarse crumbs. Add the ice water, 1 tablespoon at a time, working it in with your hands. Add only as much as you need to make a smooth ball. Wrap the dough in plastic wrap and refrigerate for at least 30 minutes.

Turn the dough onto a lightly floured work surface. Roll it out into a rectangle about 24 × 8 inches and ⅛ inch thick. With a sharp knife, cut 12 four-inch squares. Set aside.

1½ pounds sweet potatoes

1 tablespoon vegetable oil

Salt and freshly ground black pepper to taste

2 cups bleached all-purpose flour

Pinch of salt

1 tablespoon plus 2 teaspoons granulated sugar

¾ cup vegetable shortening

3 to 4 tablespoons ice water

1 large egg yolk

¼ cup Steen's 100% Pure Cane Syrup

1 teaspoon ground cinnamon

¼ teaspoon grated nutmeg

2 splashes of bourbon

Vegetable oil for deep frying

1 cup confectioners' sugar

2 to 3 tablespoons milk

Peel the potatoes and put the flesh in a large mixing bowl. Add the egg yolk, cane syrup, cinnamon, nutmeg, and a splash of the bourbon and mix well. Place about ¼ cup of the filling in the center of each pastry square. Fold one corner to the opposite corner to form a triangle. Using the tines of a fork, crimp the edges to seal.

Heat 4 inches of oil in a large, heavy pot or electric fryer to 360°F. Fry the pies, 2 or 3 at a time, until golden brown, turning them once. Remove the pies and drain on paper towels. Sprinkle with the remaining 2 teaspoons granulated sugar.

Combine the confectioners' sugar, the milk, and the remaining splash of bourbon in a medium-size mixing bowl and mix until smooth. Drizzle over the hot pies and serve immediately.

Hello Dolly Ice Cream Sandwich

Makes 10 servings

Aunt Gram and Uncle Consie, Felicia's relatives, have huge pecan trees on their property near Jonesboro, Arkansas. They have so many pecans that they had to come up with some ideas of what to do with them and here's one. First, you make a bunch of bar cookies and keep them in an airtight container. When company drops by, you get out some chocolate ice cream and make these ice cream sandwiches. Problem solved.

Hey now, these are rich—bet you can eat only one!

½ pound (2 sticks) unsalted butter, melted

4 cups graham cracker crumbs

2 tablespoons firmly packed light brown
   sugar

2 cups pecan pieces

One 12-ounce bag semisweet chocolate
   chips

One 7-ounce bag sweetened flaked coconut

One 10-ounce bag peanut butter chips

Two 14-ounce cans sweetened
   condensed milk

10 large scoops Chocolate Ice Cream
   (page 241), softened a bit, or use regular
   store-bought ice cream

½ cup Chocolate Sauce (page 73)

Preheat the oven to 350°F.

Combine the butter, graham cracker crumbs, and brown sugar in a large bowl, mixing well. Press the mixture against the bottom and sides of a 12 × 17-inch baking pan. Sprinkle the pecans over the crust. Sprinkle the chocolate chips over the pecans. Sprinkle the coconut over the chocolate chips. Sprinkle the peanut butter chips over the coconut. Drizzle the condensed milk evenly over the top of the chips. Bake until the edges are brown and crusty and the coconut is lightly toasted, 20 to 25 minutes. Remove from the oven and let cool completely.

Cut into 20 squares. Put 1 piece on each of 10 plates. Place a scoop of ice cream on top of each cookie. Top the ice cream with the remaining cookies. Drizzle with the chocolate sauce and serve.

Chocolate Sauce

Makes 1½ cups

Combine the half-and-half, butter, and corn syrup in a small, heavy saucepan over medium heat. Cook, stirring, until a thin paperlike skin appears on the top. *Do not boil.* Add the chocolate chips and vanilla and stir until the chocolate melts and the mixture is smooth. Remove from the heat and let cool.

The sauce can be refrigerated in an airtight container for several days, but it must be returned to room temperature before using.

¾ **cup half-and-half**

1 **tablespoon unsalted butter**

2 **tablespoons light corn syrup**

One 12-ounce bag semisweet chocolate chips

¼ **teaspoon pure vanilla extract**

Executive chef Susan Stockton and the *Emeril Live* kitchen brigade

73

Emerilized Starters

I like the idea of appetizers, a little something before the

main feature of a meal, to get the

gastric juices flowing. When friends

come over, setting out some

munchies or starters gives everyone

a little time to enjoy a glass of wine,

do a little visiting, relax.

For the guests at my

restaurants who choose to allow the

chef carte blanche in preparing their meals, or perhaps for

guests celebrating a special occasion, the kitchen sends

out what we call an *amuse-bouche,* which literally translates into "amuses the mouth." In the old, old days, the chef would present to the king (I told you it was in the old days) a small taste of the meal that he was preparing to get his approval before serving the meal to his guests. These days we serve this little tidbit to whet the taste buds.

The starters in this chapter are way over the top, but who wants to nibble on chips and dips all the time? I think these are fun because taste-teasers are a way to introduce new ideas and get everybody excited about what's coming up in the meal. Now, don't you go giving your guests hot dogs after these starters!

Cook Richard Graham and sous-chef Tom Wolfe at Emeril's Restaurant in New Orleans

Cheese Fondue

Makes about 2 cups; 4 servings

Fondue *is the French word for "melt." Fondue au fromage, a classic dish we learned from the Swiss, consists of melted cheese (usually Gruyère) combined with wine, kirsch (a cherry brandy), and seasonings. It was quite popular in the United States in the 1960s and I'm glad it's making a comeback.*

Go and get yourself a fondue pot at one of those fancy cooking shops, make some fondue, make some friends. My friend Rock likes to tell the story about how he used to get on a girl's good side back in college: He'd invite her over to his house to eat fondue out of his avocado-green enameled fondue pot. What a man!

Rub the inside of a medium-size saucepan with the garlic and discard. Add the wine and lemon juice and heat for 1 minute over medium heat. Add the cheese cubes to the saucepan and cook the mixture, stirring constantly, until the cheese melts completely, 2 to 3 minutes.

Combine the cornstarch and kirsch in a small bowl. Stir into the cheese mixture and continue to cook until it is smooth and slightly thick, about 3 minutes. Season with salt, pepper, and nutmeg.

Serve in a fondue pot, or use a flameproof dish set over a small candle. Serve with a platter of accompaniments.

1 clove garlic, crushed

1 cup dry white wine

3 tablespoons fresh lemon juice

8 ounces Gruyère cheese, cut into small cubes

2 teaspoons cornstarch

1 tablespoon kirsch, or other cherry brandy

Salt and freshly ground black pepper to taste

⅛ teaspoon freshly grated nutmeg

Accompaniments (page 78)

continued

Accompaniments to Cheese Fondue

Makes about 4 servings

½ pound new or small red potatoes, scrubbed and quartered

1 bunch baby carrots, peeled

3 ripe plum tomatoes, halved lengthwise

1 medium-size yellow onion, peeled and quartered

¼ cup olive oil

Salt and freshly ground black pepper to taste

One 12-inch-long loaf French bread, cut into bite-size cubes

Wooden skewers or fondue forks

Preheat the oven to 400°F. Line 2 baking sheets with parchment or waxed paper.

In a large mixing bowl, toss the potatoes, carrots, tomatoes, and onion with 2 tablespoons of the olive oil. Season with salt and pepper. Put the vegetables on the prepared baking sheets. Roast the vegetables until golden brown and very tender, 20 to 25 minutes.

Toss the bread cubes with the remaining 2 tablespoons olive oil. Season with salt and pepper. Place them on a baking sheet and bake until golden, 3 to 4 minutes.

Arrange the roasted vegetables and bread on a platter and serve with the fondue, dunking them in the cheese with a skewer or fondue fork.

Goat Cheese and Leek Cake with Lentil Salad

Makes 4 servings

To satisfy all you vegetarians, I put this on the menu at Emeril's. But even nonvegetarians have taken a liking to it and you'll understand why once you've tasted it. Chèvre is the fancy-schmancy word for goat cheese. Call it whatever you want, hey, I don't care—it still tastes the same, whatever you call it. And does it taste good! It has a tart flavor that combines well with the mild and subtle leeks. Remember to slit the leeks from top to bottom and wash well to remove all the dirt trapped between the leaves.

I added the lentils because they're good and good for you—rich in iron and vitamins A and B.

Heat 2 tablespoons of the olive oil in a medium-size sauté pan over medium heat. Add the leeks, season with salt and pepper, and cook, stirring, for 2 minutes. Add the garlic and cook for 1 minute. Pour the mixture into a medium-size mixing bowl and stir in the cheese and wine. Season again with salt and pepper and mix well. Form the mixture into 8 cakes, about ¼ cup each, about 1½ inches thick.

Put the flour in a shallow bowl and season with Essence. Put the eggs in another shallow bowl. In a third shallow bowl put the bread crumbs and season with Essence. Dredge the cakes first in the seasoned flour, coating completely and tapping off any excess, then dip the cakes in the eggs, letting the excess drip off. Dredge in the seasoned bread crumbs, coating both sides.

In another medium-size sauté pan, heat the remaining 2 tablespoons olive oil over medium heat. Pan-fry the cakes until golden brown, 2 to 3 minutes on each side. Drain on paper towels. Sprinkle with Essence and keep warm.

¼ cup olive oil

1 cup chopped leeks (white part only)

Salt and freshly ground black pepper to taste

2 teaspoons chopped garlic

1 pound *chèvre* cheese, crumbled

2 tablespoons dry white wine

1 cup bleached all-purpose flour

Essence to taste (page 7)

2 large eggs, beaten

1 cup fine dried bread crumbs

½ pound sliced bacon, chopped

½ cup chopped yellow onions

1 cup dried lentils, rinsed, picked over, and boiled in water to cover until slightly tender, then drained and cooled under cold running water

¼ cup balsamic vinegar

2 tablespoons thinly sliced fresh basil leaves

1 tablespoon snipped fresh chives

In another medium-size sauté pan, fry the bacon until crisp. Add the onions and lentils, season with salt and pepper, and cook, stirring, for 2 minutes. Stir in the vinegar and basil and remove from the heat.

To serve, place 2 of the cakes in the center of each dinner plate. Spoon the lentil mixture around the cakes and garnish with the chives.

Hearts of Palm Strudels
with Rémoulade Dipping Sauce

Makes 4 servings

Heart of palm is the edible inner portion of the stem of the cabbage palm tree, which grows in many tropical climates and, get this, it's Florida's state tree. Now aren't you glad you know that? I don't care where they come from, I just know that they're one of my favorite foods. Usually you find them in salads, but I like the flavor and texture so much I keep experimenting with them. One day I wrapped them in phyllo dough, then doused them with a spicy rémoulade sauce, a New Orleans favorite, and they got rave reviews. See what you think.

8 canned hearts of palm

Salt and pepper to taste

8 sheets phyllo dough (look for it in the frozen foods section of your supermarket)

6 tablespoons unsalted butter, melted

¾ cup Rémoulade Sauce (page 166)

Essence to taste (page 7)

2 tablespoons chopped fresh parsley leaves

¼ cup grated Parmigiano-Reggiano cheese

Preheat the oven to 400°F. Line a baking sheet with parchment or waxed paper. Season the hearts of palm with salt and pepper. Set aside. Stack the phyllo sheets on top of one another and cut down the middle, making 16 sheets. Place 2 sheets together, one on top of another (8 stacks of 2 sheets). Brush the top sheets lightly with butter. Spread each top sheet with 1 tablespoon rémoulade sauce. Place 1 heart of palm at the bottom end of the sheets. Fold in the sides and roll all the way to the end like an egg roll. Place seam side down on the baking sheet. Brush all with the remaining butter and sprinkle with Essence. Bake until golden, 10 to 12 minutes.

To serve, spoon a small amount of the remaining rémoulade in the center of each plate. Place 2 strudels on top of each pool of sauce and sprinkle with the parsley and cheese.

Truffle Chips

Makes 4 to 6 servings

In New Orleans we have Zapp's potato chips, made in nearby Gramercy, located on the mighty Mississippi River, which come in many different flavors, and I love them all. What makes them so good is that whatever flavor you try, your mouth is bammed with taste—my kind of chip. I decided to make my own and kick them up with a little truffle oil. Yeah, babe!

If you have one, use a mandoline to slice the potatoes paper-thin. Soak the slices in cool water for 30 minutes and drain. Pat dry completely with paper towels.

In a large, heavy, deep pot or electric fryer, heat 4 inches of vegetable oil to 360°F. Deep-fry the potatoes until golden brown, 3 to 5 minutes. Drain on paper towels. Season with salt and pepper.

Transfer the potatoes to a large mixing bowl and toss with the truffle oil and cheese. Serve immediately.

2 pounds new or small red potatoes, scrubbed

Vegetable oil for deep frying

Salt and freshly ground black pepper to taste

1 tablespoon white truffle oil (available in specialty food stores)

1 cup freshly grated Parmigiano-Reggiano cheese

General manager Tony Lott inspecting the waiters at Emeril's Restaurant before service

Prosciutto and Mushroom Ravioli with Fried Sage

Makes 4 servings

Proscuitto is ham that has been cured by salting and air-drying, as opposed to being smoked. Now you can really impress your friends with this tidbit of information.

Italian food always excites me for the simple reason that the ingredients are my kind of stuff–prosciutto, mushrooms, cheese–see what I mean?

If you can't find fresh pasta sheets, use your favorite pasta recipe and make your own.

2 tablespoons plus 1 teaspoon olive oil

2 tablespoons minced shallots

⅓ pound assorted exotic mushrooms, such as oysters, shiitakes, and/or chanterelles, wiped clean and sliced (about 2 cups)

Salt and freshly ground black pepper to taste

2 teaspoons chopped garlic

½ pound sliced prosciutto, julienned

1 cup freshly grated Parmigiano-Reggiano cheese

6 cups water

1 sheet (12 inches square) fresh pasta (available at specialty markets)

2 tablespoons white truffle oil (available at specialty markets)

4 tablespoons (½ stick) unsalted butter

12 fresh sage leaves

1 tablespoon snipped fresh chives

Heat 2 tablespoons of the olive oil in a medium-size sauté pan over medium heat. Add the shallots and cook, stirring, for 30 seconds. Add the mushrooms and cook, stirring, for 2 minutes, then season with salt and pepper. Add the garlic and prosciutto, and cook, stirring, for 1 minute. Remove from the heat and pour into a medium-size mixing bowl. Stir in ¾ cup of the cheese and let cool completely.

Place the water in a large saucepan, salt it, and add the remaining 1 teaspoon olive oil. Bring to a boil. With a sharp knife, cut the pasta sheet into sixteen 3-inch squares.

Using your fingers, lightly wet the edges of each square.

Spoon 1 tablespoon of the mushroom mixture into the center of 8 of the squares. Place the remaining pasta squares over the fillings and press the edges with the tines of a fork to seal.

Drop the ravioli into the boiling water and cook until they rise to the surface, 3 to 4 minutes, then cook for another 2 minutes. With a slotted spoon, remove the ravioli and drain on paper towels.

Toss the ravioli with the truffle oil in a large mixing bowl. Season with salt and pepper.

Heat the butter in a large sauté pan over medium heat. Add the sage leaves and cook for 30 seconds. Add the ravioli to the pan and cook, stirring, for 1 minute.

Serve in a shallow bowl garnished with the remaining ¼ cup cheese and the chives.

**Sommelier Julio Hernandez in the
wine room at Emeril's Restaurant**

Gnocchi au Gratin with Orleans Cream Sauce

Makes 6 servings

When I'm in New York City, I go to a place called Saint Ambroeus, where they take great care of me, and where I've eaten some of the best gnocchi ever. When I'm away from the city, I have to make my own gnocchi and I give it my own stroke, like this, served with a New Orleans–style sauce.

1 pound Idaho potatoes, peeled and diced

1 teaspoon salt

2 tablespoons olive oil

1 pound tasso or smoked sausage, finely chopped

1 cup chopped green onions (green part only)

1 cup peeled, seeded, and chopped tomatoes, fresh or canned

2 tablespoons minced shallots

1 tablespoon minced garlic

Essence to taste (page 7)

1 quart heavy cream

1 tablespoon Worcestershire sauce

1 tablespoon Crystal Hot Sauce or the hot sauce of your choice

4 tablespoons (½ stick) unsalted butter

1 cup bleached all-purpose flour

2 large egg yolks

Salt and freshly ground black pepper to taste

2 quarts salted water for cooking the gnocchi

¾ cup freshly grated Parmigiano-Reggiano cheese

1 tablespoon snipped fresh chives

Preheat the oven to 400°F.

Put the potatoes in a large saucepan and add enough water to cover. Add the salt and bring to a boil. Reduce the heat to medium and simmer, covered, until they are fork tender, about 10 minutes. Drain. Return the potatoes to the pan over high heat and let sit for several minutes to dry completely. Push the potatoes through a food mill or potato ricer. Let cool.

Heat the olive oil in a medium-size sauté pan over medium heat. Add the tasso and cook, stirring often, for 2 to 3 minutes. Add the green onions, tomatoes, shallots, and garlic. Season with Essence. Cook, stirring, for 1 minute. Add the heavy cream, Worcestershire, and hot sauce. Bring to a boil, then reduce the heat to medium and simmer, stirring occasionally, until the cream thickens and reduces by one third, 6 to 8 minutes. Set aside and keep warm.

Put the potatoes in a large mixing bowl and stir in 2 tablespoons of the butter, the flour, and egg yolks. Blend until the mixture is smooth. Season with salt and pepper.

Flour your hands and your work surface and keep them dusted throughout the rolling and cutting process. Form the mixture into a ball. Place the ball on the floured surface. Divide the dough evenly into 2 balls and roll each into a log about 1 inch thick and 20 inches long. Cut the logs crosswise into ½-inch-thick slices. With your index finger, press each piece of dough against the tines of a fork to form a decorative design.

In a large saucepan, bring the salted water to a gentle boil. Drop in the gnocchi several at a time and cook for 5 minutes. The gnocchi are done when they float to the surface and cook for another 2 minutes. Remove the gnocchi from the water with a slotted spoon and drain completely. Season with salt and pepper.

Lightly grease a large rectangular baking dish with the remaining 2 tablespoons butter. Lay the gnocchi on the bottom of the pan. Pour the sauce over the gnocchi and sprinkle with the cheese. Bake until the top is golden brown, 8 to 10 minutes. Before serving, garnish with the chives.

Sous-chef Chris Wilson at Emeril's Restaurant in New Orleans

Stuffed Morels with Crawfish Rémoulade

Makes 4 servings

The morel belongs to the same fungus species as the truffle and is an edible wild mushroom. Its spongy, honey-combed, cone-shape cap ranges in size from 2 to 4 inches high and in color from a rich tan to an extremely dark brown. The flavor of the morel is smoky, earthy, and nutty. The darker the mushroom, the stronger the flavor. Cultivated morels may appear sporadically throughout the year in specialty markets. Morels are available fresh, dried, and canned.

When we can get them fresh at Emeril's, this is one of the ways we fix 'em.

1 pound peeled crawfish tails

¼ cup minced shallots

¾ cup chopped green onions (green part only)

4 teaspoons minced garlic

½ cup minced celery

½ cup Creole or whole-grain mustard

2 cups Emeril's Mayonnaise (page 14)

3 tablespoons fresh lemon juice

Pinch of dried ground coriander

1 teaspoon Zatarain's Concentrated Crab & Shrimp Boil (optional)

1 tablespoon Crystal Hot Sauce or the hot sauce of your choice

Salt and freshly ground black pepper to taste

2 tablespoons unsalted butter

Put ½ pound of the crawfish in a food processor and pulse 2 to 3 times to chop coarsely. Add 2 tablespoons of the shallots, ½ cup of the green onions, 2 teaspoons of the garlic, and the celery, and pulse several times to mix well. Add the mustard, mayonnaise, lemon juice, coriander, crab boil, and hot sauce, pulse several times to mix, and season with salt and pepper.

Melt the butter in a large sauté pan over medium heat. Add the remaining 2 tablespoons of shallots and the chopped morels. Cook, stirring, for 1 minute, and season with salt and pepper. Add the remaining 2 teaspoons garlic, the remaining ½ pound crawfish tails, and the remaining ¼ cup green onions. Season with Essence and cook, stirring, for 2 minutes. Remove from the heat and stir in the bread crumbs. Let cool completely.

Make a small slit on 1 side of each of the whole morels. Stuff each with about 2 teaspoons of the stuffing. Press to close.

In a small mixing bowl, combine the flour and cornstarch and season with Essence. Whisk to blend. In a medium-size mixing bowl, whisk the egg and soda water together to blend. Add the flour mixture to the egg mixture and whisk until smooth.

In a large, deep, heavy pot or electric fryer, heat 4 inches of vegetable oil to 360°F.

1 cup chopped fresh morels (about 8 medium-size), plus 12 large fresh morels, wiped clean
Essence to taste (page 7)
¼ cup fine dried bread crumbs
⅔ cup bleached all-purpose flour
½ cup cornstarch
1 large egg, beaten
1 cup ice-cold soda (seltzer) water
Vegetable oil for deep frying

Dip the stuffed morels, 3 or 4 at a time, in the batter, letting the excess drip off. Fry in batches in the hot oil for 2 to 3 minutes, stirring constantly to brown evenly. Drain on paper towels.

Sprinkle with Essence and serve the morels with the crawfish sauce on the side.

Emeril Live cameramen Jay Eidt, Eric "Buck" Buchanan, and Phil Salanto

Crawfish Beignets with Tomato and Corn Tartar Sauce

Makes about 2 dozen

In late spring in Louisiana, we can get fresh crawfish, tomatoes, and corn, all of which are ideal for these savory beignets. The crunchy, hot fritters are great with the cool tartar sauce.

1 tablespoon olive oil

1 pound peeled crawfish tails, coarsely chopped

Essence to taste (page 7)

½ cup finely chopped yellow onions

¼ cup finely chopped red bell pepper

1 tablespoon plus 1 teaspoon chopped garlic

¼ cup plus 2 tablespoons chopped green onions (green part only)

1 medium-size ear fresh sweet corn, husk removed

1 teaspoon vegetable oil

Salt and freshly ground black pepper to taste

1 cup Emeril's Mayonnaise (page 14)

¼ cup peeled, seeded, and chopped tomatoes, fresh or canned

3¼ cups bleached all-purpose flour

2 teaspoons baking powder

3 large eggs

1½ cups milk

1 tablespoon finely chopped fresh parsley leaves

Heat the oven to 400°F.

Heat the olive oil in a large sauté pan over medium heat. Add the chopped crawfish and season with Essence. Cook, stirring, for 2 minutes. Add the onions and pepper and season again with Essence. Cook, stirring, for 1 minute. Remove the pan from the heat and stir in 1 tablespoon of the garlic and ¼ cup of the green onions. Let cool completely.

Rub the ear of corn with the vegetable oil and season with salt and pepper. Put it in a pie tin and roast for 20 minutes, turning the ear every 5 minutes. Remove from the oven, let cool, and, with a sharp knife, cut the kernels from the cob.

In a medium-size mixing bowl, combine the mayonnaise, tomatoes, corn, the remaining 1 teaspoon garlic, and the remaining 2 tablespoons green onions and blend well. Season with salt and pepper. Cover and refrigerate for about 20 minutes.

In a large mixing bowl, combine the flour, baking powder, eggs, and milk and whisk until smooth. Season with salt and pepper, then fold in the crawfish mixture. Stir in the parsley and hot sauce, and cover and refrigerate for 30 minutes.

2 teaspoons Crystal Hot Sauce or the hot
   sauce of your choice
Vegetable oil for frying
1 tablespoon snipped fresh chives

In a large, heavy, deep pot or an electric fryer, heat 4 inches of the vegetable oil to 360°F.

Carefully drop the batter, a heaping tablespoon at a time, into the hot oil. You should be able to do about 6 at a time. Fry the beignets, turning them around in the oil with a spoon, until golden brown, 3 to 4 minutes. Drain on paper towels, then season with Essence.

To serve, spread the tartar sauce in the center of a serving platter. Mound the beignets over the sauce and sprinkle with the chives.

Paul Fontenette, crew chief at Emeril's Restaurant in New Orleans

Caramelized Salmon with Cilantro Potato Salad

Makes 8 servings

Salmon and potatoes are two of my favorite things—served separately or together, I love 'em. I like the idea of caramelizing certain foods. It looks good and tastes fabulous. Be forewarned: when you put the sugar-coated fish in the pan, it's going to smoke up the kitchen and maybe set off your smoke alarm! Get your windows open and your kitchen fan on.

The pungent fragrance and the bright green leaves of the cilantro give a lot of bam to the combination.

1 cup Emeril's Mayonnaise (page 14)

¼ cup chopped fresh cilantro leaves

1 teaspoon chopped garlic

⅓ cup finely chopped red onion

⅓ cup finely chopped celery

Salt and freshly ground black pepper to taste

2 pounds new or small red potatoes, quartered, boiled in salted water to cover until fork tender, and drained

4 salmon fillets (about 4 ounces each), cut in half crosswise

1 cup sugar

2 tablespoons olive oil

Sprigs of fresh cilantro and parsley

In a large mixing bowl, combine the mayonnaise, cilantro, garlic, onion, and celery, mix well, and season with salt and pepper. Fold in the potatoes carefully so as not to break them up. Season again with salt and pepper. Cover and refrigerate for 1 hour.

Season each salmon fillet with salt and pepper, then dredge each in the sugar, tapping off any excess. Heat the olive oil in a large sauté pan over medium-high heat. Add the fillets and cook until the sugar caramelizes, 2 to 3 minutes on each side.

To serve, place the potato salad in the center of a serving platter. Lay the salmon on top of the salad, and garnish with cilantro and parsley sprigs.

Smoked Salmon and Brie Strudel

Makes about 12 appetizer servings

*H*ere's salmon again, but this time smoked and combined with creamy Brie cheese. While it's baking, the aroma will knock your socks off, and when you taste it, you'll know why I love this combination.

Preheat the oven to 400°F. Line a baking sheet with parchment or waxed paper.

In a large mixing bowl, whisk together the dry mustard, sugar, vinegar, yellow mustard, sesame oil, soy sauce, paprika, and cayenne. Mix thoroughly and set aside.

Lay the 3 sheets of phyllo dough, stacked one on top of each other, on a flat surface. Brush the edges of the top sheet of dough with 1 tablespoon of the melted butter. In the center of the top sheet of dough, spread one fourth of the mustard sauce in a circle. Sprinkle with the herbs. Set aside.

Season the cheese and salmon slices with salt and pepper. Wrap the Brie with the sliced salmon, allowing the salmon slices to overlap. Place the salmon-wrapped Brie in the center of the mustard-herb circle. Fold two of the ends of phyllo in toward the center of the dough. Fold the remaining ends in, forming a package, and seal it completely. Place it, seam side down, on the baking sheet. Lightly brush the dough with the remaining 2 tablespoons melted butter. Bake until golden brown, 6 to 8 minutes. Cool for several minutes before slicing to serve.

Toss the bread slices with the olive oil in a large mixing bowl. Season with salt and pepper. Lay the croutons on a baking sheet and bake until golden brown, 4 to 6 minutes.

Serve the cheese on a platter with the croutons and the remaining mustard sauce.

---

3 tablespoons dry mustard

½ cup sugar

¼ cup rice wine vinegar

¼ cup prepared yellow mustard

1 tablespoon sesame oil

2 tablespoons soy sauce

1½ teaspoons sweet paprika

Cayenne to taste

3 sheets phyllo dough (look for it in the
    frozen foods section of the supermarket)

3 tablespoons unsalted butter, melted

¼ cup chopped fresh herbs, such as basil,
    chervil, parsley, and tarragon

One ½-pound wheel Brie cheese

½ pound sliced smoked salmon

Twenty-four 1-inch-thick slices French
    baguette

¼ cup olive oil

Tempura Soft-Shells with Oriental Salad and Citrus Gastrique

Makes 4 servings

Tempura is a traditional Japanese batter, and the lightest of all batters. I love Asian food and this classic coating, teamed up with local Louisiana soft-shell crabs, the sesame flavor from the salad, and the sweetness from the gastrique, makes for an unbeatable combination of flavors. What's a gastrique? It's simply equal parts sugar and vinegar reduced to a syrup consistency. The juice from lemons, limes, and blood oranges can be substituted for the vinegar if you want to experiment with other flavors.

1 cup sugar

½ cup rice wine vinegar

¼ cup fresh orange juice

¼ cup fresh lemon juice

1 tablespoon olive oil

½ cup thin red bell pepper strips

½ cup thin yellow bell pepper strips

¼ cup chopped red onion

Salt and freshly ground black pepper to
   taste

½ cup thin Chinese cabbage strips

2 teaspoons chopped garlic

¼ pound angel hair pasta, cooked
   according to package instructions and
   tossed with 1 tablespoon olive oil

2 tablespoons sesame oil

1 tablespoon soy sauce

2 tablespoons chopped fresh cilantro leaves

¼ cup chopped peanuts

4 large soft-shell crabs

Vegetable oil for deep frying

In a small nonreactive saucepan, combine the sugar, vinegar, and fruit juices, bring to a boil, and cook until reduced by three-fourths, or the mixture has thickened like syrup. Remove from the heat and pour the mixture into a small glass bowl. Let cool completely.

Heat the olive oil in a medium-size sauté pan over medium heat. Add the bell peppers and onion and season with salt and pepper. Cook, stirring for 2 minutes. Add the cabbage and cook, stirring, for 2 minutes. Season again with salt and pepper. Remove from the heat and stir in the garlic. Pour the mixture into a medium-size mixing bowl and let cool. Add the pasta and toss well. Add the sesame oil, soy sauce, cilantro, and peanuts, season with salt and pepper, and toss again. Set aside.

To clean the crabs, use a pair of kitchen shears to cut them across the face. Remove the eye sockets and the lower mouth. Season with salt and pepper.

In a large, heavy, deep pot or an electric fryer heat 6 inches of vegetable oil to 360°F.

In a medium-size mixing bowl, combine the flour, cornstarch, egg, and soda water and mix well to make a smooth batter. Season with salt and pepper. Dip each crab into the tempura batter, shaking off any excess. Carefully holding the top of each crab, drag the legs through the oil for 5 seconds to allow the individual legs to fry separately. Then carefully flip the crabs top side down into the oil. Fry until golden brown, 2 to 3 minutes. Turn the crabs over with tongs and continue frying for another 2 to 3 minutes. Drain on paper towels. Season with Essence.

⅔ cup bleached all-purpose flour

½ cup cornstarch

1 large egg, beaten

1 cup ice-cold soda (seltzer) water

Essence to taste (page 7)

1 tablespoon finely chopped fresh parsley leaves

To serve, mound the cabbage mixture in the center of a platter. Arrange the crabs around the cabbage mixture. Drizzle the gastrique over the entire platter and garnish with the parsley.

Emerilized Tuna Tartare

Makes 4 servings

Once or twice a year I spend some time in Hawaii and I love the food, so here's my kicked-up version of tuna tartare. Ahi is the Hawaiian name for yellowfin tuna, but, hey, you can use any really fresh fish to make this.

If you do use tuna, remember it has to be fresh, fresh, fresh!

Wasabi powder (Chinese horseradish) and wonton wrappers are available in many Asian and other specialty markets.

To fry the wonton wrappers, heat 2 inches of vegetable oil in a large skillet over medium-high heat. Fry two at a time until golden brown, about 1 minute. Remove and drain on paper towels and sprinkle with salt and pepper.

1 pound sashimi-grade ahi

Salt and freshly ground white pepper to
    taste

2 tablespoons minced shallots

2 tablespoons finely chopped fresh parsley
    leaves

1 tablespoon Dijon mustard

6 tablespoons fresh lemon juice

¼ cup extra virgin olive oil

1 medium-size ripe Haas avocado, peeled,
    pitted, and cut into small dice

1 cup sour cream

2 teaspoons wasabi powder dissolved in
    2 tablespoons water

12 fried wonton wrappers

¼ cup small-diced red onion

Cut the ahi into small dice and put it in a medium-size mixing bowl. Season with salt and pepper. Whisk the shallots, parsley, mustard, lemon juice, and olive oil together in a small mixing bowl and season with salt and pepper. Toss the tuna with the vinaigrette and mix well. Cover and refrigerate the mixture for at least 1 hour.

Season the avocado dice with salt and pepper.

Combine the sour cream with the wasabi mixture and season with salt and pepper.

To serve, place a wonton in the center of an appetizer plate. Spread about a tablespoon of the tartare on top of the wonton. Spoon a dollop of the wasabi cream on top of the tartare, then scatter around a little of the avocado and red onion. Top with a wonton and repeat with tartare, wasabi cream, avocado, and red onion. Top with a third wonton, then drizzle with sesame oil and dot with the caviar and chives. Repeat the process for the other 3 sandwiches.

2 tablespoons sesame oil

1 ounce sevruga caviar

1 tablespoon snipped fresh chives

Cameraman on the
***Emeril Live* set**

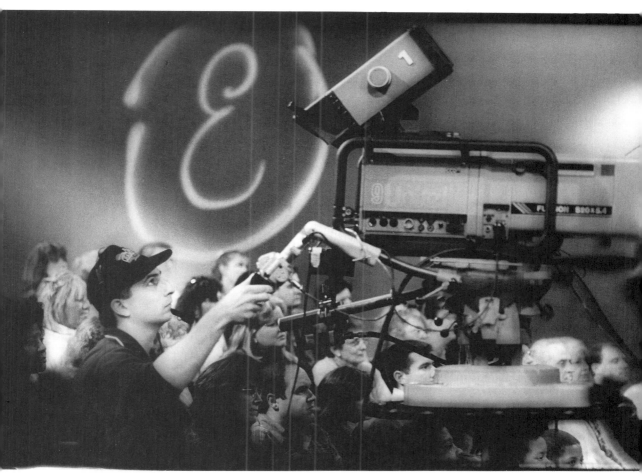

Salad Sensations

Don't you just hate those drab salads that have just plain

old lettuce and slices of tomatoes

that look like orange rubber? I

know I do. Hey, salads don't have

to be boring, they can be wild!

Over the years I've made a solemn

promise never to serve ho-hum

salads either at my restaurants or in my home. You just

have to be a little creative. Look around, prowl the

produce section, and think about adding cheeses or

meats or seafood. There's a wealth of fresh, exotic, and

unusual ingredients on the market just waiting to be used. Experiment—try some of these out on your mother-in-law, or your boss. They'll tell you what works, believe me.

These are some of my tried-and-true recipes that I've used over the years and I've never had one sent back—yet!

Leo Verde, manager, at the
pre-meal meeting at Emeril's
Restaurant in New Orleans

Carpaccio and Artichoke Salad

Makes 4 servings

Carpaccio is an appetizer of raw beef sliced very thin—really shaved—and served with drizzles of olive oil and lemon juice, or with a mayonnaise-type sauce. I've heard it was made famous by Harry's American Bar in Venice, where it was created for a countess who could not eat cooked meat. Whatever! Here's a version, served with artichokes, that I enjoy at a favorite spot of mine in New York City.

Pound the slices of filet between 2 sheets of plastic wrap with a meat mallet until paper thin. Arrange 2 slices on a serving plate and season with salt and pepper.

Divide the artichoke slices into 4 equal portions and arrange on top of the beef. Season with salt and pepper. Drizzle each plate with 2 tablespoons of the olive oil, season with salt and pepper, then squeeze a quarter of the lemon over each.

With a cheese shaver or vegetable peeler, shave the cheese over each serving. Serve immediately.

8 ounces filet mignon steak, cut evenly into
    8 thin slices
Salt and freshly ground black pepper to
    taste
1 cup thinly sliced artichoke bottoms
½ cup extra virgin olive oil
1 large lemon, quartered
One 4-ounce block Parmigiano-Reggiano
    cheese

Melissa Roberts,
associate producer for
Emeril Live

Herb-Tossed White Asparagus, Fresh Crabmeat, and Grilled Radicchio Salad

Makes 4 servings

I love asparagus, not just the fresh, tender green ones, but also the large white ones favored by Europeans. They are becoming more and more available in the United States, and when I can get them, I love to play around experimenting. This is one salad I especially like. The combination of the asparagus, crabmeat, and radicchio makes it pretty, too.

White asparagus has a thick, woody skin that must be peeled, which is easily done with a vegetable peeler or small knife. Trim off the woody end of the stem as well.

If you don't have a grill, you can skip this part of the procedure. You can thinly slice the radicchio and toss it with salt and pepper, then arrange it with the asparagus and sprinkle with the crabmeat and proceed with the rest of the recipe.

²⁄₃ cup extra virgin olive oil

6 tablespoons fresh lemon juice

½ cup chopped fresh herbs, such as parsley, basil, chervil, and/or tarragon

Salt and freshly ground black pepper to taste

½ pound fresh white asparagus, trimmed, blanched until tender, 6 to 8 minutes in salted boiling water, cooled in ice water, drained, then cut in half lengthwise

1 head radicchio (9 to 10 ounces), washed and quartered

2 tablespoons olive oil

Preheat the grill to medium heat.

In a small mixing bowl, combine the extra virgin olive oil and lemon juice. Whisk in the herbs and season with salt and pepper. Pour off ¼ cup of the dressing and set aside.

Place the asparagus in a square glass dish. Pour the remaining vinaigrette over the asparagus, cover, and refrigerate for 30 minutes.

Brush the radicchio with the 2 tablespoons olive oil and season with salt and pepper. Place on the grill, core side down, and cook for 1 to

2 minutes on each side. Remove and thinly slice. Season with salt and pepper and set aside.

In a medium-size mixing bowl, toss the crabmeat with the reserved ¼ cup vinaigrette, the shallots, and the garlic, and season with salt and pepper.

To serve, fan out the leaves of the radicchio and stuff the crabmeat between the leaves. Remove the asparagus from the vinaigrette, reserving the vinaigrette. Arrange the asparagus on the bottom of a large serving platter. Place the radicchio over the asparagus. Drizzle the entire platter with the reserved vinaigrette and sprinkle with the cheese and parsley. Serve immediately.

1 pound fresh jumbo lump crabmeat, picked over for shells and cartilage
2 tablespoons minced shallots
1 tablespoon minced garlic
2 tablespoons freshly grated Parmigiano-Reggiano cheese
1 tablespoon chopped fresh parsley leaves

Emeril's BLT Salad

Makes 4 servings

Who doesn't like a bacon, lettuce, and tomato sandwich? If you don't, skip this recipe and go fix a baloney sandwich. But, hey, you might change your mind after you taste this really kicked-up version of a BLT. And we are going to start from scratch and make our own bread. The bread can be grilled on an indoor grill or an outdoor one. Get one of those hibachis! Use your imagination!

1 envelope (¼ ounce) active dry yeast

¾ cup warm water (about 110°F)

¼ cup olive oil

2 tablespoons finely chopped fresh basil leaves

1 tablespoon minced garlic

2 cups bleached all-purpose flour

¼ cup yellow cornmeal

1 tablespoon kosher salt

4 cups assorted baby salad greens, such as romaine, frisée, red oak leaf, and radicchio, washed and patted dry

½ recipe Saffron Aioli (page 14)

Salt and freshly ground black pepper to taste

2 ripe beefsteak tomatoes, cut crosswise into ¼-inch-thick slices

12 slices bacon, crisp fried

½ pound Fontina cheese, cut into 8 slices

1 tablespoon freshly chopped parsley leaves

Combine the yeast and water in a large mixing bowl of an electric mixer fitted with a dough hook. Whisk until the yeast is dissolved. Mix in 3 tablespoons of the olive oil, the basil, garlic, flour, cornmeal, and ½ tablespoon of the kosher salt. With the mixer on medium speed, mix until the dough pulls away from the sides of the bowl and forms a ball. Turn the dough out onto a floured surface and knead until it forms a smooth ball.

Lightly oil the inside of another large mixing bowl. Place the dough in the bowl and turn to oil all sides. Cover the bowl with a clean kitchen cloth and put it in a warm, draft-free place. Let rise until it doubles in size, about 1½ hours.

Preheat the grill to medium heat.

Remove the dough from the bowl, invert it onto a heavily floured work surface, and punch it down. Divide the dough into 4 equal portions and form each into a ball. With your fingers, press each ball into a round about ¼ inch thick. Brush the rounds with the remaining 1 tablespoon olive oil. Place on the hot grill until cooked all the way through, 3 to 4 minutes on each side. Remove and sprinkle with the remaining ½ tablespoon kosher salt.

In a large mixing bowl, toss the salad greens with ¼ cup of the aioli dressing. Season with salt and pepper. Season the tomato slices with salt and pepper.

To serve, spoon the remaining dressing in the center of each plate and on the rim. Slice the flat breads in half crosswise.

For each sandwich, tuck in 2 slices of tomato, 3 slices of bacon, 2 slices of cheese, and some of the lettuce and place on top of the dressing and sprinkle with parsley.

Chicken and Pineapple Salad

Makes 2 servings

*H*ey, we're gonna make us some boats, yeah, pineapple boats, and fill 'em with grilled chicken, pineapple, walnuts, and some other stuff. You'll think you're in Hawaii on the island of Lanai, called the Pineapple Island. Aloha!*

No kidding, these are great for summertime parties, or just for you and your honey to enjoy on the patio.

To roast the walnuts, preheat the oven to 375°F. Place the nuts on a baking sheet and roast until golden and fragrant, 5 to 6 minutes. Watch carefully to be sure they don't burn.

2 skinless boneless chicken breast halves
   (about 6 ounces each)
Salt and freshly ground white pepper to
   taste
1 tablespoon olive oil
1 medium-size pineapple
¼ cup walnut oil
1 tablespoon chopped fresh chervil leaves
½ cup minced red onions
½ cup minced celery
½ teaspoon minced garlic
½ cup chopped roasted walnuts
1 teaspoon finely chopped fresh parsley
   leaves

Preheat a grill to medium heat.

Season the chicken breasts with salt and pepper and rub them with ½ tablespoon of the oil. Grill the chicken, turning once, until the juices run clear, 12 to 15 minutes. Remove and cut into ½-inch dice.

With a sharp knife, split the pineapple in half lengthwise, leaving the plume. Cut a thin slice from the bottom of each half so that it sits flat for serving. With a small sharp knife, cut the core from the center of the halved pineapple. With a serrated grapefruit knife, cut out the flesh and cut crosswise into ½-inch-thick slices. Cover the pineapple boats with plastic wrap and refrigerate.

Season the pineapple slices with salt and pepper and rub with the remaining ½ tablespoon olive oil. Grill the pineapple slices until just lightly golden, 1 to 2 minutes on each side. Remove and let cool.

Put 2 slices of the pineapple in a medium-size mixing bowl; dice the rest and combine with the chicken. With the back of a fork, mash the 2 slices against the side of the bowl, add the walnut oil, and stir to blend. Add the chervil and season with salt and pepper. Pour the mixture into a large salad bowl, add the chicken and pineapple dice, the onions, celery, garlic, and walnuts, and toss to mix thoroughly. Cover and chill for at least 1 hour.

When ready to serve, divide the chicken-pineapple mixture into 2 equal portions and spoon into the pineapple boats. Garnish with the parsley.

Molasses Duck Salad

Makes 4 servings

If you really want to have something new and different, well, you need to try this combination—crispy duck, fresh spinach, crunchy pecans, and creamy Maytag blue cheese (see Source Guide). The warm dressing spiked with garlic and mustard is a killer.

Be forewarned: this recipe takes 3 days to prepare.

1 whole boneless duck breast, cut in half (about 1 pound)

¼ cup kosher salt

¼ cup cracked black peppercorns

½ cup plus 2 tablespoons dark molasses

4 cloves garlic, peeled

8 dried juniper berries

8 black whole peppercorns

2 tablespoons plus 1 teaspoon olive oil

2 tablespoons minced shallots

1 teaspoon minced garlic

1 teaspoon Dijon mustard

2 tablespoons rice wine vinegar

Salt and freshly ground black pepper to taste

4 cups fresh spinach leaves, washed well and tough stems removed

½ cup pecan pieces, toasted (see headnote on page 104)

½ cup thinly sliced red onion

4 ounces Maytag blue or other blue cheese, crumbled

Rub the duck breast with the kosher salt and cracked pepper. Wrap in plastic wrap and refrigerate for 24 hours.

Remove the duck breast from the refrigerator and rinse thoroughly with cool water to remove the salt and pepper. Place the meat in a small glass container and cover with ½ cup of the molasses, the garlic cloves, juniper berries, and whole peppercorns. Cover and refrigerate for 48 hours.

Remove the duck from the refrigerator and drain off the marinade.

Preheat the oven to 400°F.

Heat 1 teaspoon of the olive oil in a large oven-proof sauté pan over medium heat. Place the duck breast, skin side down, in the pan and cook until the skin is crispy and brown, 10 minutes. Turn the meat over and cook for 10 minutes more. Transfer the pan to the oven. Roast for about 5 minutes for medium rare; 8 minutes for medium; 10 minutes for well done. Remove the pan from the oven, transfer the meat to a cutting board, and let it rest for about 2 minutes before cutting at an angle into ¼-inch-thick slices.

In the sauté pan, over low heat, combine the remaining 2 tablespoons molasses, the shallots, minced garlic, mustard, the remaining 2 tablespoons olive oil, and the vinegar. Whisk until the mixture is emulsified, about 2 minutes. Season with salt and pepper. Remove from the heat, add the spinach, and toss to coat evenly.

To serve, mound the greens in the center of the plate. Arrange the duck slices around the greens, and sprinkle with the pecans, red onion, and blue cheese.

Haricots Verts and Horseradish Salad

Makes 8 servings

Haricots verts is the French term for "green string beans," and they're a bit different from our American ones. They're smaller, very tender, slender, and sought after because of their intense taste. It's this flavor that I really get a kick out of and you don't have to do too much to them—just toss them with a horseradish dressing and serve with bacon and hard-boiled eggs. My friend Brenda showed me how to do this and I owe her one.

Put the water in a large saucepan, add salt, and bring to a boil over medium-high heat. Add the beans and cook for 2 minutes. Remove them from the water and shock in an ice bath to stop the cooking. Drain and pat dry.

In a small mixing bowl, whisk together the horseradish, sour cream, mayonnaise, onion, and garlic, then season with the Worcestershire sauce, salt, and pepper. Toss the haricots verts with the horseradish mixture. Season again with salt and pepper. Cover and refrigerate for 8 hours.

To serve, mound the beans on a serving platter. Sprinkle with the bacon, eggs, and parsley.

6 cups water

Salt

2½ pounds fresh haricots verts, or small green beans, ends trimmed

2 tablespoons prepared horseradish

2 tablespoons sour cream

¼ cup Emeril's Mayonnaise (page 14)

¼ cup minced red onion

2 teaspoons minced garlic

⅛ teaspoon Worcestershire sauce

Freshly ground black pepper to taste

½ pound sliced bacon, chopped and crisp fried

3 hard-boiled eggs, shelled and chopped

3 tablespoons finely chopped fresh parsley leaves

107

Pecan-Crusted Mozzarella with Baby Greens

Makes 4 servings

First of all, you need to get the best fresh mozzarella you can find. The best comes from Italy where it and its cousin provolone are pasta filata, *which means pulled or stretched curd, a cheese-making technique that is uniquely Italian. Tell that to your friends and impress 'em.*

At one time, mozzarella was made only from the milk of water buffaloes, but today, the majority is made with cow's milk. Don't buy that factory-produced stuff; buy only one that's packed in whey or water—it's often labeled "Italian style." Stay away from mozzarella if it smells sour, has yellowed, or looks dried out. And once you've bought it, don't keep it too long in the icebox. Think of it as fresh milk.

Crusted with pecans, then fried and served with spinach, this is one of the best ways to enjoy really fine mozzarella.

2 cups pecan pieces, toasted (see headnote on page 104)

1½ cups bleached all-purpose flour

Essence to taste (page 7)

1 pound fresh mozzarella cheese, cut into eight ¼-inch-thick slices

Salt and freshly ground white and black peppercorns to taste

1 large egg beaten with 1 tablespoon milk

½ cup plus 3 tablespoons olive oil

1 medium-size yellow onion, thinly sliced

1 medium-size red onion, thinly sliced

In a food processor, finely chop the pecans. Add about ½ cup of the flour, or enough to bind the pecans and form a coarse meal. Season with Essence.

In a shallow bowl, season the remaining flour with Essence.

Season both sides of the cheese slices with salt and white and black peppers. Dredge each slice in the flour, tapping off any excess, then dip each slice in the egg wash, letting the excess drip off; dredge the slices in the pecan meal to coat both sides. Set aside.

In a medium-size saucepan, heat 1 tablespoon of the olive oil over medium heat. Add the onions and cook, stirring, until they caramelize, 10 to 12 minutes. Add the shallots and garlic and cook, stirring for 1 minute. Whisk in ½ cup of the olive oil, the vinegar, and the honey and season with salt and black pepper. Remove from the heat.

2 tablespoons minced shallots

1 tablespoon minced garlic

¼ cup rice wine vinegar

1 tablespoon honey

8 cups fresh spinach, well washed and tough stems removed, and torn into small pieces

In a large sauté pan over medium heat, heat the remaining 2 tablespoons olive oil. Pan-fry the cheese until the crust is golden, 1 to 2 minutes on each side. Drain on paper towels. Season with Essence.

Toss the spinach with the honey-onion dressing and season with salt and pepper. To serve, divide the greens into 4 equal portions and put in the center of 4 salad plates. Arrange 2 slices of cheese around the greens on each plate.

Sean Dowd, production manager for *Emeril Live*, and Emeril's dad, Mr. John

Exotic Mushroom Flan with Warm Spinach Salad

Makes 12 servings

Anybody who knows me well knows that I have a weakness for mushrooms. Each one has its own distinct flavor and I love to combine several kinds to get the full impact of taste. Now don't y'all go rooting around in the woods picking mushrooms unless you know what you're doing. Do some investigating in your area and see what's available to you at respected markets.

We have a place north of New Orleans, across Lake Pontchartrain, called Chicory Farm, which supplies my restaurants with some of the best mushrooms I've ever had. You might want to experiment with different kinds to find the ones you like best.

2 tablespoons olive oil

1 pound assorted exotic mushrooms, such as shiitakes, chanterelles, and oysters, wiped clean and sliced (about 6 cups)

Salt and freshly ground black pepper to taste

½ cup minced yellow onions

1 tablespoon chopped garlic

1 tablespoon chopped fresh thyme leaves

1 tablespoon chopped fresh parsley leaves

8 large egg yolks

1 quart heavy cream

1 cup freshly grated Parmigiano-Reggiano cheese

¼ teaspoon freshly grated nutmeg

6 slices bacon, chopped

Preheat the oven to 350°F. Lightly butter twelve 4-ounce ramekins.

In a medium-size sauté pan, heat the olive oil over medium heat. Add the mushrooms and cook, stirring, for 2 minutes, then season with salt and pepper. Add the yellow onions and garlic, and cook, stirring, for 1 minute. Remove from the heat, stir in the herbs, and let cool.

In a large mixing bowl, combine the egg yolks and heavy cream and whisk to blend. Stir in the cheese, nutmeg, and the mushroom mixture. Spoon the mixture into the ramekins. Place the ramekins in a baking pan and fill the pan with enough water to come halfway up the sides of the ramekins. Bake until the flans set, 50 to 55 minutes.

In a medium-size sauté pan, fry the bacon until crispy, about 10 minutes. Transfer the bacon and ¼ cup of the bacon grease to a large mixing bowl. Add the vinegar, mix, and season with salt and pepper. Add the spinach and red onions and toss to coat evenly.

3 tablespoons balsamic vinegar
One 10-ounce bag fresh spinach, well
washed and tough stems removed
½ cup thinly sliced red onions

To serve, gently loosen the mushroom flans with a knife and invert each onto a plate. Mound a small amount of the spinach salad in the center of each flan and serve.

Emeril's Panzanella

Makes 4 servings

The Italians know how to enjoy good food and they have an incredible talent for using the simplest ingredients to make something as delicious as this. All you really need is fresh components–basil leaves, tomatoes, mozzarella–and crusty bread fried in olive oil.

Susan Stockton, who works in my kitchen at the Food Network, berated me for adding the salami to this traditional salad, but, hey, I just wanted to kick it up a notch. Forgive me, Susan?

2 cups olive oil

4 cups cubed Italian or French bread

Salt and freshly ground black pepper to taste

3 tablespoons finely chopped fresh basil leaves

3 tablespoons extra virgin olive oil

1 tablespoon balsamic vinegar

1 teaspoon minced garlic

4 ripe plum tomatoes, cut into ¼-inch slices

3 tablespoons chopped red onion

½ pound fresh mozzarella cheese, cut into ½-inch cubes

½ pound salami in 1 piece, cut into ½-inch cubes

Heat the oil to hot but not smoking in a large sauté pan over medium heat. Fry the bread in batches and cook until golden, 3 to 4 minutes, stirring often to keep the cubes from sticking. Remove with a slotted spoon and drain on paper towels. Season with salt and pepper. Set aside.

Toss the remaining ingredients together in a mixing bowl. Season with salt and pepper. Add the bread cubes and toss again.

Arrange the salad on a serving platter and pass to serve.

The salad can be made ahead of time and chilled. If this is done, add the bread just before serving.

Creole Tomato Salad

Makes 6 servings

Creole tomatoes, grown in the alluvial soil along the Mississippi River in Plaquemines Parish, south of New Orleans, are especially prized in the New Orleans area. Available roughly from May to July, they have a distinctive and delicious taste that's hard to describe. Any variety of tomato is considered Creole as long as it's grown in the soil of the Mississippi Delta. There is also a Creole variety that is grown in home gardens all over the state. These, too, are quite good but lack some of the flavor.

You know what kind of tomatoes are prized in your area, so be sure to get the very best of the best to make this salad that's so enjoyable in the warm summer months. Don't be afraid to combine several kinds of tomatoes if there's an assortment in your locale.

In a small mixing bowl, combine the olive oil, vinegar, garlic, and herbs. Whisk until well blended, then season with salt and pepper.

Cut the tomatoes into ½-inch-thick slices. Cut the onion into thin slices or rings. Slice the avocados lengthwise into ½-inch-thick slices. Season both sides of all of them with salt and pepper.

To serve, arrange the tomatoes, onion, and avocados on a large platter along with the cheese and drizzle with the dressing.

½ cup extra virgin olive oil

¼ cup balsamic vinegar

1 teaspoon minced garlic

2 tablespoons chopped fresh herbs, such as parsley, basil, chervil, and/or tarragon

Salt and freshly ground black pepper to taste

2 pounds ripe Creole or other good-quality tomatoes

1 large sweet onion, such as Vidalia, Maui, or Walla Walla

2 medium-size ripe Haas avocados, peeled and pitted

¾ pound fresh mozzarella cheese, cut into six ½-inch-thick slices

Emeril's Poke Salad
with Sesame Vinaigrette

Makes 6 servings

Now don't get this confused with pokeweed, sometimes called "poke," which is found in the wild in the eastern United States. Then there's the Hawaiian word poke (pronounced POE-kay), which means to slice or cut crosswise into pieces. The poke I'm talking about is an old-time Hawaiian dish that I learned about from my dear friend Sam Choy, who's the Hawaiians' answer to Paul Prudhomme. Anyway, poke in Hawaii usually consists of sliced raw fish, limu (seaweed), fresh red chile pepper, Hawaiian sea salt, and 'inamonia (roasted, ground, and salted kukui nuts). Those wonderful Hawaiians eat this with just about anything, sort of like our rice and gravy in south Louisiana.

You can get the seaweed at most Asian markets. If you get the dried kind, you'll have to reconstitute it in warm water. Either fresh or dried will do just fine.

Here's my take on poke, a salad that will give you a real sensation! And please use fresh, fresh fish for this!

In a medium-size mixing bowl, combine 3 tablespoons of the sesame oil with the next six ingredients and whisk well. Season with salt and pepper.

In another mixing bowl, combine the nuts, seaweed, jalapeños, and onions. Add the ahi and mix well. Season with salt and pepper.

Combine the salad dressing with the ahi mixture. Toss the radicchio with the remaining 2 teaspoons sesame oil.

To serve, arrange the radicchio in the center of a serving platter. Mound the salad in the center and garnish with the chives.

3 tablespoons plus 2 teaspoons sesame oil

¼ cup soy sauce

2 tablespoons honey

2 teaspoons minced shallots

1 tablespoon minced garlic

1 teaspoon chopped fresh cilantro leaves

2 tablespoons black sesame seeds or regular sesame seeds

Salt and freshly ground black pepper to taste

3 tablespoons crushed macadamia nuts

2 tablespoons fresh or reconstituted dried seaweed, coarsely chopped

2 red jalapeño peppers, seeded and minced

½ cup finely chopped Maui or other sweet onions like Vidalia or Walla Walla

2 pounds sashimi-grade ahi fillet, cut into bite-size pieces

1 head radicchio (9 to 10 ounces), washed and julienned

1 tablespoon snipped fresh chives

Rochelle Brown, *Emeril Live* producer

Vegetable World

Although I don't think I'll ever be a strict vegetarian, I do

like vegetables and I like them

prepared in any number of ways.

My daughter Jill is a vegetarian

and keeps me on my toes thinking

up new ideas and I hope I pass

muster because she's a tough cookie.

When preparing vegetables, think of using different

textures and flavors together, like vegetables with tart

goat cheese, or a custard made with roasted vegetables,

or an eggplant in a soup bammed with lots of garlic.

In this chapter you'll find mushrooms in combination with tomatoes, spinach, cheeses, and pasta because those are the flavors I like, and I think you will too. The mushroom-and-potato lasagna will knock your socks off! The portobello sandwich is a killer, and the oven-roasted tomatoes with risotto is beautiful.

**Emeril with Emeril's
chef de cuisine,
Bernard Carmouche**

Roasted Eggplant and Garlic Soup

Makes 4 to 6 servings

Eggplant is used a lot in Louisiana, especially during the summer when the season is at its peak. The locals like them fried, smothered, stuffed, and like this, cooked in a soup smacked with garlic and fresh herbs, then pureed.

Preheat the oven to 400°F.

In a small mixing bowl, combine the roasted garlic, herbs, and 1 tablespoon of the olive oil, season with salt and pepper, and mix well.

Cut the eggplant in half lengthwise and smear the garlic-herb mixture over the flesh of each half. Put the eggplant on a baking sheet and bake until tender, about 30 minutes. Remove from the oven and let cool.

With a spoon, remove the flesh from the eggplant and discard the skin.

Toss the cubed bread in a small mixing bowl with 2 tablespoons of the olive oil and season with salt and pepper. Place on a baking sheet and bake until lightly toasted, 2 to 3 minutes. Remove from the oven and set aside.

1 cup Roasted Garlic (page 15)

½ cup chopped assorted fresh herbs, such as basil, oregano, and parsley

¼ cup olive oil

Salt and freshly ground black pepper to taste

2 large eggplant (about 1 pound each)

1 cup cubed French bread

1 cup minced yellow onions

1 tablespoon chopped garlic

1½ quarts Chicken Stock (page 8) or canned chicken broth

1 cup heavy cream

¼ cup freshly grated Parmigiano-Reggiano cheese

1 tablespoon chopped fresh parsley leaves

Heat the remaining tablespoon olive oil in a large saucepan over medium heat. Add the onions, season with salt and pepper, and cook, stirring, until limp, about 5 minutes. Add the eggplant and chopped garlic and continue to cook, stirring, for 2 minutes. Add the stock and bring to a boil. Reduce the heat to medium-low and simmer for 10 minutes. In batches in a blender or with a handheld blender, puree the soup until smooth. Stir in the heavy cream, increase the heat to medium, and simmer for 3 minutes, then season with salt and pepper.

To serve, ladle into soup bowls and sprinkle with the croutons, cheese, and parsley.

Vegetable and Goat Cheese Empanada with Roasted Tomatillo Sauce

Makes 4 servings

*H*ere I'm using an assortment of vegetables to make an empanada, which is a pie, or tart, and dressing it up with a roasted tomatillo sauce. It was on the menu at Emeril's for a while and it got to be so popular that we still get requests for it.

Masa harina is flour made from dried masa, which are corn kernels that have been cooked in limewater. It is usually available in large supermarkets and specialty shops.

1 cup masa harina flour

½ cup bleached all-purpose flour

½ cup yellow cornmeal

½ teaspoon baking powder

Essence to taste (page 7)

1 small fresh jalapeño, seeded and minced

Salt and freshly ground black pepper to taste

2½ tablespoons unsalted butter

1 cup warm water, as needed

2 cups assorted diced vegetables, such as
    yellow squash, zucchini, eggplant,
    endive, red onion, red and yellow bell
    peppers

2 tablespoons olive oil

¼ to 1 cup crumbled goat cheese (as
    needed), at room temperature

1 recipe Roasted Garlic Puree (page 121)

1 tablespoon finely chopped fresh cilantro
    leaves

Three 6-inch corn tortillas, cut into strips
    and deep-fried until crisp

To make the empanadas, combine the masa harina and all-purpose flour, cornmeal, baking powder, Essence, and jalapeño in a large mixing bowl. Season with salt and pepper and mix well. Add the butter and work it in with your hands until the mixture resembles coarse crumbs. Add the water, a little at a time, and work it in with your hands. Add only as much as you need to make a smooth ball. Form the dough into a log about 12 inches long by 3 inches across. Wrap in plastic wrap and refrigerate for 20 minutes.

Remove the dough from the refrigerator. Divide the log into 4 equal sections (each about 3 inches long), and carefully roll each out between sheets of plastic wrap to an 8-inch circle, about ¼ inch thick.

Preheat the oven to 375°F.

Season the assorted vegetables with Essence. Heat the olive oil in a large sauté pan over medium-high heat. Add the vegetables and cook, stirring often, until they are slightly limp, about 1 minute. Remove and put into a medium-size mixing bowl. Add enough cheese to bind the vegetables. Season with salt and pepper. Add the garlic puree, cilantro, and fried tortilla strips and toss to mix.

1 large egg, beaten

1 cup Roasted Tomatillo Sauce (below)

1 recipe Avocado Puree (page 122)

4 sprigs fresh cilantro

Spoon about ¾ cup of the filling into the center of each of the dough rounds. Fold over to form a half-moon and crimp the edges to seal. On a parchment-lined baking sheet, place the empanadas about 2 inches apart and brush with the egg. Bake until golden brown, about 30 minutes.

To serve, place the empanadas on serving plates, drizzle with the tomatillo sauce and avocado puree, and garnish with the cilantro sprigs.

Roasted Garlic Puree

Makes ¼ cup

Combine the ingredients in a food processor or blender and process until smooth.

2 recipes Roasted Garlic (page 15)

1 tablespoon olive oil

Salt and freshly ground black pepper to
    taste

Roasted Tomatillo Sauce

Makes about 2 cups

Preheat the oven to 400°F.

Combine all of the ingredients except the water in a large mixing bowl and toss to mix. Then spread the mixture evenly on a baking sheet and roast for 30 minutes. Remove from the oven, pour everything into a food processor or blender, add the water, and process until smooth.

1 pound fresh tomatillos, husks removed

½ medium-size yellow onion, thinly sliced

6 cloves garlic, peeled

2 tablespoons olive oil

Salt and freshly ground black pepper to
    taste

½ cup water

Avocado Puree

Makes about ¾ cup

1 medium-size ripe Haas avocado, peeled, pitted, and chopped
2 tablespoons fresh lime juice
2 tablespoons heavy cream
Salt and freshly ground black pepper to taste

In a blender or food processor, process the avocado until smooth. Add the lime juice and heavy cream and season with salt and pepper. Pulse once or twice to blend.

Vegetable Quesadilla with Caramelized Onion Marmalade and Cilantro Sour Cream

Makes 4 servings

Quesadilla is the Spanish word for "little cheese bites." In Mexico, it is a small fried turnover made with fresh dough that has been stuffed with a variety of ingredients and almost always contains cheese. This one is filled with vegetables and cheese, then, after it's cooked, it's served with a wonderful onion marmalade and sour cream flavored with cilantro. Chihuahua!

Heat 2 tablespoons of the olive oil in a medium-size sauté pan over high heat. Add the onions, season with salt and pepper, and cook, stirring often, until they caramelize, 8 to 10 minutes. Add the garlic, parsley, and vinegar and cook, stirring, for about 1 minute. Set aside.

Combine the grilled vegetables in a medium-size mixing bowl and season with salt and pepper. Divide the mixture into 4 equal portions and spread on 4 of the tortillas, leaving about a 1-inch border all around. Sprinkle the vegetables with equal amounts of the cheese, then top with the remaining tortillas. Gently press the edges together to seal.

Heat 1 teaspoon of the olive oil in a large non-stick skillet over medium-high heat. Carefully lay a quesadilla in the center of the skillet and cook until lightly browned, about 1 minute. Then, with a wide spatula, turn the quesadilla over and cook until lightly golden, 1 to 2 minutes. Repeat the procedure using the remaining oil.

To serve, cut the quesadillas into 4 wedges. Arrange on individual plates and top with the onion marmalade and cilantro sour cream.

2 tablespoons plus 4 teaspoons olive oil
¾ cup chopped yellow onions
Salt and freshly ground black pepper to taste
1 teaspoon minced garlic
1 tablespoon finely chopped fresh parsley leaves
1 tablespoon rice wine vinegar
1 cup assorted julienned grilled vegetables, such as red onion, bell pepper, yellow squash, and tomato
8 medium-size flour tortillas
¼ pound grated Maytag or other white Cheddar cheese
1 recipe Cilantro Sour Cream (below)

Cilantro Sour Cream

Makes about ¼ cup

Combine the sour cream and cilantro in a small mixing bowl and stir to mix. Season with salt and pepper.

¼ cup sour cream
1 tablespoon chopped fresh cilantro leaves
Salt and freshly ground black pepper to taste

Vegetable Custard Tart

Makes one 10-inch tart; 8 servings

This is more like a thick quiche than a tart, and it's great to serve on a brunch menu, or to pack up in your picnic basket. The flavor of the roasted vegetables with the creamy custard is something I really like.

¼ pound assorted wild and exotic mushrooms, such as shiitakes, chanterelles, oysters, and/or hedgehogs, wiped clean and sliced

Five ½-inch-thick slices red onion

Five ½-inch-thick slices eggplant

Ten ½-inch-thick slices zucchini

Ten ½-inch-thick slices yellow squash

¼ cup olive oil

Salt and freshly ground black pepper to taste

4 large egg yolks

2 cups heavy cream

½ cup freshly grated Parmigiano-Reggiano cheese

1 tablespoon chopped fresh parsley leaves

Dash of Worcestershire sauce

Dash of hot sauce

½ recipe Basic Savory Piecrust (page 168), rolled out ⅛ inch thick

Preheat the oven to 400°F.

Put the mushrooms and vegetables in a large mixing bowl, add the olive oil, and season with salt and pepper. Toss to coat. Spread the vegetables evenly on a large baking sheet and roast until lightly golden, about 20 minutes. Remove from the oven and let cool.

Reduce the oven temperature to 350°F.

In another large mixing bowl, combine the egg yolks and heavy cream and whisk well. Add the cheese, parsley, Worcestershire, and hot sauce, and season with salt and pepper. Whisk to blend.

Line a deep 10-inch pie pan with the piecrust and crimp the edges. Arrange the vegetables evenly in the bottom of the pan. Pour the egg mixture evenly over the top. Bake until the center sets and the top is golden, about 50 minutes. Remove from the oven and let cool for 5 minutes before slicing to serve.

Oven-Roasted Tomatoes with Mushroom Risotto and Fresh Mozzarella Cheese

Makes 8 servings

*S*tuffing the tomatoes with mushroom risotto makes an outstanding pre-sentation as a side dish for pork, beef, or poultry. Vegetarians can adapt it by substituting a vegetable stock for the chicken stock. The stock can be made with mushroom stems, onions, celery, and any kinds of veg-etables you have hanging around. Easy enough, huh?

Preheat the oven to 400°F.

Rub the tomatoes with 1 tablespoon of the olive oil and season with Essence. Place on a baking sheet and roast for 15 minutes. Remove from the oven and set aside.

Heat the remaining tablespoon olive oil in a large sauté pan over medium heat. Add the shallots and onions, season with salt and pepper, and cook, stirring, until the onions are slightly soft, about 3 minutes. Add the stock and garlic, bring to a boil, then reduce the heat to medium-low and simmer for about 6 minutes. Add the rice and simmer for 10 minutes, stirring constantly. Add the mushrooms and continue to simmer, stirring constantly, until the mixture is creamy and bubbly, about 8 minutes. Stir in the butter and heavy cream, and simmer until creamy, 2 minutes, stirring constantly. Season with salt and pepper.

Spoon the risotto into the center of each tomato, top each with a slice of mozzarella cheese, and bake until the cheese melts and browns a bit. Remove from the oven and place each tomato on a serving plate. Drizzle each with 2 tablespoons of the veal reduction and garnish with the basil.

8 large ripe Creole or beefsteak tomatoes, peeled and pulp removed

2 tablespoons olive oil

Essence to taste (page 7)

2 tablespoons chopped shallots

½ cup chopped yellow onions

Salt and freshly ground black pepper to taste

6 cups Chicken Stock (page 8) or canned chicken broth

2 teaspoons chopped garlic

1 pound (2 cups) Arborio rice

⅓ pound assorted exotic mushrooms, such as shiitakes, chanterelles, and oysters, wiped clean and chopped (about 2 cups)

1 tablespoon unsalted butter

¼ recipe heavy cream

¼ pound fresh mozzarella cheese, cut into 8 slices

1 recipe Veal Reduction (page 10)

¼ cup chopped fresh basil leaves

Confit of Exotic Mushrooms
with Pasta Rags

Makes 4 servings

There are times my staff calls me the mushroom maniac because I'm wild about wild and exotic mushrooms. They are mysterious to me. They grow in the dark, some look real weird, and they all have great flavor. Wild mushrooms, like chanterelles, grow—where else?—in the wild. Exotic mushrooms, like shiitakes and oyster mushrooms, are cultivated and are available in many supermarkets and gourmet shops.

I just can't get enough mushrooms and, as you can see, I'll try just about anything with them. You just can't go wrong, in my opinion, with mushrooms.

This recipe takes a little time to get it all together, but I don't mind because the result is beautiful! First you have to make a confit of mushrooms before you combine it with the pasta. The confit recipe follows the main recipe.

Oh, the pasta rags are nothing more than pasta sheets torn into pieces to look like little rags—at least that's what they look like to me. If you can't get, or make, fresh pasta, you can substitute lasagna sheets and simply cut them into pieces.

The black truffle is the most famous of all truffles and it is found by hunters who send out their pigs or dogs to sniff them out underground. Black truffles have an extremely pungent flesh, and for that reason only a small amount is needed to flavor this dish. Be aware that they are extremely expensive.

To shave the truffle, I recommend using a truffle slicer, a small kitchen gadget with an adjustable blade mounted on a stainless steel frame. The blade is held at a 45-degree angle and the truffle is pressed down and across it, allowing the blade to shave off slivers and slices. But, in a pinch, you can use a handheld (small) mandoline.

Bring a large pot of salted water to a boil. Drop the pasta into the hot water and cook until tender, 3 to 4 minutes, or longer for the dried lasagna. Drain. Transfer the pasta to a large mixing bowl and toss with 1 tablespoon of the confit oil, then season with salt and white pepper. Set aside.

Heat the remaining tablespoon confit oil in a large sauté pan over medium heat. Add the mushroom confit and cook, stirring, for 1 minute. Add the shallots and garlic and cook, stirring, for another minute. Remove from the heat and pour over the pasta. Add the ¼ pound grated cheese and toss to mix evenly, then season with salt and black pepper. Drizzle with the truffle oil.

To serve, mound the pasta in the center of a large serving platter. Shave the truffle over the pasta and garnish with more cheese and the chives.

Salt

½ pound fresh pasta sheets torn or cut into random pieces, or ½ pound lasagna sheets, broken into pieces

2 tablespoons oil from Duck Confit (page 175)

Freshly ground white pepper to taste

1 recipe Confit of Exotic Mushrooms (page 128)

2 tablespoons minced shallots

1 tablespoon minced garlic

¼ pound freshly grated Parmigiano-Reggiano cheese, plus more for garnish

Freshly ground black pepper to taste

1 tablespoon white truffle oil (available in specialty food stores)

1 small fresh black truffle (available in specialty food stores), brushed clean

1 tablespoon snipped fresh chives

continued

Confit of Exotic Mushrooms

Makes about 1 pound

You've probably heard of confits made with duck or goose; a confit is something that has been cooked in its own fat. Well, obviously, mushrooms don't have any fat, so we're going to have to improvise with some good-quality olive oil. All we're doing is slow-baking the mushrooms in the olive oil.

5 cups good-quality olive oil

2 pounds assorted wild and exotic
    mushrooms, such as shiitakes, oysters,
    chanterelles, cloud ears, and hedgehogs,
    wiped clean and coarsely chopped (about
    10 cups)

1 recipe Bouquet Garni (page 7)

2 heads garlic, split in half crosswise

Salt and freshly ground black pepper to
    taste

Preheat the oven to 200°F.

Pour the oil into a large roasting pan and add the mushrooms, spreading them out evenly and pressing them down gently. Add the bouquet garni and submerge in the oil.

Separate the split garlic head into cloves and submerge them in the oil-mushroom mixture. Season with salt and pepper. Cover the pan with a sheet of heavy-duty aluminum foil and slow-bake for 2 hours.

Drain the mushrooms, reserving the oil.

Lasagna of Exotic Mushrooms

Makes about 8 servings

I think you'll like this lasagna made with potatoes rather than pasta. I've suggested using 3 types of potatoes, but you can use just 1 kind—it's up to you. I kinda like the different kinds of potato because of the assortment of flavors and the appearance of the final dish: a layer of mushroom-tomato mixture, a layer of potatoes, a layer of the cheese mixture—just continue layering until you've used all the ingredients. I suggest you end up with the mushroom-tomato mixture, then top with a sprinkling of grated cheese.

Preheat the oven to 350°F. Lightly oil a 13 × 9-inch baking dish.

In a large sauté pan, heat the olive oil over medium heat. Add the onions and season with salt and pepper. Add the prosciutto and cook, stirring, until the onions are soft and lightly golden, about 5 minutes. Stir in ¼ cup of the parsley, the shallots, garlic, and mushrooms. Season with salt and pepper and cook, stirring, until the mushrooms are slightly limp, about 2 minutes. Add the wine and cook, stirring, for 6 minutes. Add the tomatoes, season with salt and pepper, and cook, stirring, for 10 minutes, then season again with salt and pepper and add the basil and oregano. Stir to mix. Remove from the heat.

In a large mixing bowl, combine the ricotta cheese, egg, remaining ¼ cup parsley, ½ cup of the grated Parmigiano, grated mozzarella, and heavy cream. Season with salt and pepper.

Spoon 1 cup of the mushroom-tomato mixture into the baking dish and spread evenly over the bottom. Then arrange the Idaho potatoes in a single layer, slightly overlapping. Spread 1 cup of the cheese mixture over the potatoes. Repeat with another cup of the mushroom-tomato mixture, then a layer of sweet potatoes, 1 cup of the cheese mixture, then another cup of mushroom-tomato mixture, a layer of red potatoes, and another layer of the cheese mixture;

2 tablespoons olive oil

1 cup minced yellow onions

Salt and freshly ground black pepper to taste

2 ounces sliced prosciutto, finely chopped

½ cup finely chopped fresh parsley leaves

2 tablespoons minced shallots

2 tablespoons minced garlic

1 pound assorted wild and exotic mushrooms, such as chanterelles, oysters, shiitakes, and lobster mushrooms, wiped clean and coarsely chopped (about 5 cups)

⅔ cup dry white wine

2 pounds canned crushed tomatoes, undrained

2 tablespoons thinly sliced fresh basil leaves

1 tablespoon chopped fresh oregano leaves

2 cups fresh ricotta cheese

1 large egg

2 cups freshly grated Parmigiano-Reggiano cheese, plus more for garnish

2 cups grated fresh mozzarella cheese

1 cup heavy cream

2 pounds assorted potatoes, such as Idaho, red, and sweet, peeled and thinly sliced

finish with a layer of the mushroom-tomato mixture. Sprinkle with the remaining 1½ cups Parmigiano. Cover the lasagna with a sheet of aluminum foil and bake for 30 minutes. Remove the foil and bake until the top is golden brown, 10 to 15 minutes.

Remove from the oven and let rest for 10 minutes before cutting. Place a portion of the lasagna in the center of each plate. Garnish with grated cheese.

Portobello Sandwich with
Mashed Root Vegetable Mushroom Stew

Makes 4 servings

A portobello is an extremely large, dark brown mushroom that is simply the fully mature form of the crimini, which in turn is a variation of the common cultivated white mushroom. The name "portobello" began to be used in the 1980s as a marketing ploy to popularize this mushroom. The portobello mushroom, which easily measures six inches in diameter, has an open, flat cap. Because it's the eldest of the mushroom species, the portobello's gills are fully exposed, which means that some of the mushroom's moisture has evaporated. The reduced moisture concentrates and enriches the flavor and creates a dense, meaty texture. Portobellos can be found in gourmet produce markets as well as in many supermarkets. The stems are very woody and need to be removed.

Since they are so large, I find portobellos ideal for making sandwiches. Put some filling—mashed root vegetables in this case—in between two of 'em, grill, then top 'em with a mushroom stew. Blow your mind!

1 medium-size carrot, chopped

1 medium-size parsnip, peeled and chopped

1 small sweet potato, peeled and diced

5 tablespoons olive oil

Salt and freshly ground white pepper to taste

1½ pounds Idaho potatoes, peeled and diced

½ cup heavy cream

4 tablespoons (½ stick) unsalted butter

Preheat the oven to 400°F. Preheat the grill.

In a medium-size mixing bowl, toss the carrot, parsnip, and sweet potato with 1 tablespoon of the olive oil, then season with salt and pepper. Put the vegetables on a baking sheet and roast until tender, about 40 minutes.

Put the Idaho potatoes in a large saucepan, cover with water, and season with salt. Bring to a boil, reduce the heat to medium and cook until fork tender, about 10 minutes. Drain and return to the saucepan and over low heat let the potatoes dry for 1 minute. Add the roasted vegetables and mash with a potato masher, leaving some small lumps. Season with salt and pepper. Add the heavy cream and 2 table-spoons of the butter and mix well. Season again with salt and pepper.

Drizzle the portobellos with 1 tablespoon of the olive oil and season with salt and pepper. Grill for 3 to 4 minutes on each side. Spread one quarter of the potato mixture over the gill side of 4 of the portobellos. Top with the remaining ones to form sandwiches.

Put the sandwiches on a baking sheet and bake for 6 minutes.

In a large sauté pan, heat the remaining 3 tablespoons olive oil over medium heat. Add the onions, season with salt and pepper, and cook, stirring, for 2 minutes. Add the sliced mushrooms and garlic, season with salt and pepper, and cook, stir-ring, for 3 to 4 minutes. Add the parsley and veal reduction and bring to a boil. Reduce the heat to medium-low and simmer for 2 minutes. Remove from the heat and stir in the remaining 2 tablespoons butter.

To serve, spoon some of the mushroom stew in the center of each plate. Place the portobello sandwich on top of the stew, then top with more stew and garnish with the shaved cheese.

8 fresh portobello mushrooms, stemmed
   and wiped clean

½ cup minced yellow onions

¼ pound assorted wild and exotic
   mushrooms, such as shiitakes, oysters,
   and chanterelles, wiped clean and sliced
   (about 4 cups)

1 tablespoon chopped garlic

1 tablespoon chopped fresh parsley leaves

2 cups Veal Reduction (page 10)

¼ pound shaved Parmigiano-Reggiano
   cheese

Essence of Emeril director, Dini Diskin-Zimmerman, and Emeril

Emeril's Potato Truffle Charlotte

Makes 8 servings

Besides mushrooms, I love potatoes. There are many different kinds and they are so versatile. Let me tell you a little about these suckers!

The ancient Incas were cultivating these humble tubers thousands of years ago. However, because potatoes belong to the nightshade family, they were thought to be poisonous and were not readily accepted in Europe. But Sir Walter Raleigh planted them on property he owned in Ireland, and the Irish knew a good thing when they saw it. Hundreds of years later, Irishmen were growing and consuming potatoes in great quantities.

There are a great number of varieties grown around the world today. In the United States, the potato is divided into four basic categories: russet, long white, round white, and round red. The russet or Idaho is long, slightly rounded, and has a brown, rough skin and numerous "eyes." Its low moisture and high starch contents not only give it superior baking qualities but make it excellent for french fries.

Long white potatoes have a shape similar to the russet, but they are thin, pale, gray-brown skinned and have almost imperceptible eyes. They are sometimes called white rose or California long whites, and can be baked, boiled, and fried. What are called ginger potatoes are the thumb-size baby long white potatoes.

The round white and round red potatoes are commonly referred to as boiling potatoes, since they contain less starch and more moisture, making them perfect for boiling.

Yukon Gold potatoes have a skin and flesh that ranges from buttery

*yellow to golden. These boiling potatoes have a moist, almost succulent tex-
ture and make excellent mashed potatoes. New potatoes are simply young
potatoes, whatever the type. They haven't had time to convert their sugar
fully into starch and consequently have a crisp, waxy texture and thin, unde-
veloped wispy skins. New potatoes are small enough to cook whole and are
excellent boiled or pan-roasted.*

Now, aren't you glad I told you all this?

*For this next recipe, we're going to use the Yukon Golds to make a
dish that I like to serve as a side to steaks or a whole beef tenderloin, but it's
good with chicken too.*

Preheat the oven to 400°F.

Put the Yukon Gold potatoes in a large saucepan, cover with water, season with salt, and bring to a boil over high heat. Reduce the heat to medium and simmer until tender, 8 to 10 minutes. Remove from the heat and drain. Return the potatoes to the saucepan and, over low heat, let the potatoes dry for about 1 minute. Add the butter, heavy cream, and truffle oil. With a hand masher, mash and stir the mixture until almost smooth, leaving a few small lumps. Season with salt and pepper.

Using a mandoline, if you have one, cut the Idaho potatoes into shoestrings. (If you don't have a mandoline, simply coarsely grate them.) Rinse under cold water and pat dry. In a large mixing bowl, toss the potatoes with the olive oil and season with salt and pepper.

2 pounds Yukon Gold potatoes, peeled and
   quartered

Salt

4 tablespoons (½ stick) unsalted butter

½ cup heavy cream

White truffle oil to taste (available in
   specialty food stores)

Freshly ground black pepper to taste

1 pound Idaho potatoes, peeled

2 tablespoons olive oil

½ cup freshly grated Parmigiano-Reggiano
   cheese

2 black truffles (available in specialty food
   stores), brushed clean

1 tablespoon snipped fresh chives

Heat the pan over medium heat, then add the shoestring potatoes, spreading them evenly on the bottom of the skillet, then, using your fingers, press them up the sides of the skillet about 2 inches. Cook over medium heat until golden brown, 5 to 6 minutes. Flip the potatoes over and continue to cook until golden brown.

Gently transfer the potato pancake to a baking sheet lined with parchment paper. Spoon the mashed potatoes evenly over the potato crust, leaving a ½-inch border. Sprinkle with the cheese. Place in the oven and bake until the cheese has melted and the potatoes are heated through, about 5 minutes.

Shave the truffles over the tart. Carefully slide the tart onto a serving platter, garnish with the chives, then slice into wedges to serve.

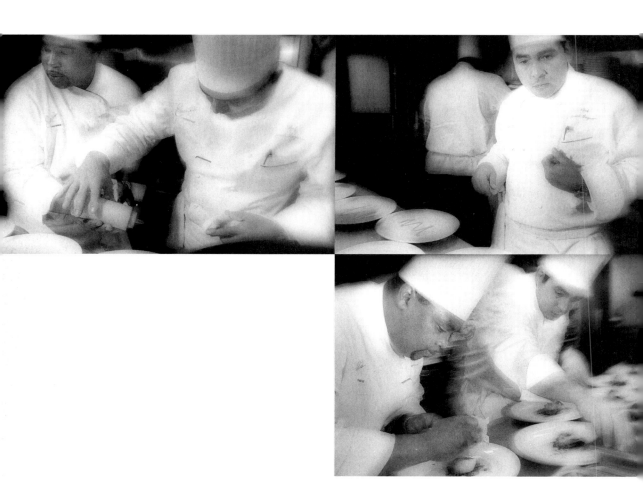

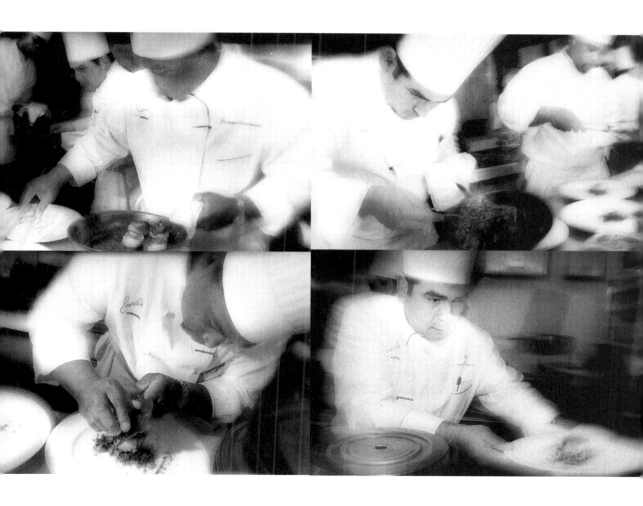

Emeril's

Fish Market

When I have some free time, it's hard to decide whether

to go fishing or play a round of

golf. Well, to be honest, I usually

choose to get out on the open

waters of the Gulf of Mexico, or

any body of water for that matter.

Seafood has fascinated me ever

since I was a child when I first stared a cod in the eye.

Growing up in Fall River, we had not only cod but

haddock, as well as shrimp, clams, mussels, and, of

course, lobster from the Atlantic. And what was intriguing

to me was how versatile fish and shellfish are. You can bake 'em, fry 'em, broil and bake, grill and poach, boil or steam. Get my drift?

When I moved to New Orleans, I was introduced to a whole new cast of seafood. Down here we have crawfish, crabs, oysters, redfish, snapper, and fresh-water catfish and bass. And you should see what they do with seafood around here. Fantastic!

I guess the point I'm trying to make is that, whatever coast you live on, there's fresh fish and seafood. Hey, everybody thought I was crazy when I opened Emeril's New Orleans Fish House in Las Vegas in the middle of the desert! See, you don't even have to live on the coast. These days seafood suppliers are doing an incredible job of getting fresh seafood all over America. Do some investigating, make friends at your local markets, or get your own fishing gear and go drop a line in some water. Learn what's in season in your locale and when you go shopping, don't be shy—sniff that fish, or the shrimp, or crabmeat. Believe me, you'll know if it's fresh or not. If it smells fishy, it's not fresh.

Ready to go on an adventure? Let's go fishing!

Emeril's parents, John and Hilda Lagasse

Provençal Fish Stew

Makes 4 servings

There are times when something as simple as this fish stew is all one needs after a long day. The first time I had it was on a fling through the absolutely charming French province of Provence, where the cuisine is superlative—my kind of food.

I try to make it to Europe once a year, looking for ideas, and this one really impressed me. The ingredients are nothing exotic or difficult to find. Anyone can make this stuff.

In a large saucepan over high heat, combine the stock, tomatoes, tomato paste, Pernod, garlic, and saffron. Bring to a boil, then reduce the heat to medium-low and simmer, uncovered, for 30 minutes. Add the fennel and cod and gently simmer until the fish flakes easily with a fork and the fennel is tender, about 5 minutes. Season with salt and pepper.

Meanwhile, preheat the oven to 400°F. In a medium-size mixing bowl, toss the bread with the olive oil and season with salt and pepper. Put the bread on a baking sheet and toast until crusty, about 5 minutes. Remove from the oven and rub each slice with the garlic halves.

To serve, place a slice of bread in the bottom of 4 soup bowls. Ladle the stew over the croutons and serve hot.

4 cups Fish Stock (page 11) or canned
    chicken broth
3 cups peeled, seeded, and chopped
    tomatoes
2 tablespoons tomato paste
1 tablespoon Pernod
1 tablespoon chopped garlic
10 saffron threads
1 cup thinly sliced fennel bulb
10 ounces cod fillet, cut into 1-inch cubes
Salt and freshly ground black pepper to
    taste
4 slices French bread about 1 inch thick
2 tablespoons olive oil
1 clove garlic, cut in half

Grilled Escolar with Crawfish Cream Sauce

Makes 4 servings

Escolar is native to the Gulf of Mexico and you don't find it too often on menus, but if and when you do, order it! You'll not find a better-tasting fish. Now don't get this escolar confused with that nasty oily fish that sometimes goes by the same name. The bad fish has scales so sharp they'll cut your hands into shreds. Don't buy it.

I'm lucky to have the New Orleans Fish House, which can supply me with escolar that literally slept in the waters the night before. If you can't get it, you can substitute any firm white-fleshed fish such as sea bass, halibut, or pompano. It's great with this crawfish cream sauce, but again, if you can't get crawfish, you can use shrimp or bay scallops. Don't make yourself crazy!

¼ cup plus 2 tablespoons olive oil

½ pound tasso or smoked sausage or ham, finely chopped

1 cup chopped yellow onions

Essence to taste (page 7)

1 pound peeled crawfish tails

1 cup peeled, seeded, and chopped fresh or canned tomatoes

1 tablespoon minced garlic

Salt and freshly ground black pepper to taste

2 cups heavy cream

1 tablespoon Worcestershire sauce

1 tablespoon Crystal Hot Sauce or the hot sauce of your choice

Heat 2 tablespoons of the olive oil in a large sauté pan over medium heat. Add the tasso and cook, stirring often, for 2 to 3 minutes. Add the yellow onions and season with Essence. Add the crawfish and cook all, stirring, for 2 minutes. Add the tomatoes and garlic, season with salt and pepper, and cook, stirring, for 3 minutes more. Add the heavy cream, Worcestershire, and hot sauce and bring to a boil, then reduce the heat to medium and simmer, stirring occasionally, until the cream thickens and reduces by one third, 6 to 8 minutes. Add the green onions. Season again with salt and pepper. Set aside and keep warm.

Season the escolar fillets with Essence. Heat the remaining ¼ cup olive oil in a large sauté pan over medium-high heat, then add the escolar and sear until the fillets are lightly golden and flake easily with a fork, 5 to 6 minutes on each side. Remove and drain on paper towels.

To serve, put equal amounts of the crawfish sauce in the center of 4 serving plates, lay a fillet on top of each, and sprinkle with the parsley.

¼ cup chopped green onions
(green part only)

4 escolar fillets (6 to 8 ounces each)

2 teaspoons chopped fresh parsley leaves

Emeril Live musician
Leonard "Doc" Gibbs

Rock Shrimp Stuffed Flounder

Makes 4 servings

Rock shrimp are caught off the Florida coast and have a delicious lobsterlike flavor. I'm finding them more and more in supermarkets and specialty food shops peeled and headed, which is fine, since they are tough to peel. Just make sure they're fresh when you buy them and use them right away.

Flounder, a flatfish that spends most of its time resting flat, half buried in sand, has long been a Louisiana favorite. For years it was featured in many local restaurants, but it's not as popular as it was once. I don't know why, because I find it very tasty and appealing. The best deal is to find flounders weighing about 1 pound, dressed, which is sufficient to serve 1 person. There are really no bones to worry about except for the center bone. As you eat, the center bone can be easily taken out. Here I've cut open a pocket on top of the fish in which to put a stuffing. Come on, give it a try! You have to be a little adventurous sometimes.

1 tablespoon olive oil

½ cup minced yellow onions

¼ cup minced celery

¼ cup minced red bell pepper

Salt and cayenne to taste

2 teaspoons chopped garlic

1 pound rock shrimp, peeled

¼ cup water

1 cup fine dried bread crumbs

2 tablespoons finely chopped fresh parsley
  leaves

Preheat the oven to 400°F. Line a baking sheet with parchment paper.

Heat the olive oil in a medium-size sauté pan over medium heat. Add the onions, celery, and pepper, season with salt and cayenne, and cook, stirring, until the vegetables are wilted, about 2 minutes. Add the garlic and shrimp and season again with salt and cayenne. Cook, stirring, for 2 minutes, then remove the pan from the heat.

Pour the mixture into a medium-size mixing bowl. Stir in the water and enough bread crumbs to bind the mixture. Add the parsley and season again to taste with salt and cayenne. Set aside.

4 whole flounders (about 1 pound each)

Essence to taste (page 7)

¼ pound (1 stick) unsalted butter, melted

Place each flounder brown side up on a cutting board. With a sharp boning knife, cut along the center bone of the fish. Carefully peel open the fish, pulling the flesh back to form a pocket. Season the outside and pocket of the fish with Essence.

Divide the stuffing mixture into 4 equal parts and fill the pocket of each flounder with it. Fold the flaps over the stuffing.

Place the fish on the prepared baking sheet. Drizzle with the melted butter and bake until the fish flakes easily with a fork, 20 to 25 minutes.

Serve immediately.

Crispy Fish with Salsify, Celery Root, and Fennel Slaw and Parsnip Creamed Potatoes

Makes 2 servings

*R*oot vegetables like salsify and celery root have a great earthy flavor. Not surprising, since they grow underground, right? Here I've paired them with fennel, which sometimes gets bad press because some people think it has an anise flavor, but the taste is sweeter and more delicate than that. The crispy fish is served on a bed of creamed potatoes coupled with parsnip, another root vegetable. This is a super dish where earth and water come together to make a wonderful match.

¼ cup chopped bacon

½ cup thinly sliced salsify, blanched for
    2 minutes in boiling water

½ cup thinly sliced celery root, blanched for
    2 minutes in boiling water

½ cup thinly sliced fennel bulb, blanched for
    2 minutes in boiling water

Salt and freshly ground black pepper to taste

2 tablespoons rice wine vinegar

1½ tablespoons sesame oil

¼ cup chopped unsalted peanuts

2 tablespoons chopped fresh chervil leaves

2 redfish fillets or any firm-fleshed white fish
    (about 6 ounces each)

Essence to taste (page 7)

½ cup bleached all-purpose flour

¼ cup olive oil for frying

1 recipe Parsnip Creamed Potatoes
    (page 145)

Fry the bacon in a medium-size sauté pan over medium heat until crispy, 6 to 8 minutes. Add the salsify, celery root, and fennel, season with salt and pepper, and cook, stirring, for 1 minute. Remove from the heat and pour into a small mixing bowl. Add the vinegar, sesame oil, peanuts, and chervil and toss well to mix. Season with salt and pepper.

Season the fillets with Essence. Put the flour in a shallow bowl and season with Essence. Dredge the fish in the seasoned flour, lightly coating each side and shaking off any excess. Heat the olive oil in a medium-size sauté pan over medium heat, then pan-fry the fish until golden brown and crispy, 2 to 3 minutes on each side. Drain on paper towels. Season with Essence.

To serve, spoon the creamed potatoes in the center of a platter. Place the fish on top of the potatoes and mound the root vegetable slaw on top of the fish.

Parsnip Creamed Potatoes

Makes 2 servings

Put the potatoes and parsnips in a large saucepan with water to cover. Season with salt, put the lid on, and bring to a boil. Reduce the heat to medium and cook until fork tender. Drain. Return the potatoes to the pan and, over low heat, stir with a fork or wire whisk to dry them. Add the butter and heavy cream, season with salt and pepper, and mix or mash well, leaving a few lumps. Serve hot.

½ pound Idaho potatoes, peeled and diced

½ pound parsnips, peeled and chopped

Salt

2 tablespoons unsalted butter

½ cup heavy cream

Freshly ground white pepper to taste

Linguiça-Crusted Roasted Salmon Cedar Plank

Makes 4 servings

Linguiça is a Portuguese sausage that's heavily flavored with garlic and can be found in some Latin American markets and many supermarkets. But if you can't find it, you can use any kind of smoked sausage. The salmon is coated with a sausage mixture, then cooked on an untreated cedar plank, which can be found at home-improvement centers and lumberyards. Just be sure it's untreated.

4 salmon fillets (about 6 ounces each)

4 teaspoons plus 1 tablespoon olive oil

Essence to taste (page 7)

4 untreated cedar planks, about 5½ × 10 inches, lightly rubbed with vegetable oil

½ pound chopped linguiça sausage or any other smoked sausage

½ cup fine dried bread crumbs

2 tablespoons grated lemon zest

2 tablespoons grated orange zest

Salt and freshly ground black pepper to taste

Preheat the oven 400°F.

Rub each fillet with a teaspoon of the olive oil and season with Essence. Heat the remaining tablespoon olive oil in a large sauté pan over high heat. Sear the salmon fillets for 1 to 2 minutes on each side. Transfer the salmon to the cedar planks and set aside.

In a large sauté pan, fry the sausage for 2 to 3 minutes over medium heat. Add the bread crumbs and mix to bind with the sausage. Stir in the lemon and orange zests and season with salt and pepper. Using your fingers, spread the sausage mixture evenly all over the top of the salmon fillets, pressing it firmly into the fish.

Place the planks on a baking sheet and bake for 14 minutes for medium-rare, 16 minutes for medium, and 18 minutes for well done.

Remove from the oven and serve immediately.

Roasted Ginger Salmon with Ginger Soy Butter Sauce

Makes 4 servings

I'm a big fan of Asian and Middle Eastern cooking, and I especially like the flavor that gingerroot brings to many dishes. Pairing ginger with fish is not something new, and I think you're going to like this dish I created.

Preheat the oven to 400°F.

In a medium-size nonreactive saucepan over medium heat, combine the soy sauce, honey, brown sugar, gingerroot, garlic, and shallots. Bring to a boil, reduce the heat to low, and simmer until the sauce is dark brown and reduced by half, 5 to 6 minutes. Remove from the heat and add the butter cubes, stirring until they have completely melted. Stir in the orange juice. Strain the sauce through a chinoise or fine-mesh sieve and season with salt and pepper. Keep the sauce warm.

In a small mixing bowl, combine the 1 cup grated gingerroot, orange zest, lemon zest, and cilantro and mix well. Add enough bread crumbs to bind the mixture. Season with salt and pepper.

Season the salmon with Essence. In a large sauté pan with an ovenproof handle, heat the olive oil over high heat. Add the salmon and sear for 2 minutes. Turn over and cover the top side of each fillet with the bread crumb mixture. Place the pan in the oven and roast 14 minutes for medium-rare, 16 minutes for medium, and 18 minutes for well done.

½ cup soy sauce

⅓ cup honey

1 tablespoon firmly packed light brown sugar

One 1-ounce piece fresh gingerroot, peeled and minced, plus 1 cup peeled and grated fresh gingerroot

1 tablespoon minced garlic

1 tablespoon minced shallots

½ pound (2 sticks) cold unsalted butter, cut into cubes

Juice of 1 orange (about ⅓ cup)

Salt and freshly ground black pepper to taste

2 tablespoons grated orange zest

2 tablespoons grated lemon zest

3 tablespoons finely chopped fresh cilantro leaves

½ to 1 cup fine dried bread crumbs, as needed

4 salmon fillets (about 6 ounces each)

Essence to taste (page 7)

2 tablespoons olive oil

To serve, spoon a small pool of the sauce in the center of a serving platter and place the salmon in the center of the sauce.

Whole Sea Bass with Niçoise Tapenade

Makes 4 servings

When you go to the fish market, specify that you want a true saltwater bass, not the freshwater species. The saltwater bass is truly delicious and has very few bones. A whole bass makes a really kicked-up presentation.

Oh, by the way, a tapenade is a thick paste made with olives, capers, anchovies, and some other good stuff that is popular in France's Provence region.

1 tablespoon dried savory

1 tablespoon dried rosemary

1 tablespoon dried thyme

1 tablespoon dried oregano

1 tablespoon dried basil

1 tablespoon dried marjoram

1 tablespoon fennel seeds

1 cup pitted niçoise olives

1 tablespoon minced garlic

1 tablespoon drained capers

3 anchovy fillets

3 tablespoons fresh lemon juice

¼ cup extra virgin olive oil

Salt and freshly ground black pepper to taste

1 whole sea bass (about 2 pounds), cleaned and scaled

1 tablespoon olive oil

Preheat the oven to 400°F. Line a baking sheet with parchment or waxed paper.

In a small mixing bowl, combine all the dried herbs and mix well. Set aside.

In a food processor or blender, combine the olives, garlic, capers, anchovies, lemon juice, and extra virgin olive oil and process until smooth. Season with salt and pepper. Set aside.

Rub the fish with plain olive oil and season with salt and pepper. Spread the olive mixture evenly over the fish and in the cavity, then press the herb mixture evenly all over the fish. Place the fish on the baking sheet and bake until the fish flakes easily with a fork, 25 to 30 minutes. Remove the fish from the oven and serve hot.

Scallops, Confit of Wild Mushrooms, and Black Truffle Dome

Makes 4 appetizer servings

Now, *don't be scared about the word* dome, *since all I'm doing really is making a kicked-up version of a good old American pot pie. It's so kicked-up we served it last New Year's Eve at Emeril's as an appetizer and it was a hit. But you can serve it anytime—maybe for your mother-in-law's birthday!*

Preheat the oven to 400°F.

In a medium-size sauté pan, heat the olive oil over medium heat. Season the scallops with salt and pepper and add to the pan. Sear for 2 minutes on each side and remove from the heat.

Season the sliced potato with salt and pepper. Divide them into 4 equal portions. Line the bottoms of four 6-ounce ramekins with the potato slices, overlapping them. Top each with a scallop, then ¼ cup of the confit, then pour in ¼ cup of the veal reduction. Drizzle each with a teaspoon of truffle oil, sprinkle with a tablespoon of the cheese, and top with shaved truffle.

Cut four 4-inch rounds out of the puff pastry and cover the top of each ramekin with one. With your fingers, press the pastry over the rims and remove any excess to seal completely. Lightly brush the pastry with the beaten egg and sprinkle with salt and pepper and the remaining 4 teaspoons cheese. Bake until golden, 10 to 12 minutes.

Garnish with the parsley and serve hot.

1 tablespoon olive oil

4 large sea or diver scallops

Salt and freshly ground black pepper to taste

1 medium-size red potato, thinly sliced

1 cup Confit of Exotic Mushrooms (page 128)

1 recipe Veal Reduction (page 10)

4 teaspoons white truffle oil (available in specialty food stores)

¼ cup plus 4 teaspoons freshly grated Parmigiano-Reggiano cheese

1 small black truffle (available in specialty food stores), wiped clean and shaved

1 sheet (11 × 14 inches) puff pastry (look for this in the frozen foods section of your supermarket)

1 large egg, lightly beaten

1 tablespoon chopped fresh parsley leaves

Chorizo-Crusted Scallops with Cilantro Guacamole and Tortilla Strips

Makes 4 appetizer servings

Here's a great combination–chorizo, scallops, guacamole, and tortilla strips–a dash of Portuguese and a little something from south of the border! Hey, now!

2 medium-size ripe Haas avocados, peeled, pitted, and seeded

3 tablespoons peeled, seeded, and finely chopped ripe tomatoes

1 small fresh jalapeño, seeded and minced

2 tablespoons finely chopped yellow onion

1 teaspoon minced garlic

3 tablespoons fresh lemon juice

3 tablespoons fresh lime juice

2 tablespoons finely chopped fresh cilantro leaves

Crystal Hot Sauce or the hot sauce of your choice to taste

Salt and freshly ground black pepper to taste

2¼ cups vegetable oil

1 cup corn tortilla strips

Essence to taste (page 7)

½ pound finely chopped chorizo sausage

1 cup fine dried bread crumbs

16 large sea scallops

½ cup bleached all-purpose flour

1 large egg, lightly beaten

1 cup Pico de Gallo (page 151)

In a medium-size mixing bowl, mash the avocados together with a fork until they are soft but still lumpy. Stir in the tomatoes, jalapeño, onion, garlic, lemon and lime juices, cilantro, and hot sauce. Season with salt and black pepper. Press a sheet of plastic wrap directly on the surface of the guacamole, forcing out any air bubbles. Refrigerate. It will keep for up to 8 hours.

In a large, heavy, deep pot or an electric fryer, heat 2 cups of the vegetable oil to 360°F. Deep-fry the tortilla strips until lightly golden and crispy, 1 to 2 minutes. Drain on paper towels, then season with Essence.

In a medium-size sauté pan, fry the chorizo over medium heat for 2 to 3 minutes. Put the chorizo and bread crumbs in a food processor and pulse several times until the mixture binds together. Season with Essence. Set aside.

Season the scallops with Essence. Put the flour in a shallow bowl and season with Essence. Put the egg in another shallow bowl and season with Essence. Dredge the scallops in the flour, shaking off any excess. Dip each scallop in the egg, letting the excess drip off. Then dredge them in the chorizo mixture, coating evenly.

Heat the remaining ¼ cup vegetable oil in a large sauté pan over medium heat. Pan-fry the scallops until golden, 2 to 3 minutes on each side. Drain on paper towels and season with Essence.

To serve, spoon equal amounts of the guacamole in the center of 4 appetizer plates. Arrange the scallops around the guacamole. Spoon the pico de gallo on top of each scallop, then pile the tortilla strips on top of the guacamole.

Pico de Gallo

Makes about 2½ cups

Combine all of the ingredients in a medium-size mixing bowl and stir to mix. Cover and chill for at least 2 hours before serving.

1½ cups peeled, seeded, and diced ripe
   tomatoes
¼ cup diced yellow onion
1 tablespoon seeded, minced fresh jalapeño
2 teaspoons chopped garlic
1 tablespoon fresh lemon juice
1 tablespoon fresh lime juice
1 tablespoon chopped fresh cilantro leaves
Salt and freshly ground black pepper to
   taste

Mussels and Fennel with Saffron Cream Sauce

Makes 2 servings

When selecting mussels at the store, make sure they are fresh and not gaping wide open. You can check by giving them a sniff, and believe me you'll know if they're not fresh. They should have a nice briny fragrance. You can clean them by brushing them with a stiff kitchen brush under cool water to get rid of any grit and sand, then pinching off the beard— that little tuft of hairs sticking out.

Herbsaint is the anise-flavored liqueur used in making that New Orleans favorite, oysters Rockefeller. When you flame it, be extremely careful and cautious. We don't want y'all catching on fire or burning yourselves! Listen to me well so you'll know how to flambé—or flame—things. Add the alcohol to the cooking pan and, being very careful, light it with a taper. Stand back so you won't burn your eyebrows off! Shake the pan a couple of times and the flames will die down as the alcohol burns off.

1 tablespoon olive oil

1½ cups thinly sliced fennel bulb
    (about ½ bulb)

1 medium-size red bell pepper, cut into
    strips

1 medium-size yellow bell pepper, cut into
    strips

Salt and freshly ground black pepper to
    taste

2 ounces Herbsaint or Pernod

1 tablespoon minced shallots

Heat the olive oil in a large sauté pan over medium heat. Add the fennel and bell peppers, and season with salt and pepper. Cook, stirring, for 2 to 3 minutes. Take the pan away from the heat and add the Herbsaint. Carefully place the pan back over the heat for about 15 seconds to get the alcohol warm, and flame, shaking the pan several times. Add the shallots, garlic, and heavy cream and stir in the saffron. Season with salt and pepper. Bring the liquid to a boil, then reduce the heat to a simmer. Add the mussels, cover the pan, and simmer until the mussels open, 3 to 4 minutes. Discard any unopened mussels.

To serve, spoon the mixture into 2 shallow bowls and garnish with the chopped parsley.

1 teaspoon minced garlic

2 cups heavy cream

Pinch of saffron threads

2 dozen live mussels, scrubbed and
   debearded

2 tablespoons chopped fresh parsley leaves

Emeril with Vinny the butcher

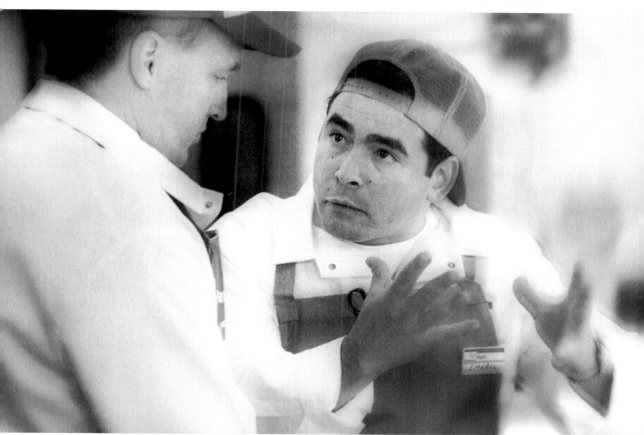

Baked Oysters with Braised Leeks and Tasso Hollandaise

Makes 4 appetizer servings

Bet you didn't know that the flavor of the oyster depends on its habitat and that oysters go by many different names, depending on where they are grown. And the oyster has a reputation as an aphrodisiac, especially in New Orleans where bumper stickers read, "Eat Louisiana oysters and love longer." That should be inspiration enough to slurp down a few on the half shell!

For those of you who are not prone to eat them raw, here are baked oysters, dazzled with some hollandaise spiced with tasso, a Louisiana smoked and seasoned ham. But if you don't have tasso, use whatever you got—smoked sausage, ham, bacon—be creative!

2 tablespoons olive oil

2 tablespoons minced shallots

1 tablespoon minced garlic

2 cups julienned leeks (white part only, well washed)

Salt and freshly ground black pepper to taste

2 tablespoons dry white wine

¼ pound tasso, finely chopped

3 large egg yolks

2 tablespoons fresh lemon juice

¼ pound (1 stick) unsalted butter, melted

1 dozen shucked oysters (reserve the shells)

1 cup fine dried bread crumbs

Essence to taste (page 7)

¼ cup freshly grated Parmigiano-Reggiano cheese

2 tablespoons chopped fresh parsley leaves

Preheat the oven to 450°F. Line a baking sheet with parchment or waxed paper.

Heat the olive oil in a medium-size sauté pan over medium heat. Add the shallots, garlic, and leeks and season with salt and pepper. Cook, stirring, for 1 to 2 minutes. Add the wine and cook until the leeks are tender, another 2 to 3 minutes. Remove from the heat and set aside.

Heat a small skillet over medium heat. Add the tasso and fry until crispy, 4 to 6 minutes. Drain on paper towels. Reserve the rendered fat in the skillet.

Prepare the bottom of a double boiler with water and bring to a gentle boil over medium heat. Combine the egg yolks and lemon juice in a stainless steel mixing bowl and season with salt and pepper. Place the bowl over the boiling water and whisk until the yolks are thick and ribbonlike, 3 to 4 minutes. Whisk the melted butter and reserved tasso fat into the egg mixture in a steady stream. Season with salt and pepper and continue whisking until the mixture thickens again. Fold in the tasso. Keep warm.

Arrange the oyster shells on the baking sheet.

Season the bread crumbs with Essence. Season the oysters with Essence. Dredge them in the bread crumbs, coating each one evenly. Place a spoonful of the leek mixture in the center of each oyster shell. Lay an oyster on top of the leek mixture. Sprinkle them with the remaining bread crumbs. Bake until the tops of the oysters are golden brown, 4 to 6 minutes.

To serve, drizzle the oysters with the hollandaise sauce and sprinkle with the cheese and parsley.

155

Sweet Water Prawns over Spinach Pappardelle with a Champagne and Salmon Roe Butter Sauce

Makes 4 to 6 servings

Sometimes there's some confusion about what are prawns and what are shrimp. Well, in some parts of the United States and Great Britain, the word prawn is used for all shrimp except tiny shrimp, which are usually called bay shrimp. Then there are times when only very large shrimp are called prawns. On the East Coast, everything is called shrimp except freshwater prawns, which are called prawns. Now that I have you really confused, you should know that scampi is a Venetian word for Dublin Bay prawns, which are really more like lobsters than shrimp. Got it? Now go get yourself some prawns, those big shrimp, and you're set.

Be forewarned, this is a rather rich dish.

2 tablespoons minced shallots

1 cup Champagne

1 pound (4 sticks) cold unsalted butter, cut into 2-inch cubes

Salt and freshly ground black pepper to taste

8 cups salted water

½ pound fresh spinach pappardelle pasta

1 teaspoon plus 2 tablespoons olive oil

2 pounds large prawns, shelled and deveined, heads left on if you can get them that way

2 tablespoons salmon roe

Preheat the oven to 400°F.

Combine the shallots and Champagne in a medium-size saucepan over medium heat and reduce the mixture to a glaze. Add the butter cubes slowly, whisking constantly until they are all melted. The sauce will thicken slightly. Strain through a fine-mesh strainer into a medium-size sauté pan. Season with salt and pepper. Set aside and keep warm.

Bring the salted water to a boil in a large saucepan. Add the pasta and cook until tender, 2 to 3 minutes. Drain. Toss the pasta in a large mixing bowl with 1 teaspoon of the olive oil. Season with salt and pepper.

Heat the remaining 2 tablespoons olive oil in a large ovenproof sauté pan over medium heat. Season the prawns with salt and pepper. Sear them for 2 minutes on each side. Transfer the pan to the oven and bake for 3 to 4 minutes.

Carefully fold the salmon roe into the Champagne sauce. Toss the pasta with the sauce.

To serve, divide the pasta into equal portions. Twirl into nests and place in the center of dinner plates. Arrange the prawns around the pasta, sprinkle with the cheese and parsley, and serve.

¼ cup freshly grated Parmigiano-Reggiano cheese

1 tablespoon finely chopped fresh parsley leaves

Emeril Live production manager Sean Dowd and soundman Jeff Lieb

Potato-Crusted Lobster Tails
on a Bed of Crawfish Mashed Potatoes

Makes 4 servings

Friends, this is an incredible dish! What could be better than lobster from Maine and crawfish from Louisiana? Don't you love it? You just got to taste this stuff!

Now don't get uptight about the potato threader we use; you can get one at a fancy-schmancy gourmet or kitchen shop (see the Source Guide), and you won't be sorry you bought one. I've had lots of fun with it, plus it's a great conversation piece!

2 tablespoons unsalted butter

½ pound peeled crawfish tails

Salt and freshly ground black pepper to taste

½ cup heavy cream

Essence to taste (page 7)

1 recipe Roasted Garlic Mashed Potatoes (page 63)

4 Maine lobster tails (about 7 ounces each), shelled

¼ cup Dijon mustard

2 large Idaho potatoes, peeled

3 tablespoons olive oil

1 tablespoon chopped fresh parsley leaves

Heat the butter in a large saucepan over medium heat. Add the crawfish tails, season with salt and pepper, and cook, stirring, for 2 minutes. Add the heavy cream and bring to a simmer. Season with Essence. Add the garlic mashed potatoes and season again with salt and pepper if needed. Set aside and keep warm.

Season the lobster tails with salt and pepper. Rub each lightly with the mustard. With a potato threader, cut the potatoes into long spiral curls. Season the curls with salt and pepper. Wrap each lobster tail tightly with the curls, then place the tails in a damp, clean kitchen cloth, roll them up tightly to adhere the potatoes to the lobster, and remove the cloth.

Heat the olive oil in a medium-size sauté pan over medium heat. Add the lobster tails and pan-fry until the potato crust is golden brown, 4 to 6 minutes on each side. Drain on paper towels, then season with Essence.

To serve, mound the crawfish-and-mashed potato mixture in the center of 4 dinner plates. Lay a lobster tail over the potatoes and garnish with the parsley.

Know Your Birds

Chicken is probably the most popular bird that lands on our dining tables. You can dress it up, or you can dress it down and, you know, I know of no one who's allergic to it or offended by it. Plus, did you ever wonder why, when people ask what something—

alligator, rabbit, snake, nutria—tastes like, everybody answers, "It tastes like chicken!" I guess poor old chicken is just neutral-tasting.

Seriously, though, chicken and duck are easy to

work with. You can find them in the supermarkets, there's really nothing exotic about them, and even little children like them.

The recipes here are some of the best in my bird repertoire. Enjoy!

Emerilized Chicken Cordon Bleu

Makes 4 servings

Chicken Cordon Bleu, as well as Veal Cordon Bleu, has been around a long time. It's simply thin scallops of chicken or veal sandwiched around a thin slice of prosciutto or other ham and Gruyère or Swiss cheese; then the stacked meat and cheese are breaded and cooked until golden.

To kick it up a notch, I use De Soto cheese, made by my friends at Chicory Farm in Louisiana, or an Emmental-style cheese, which is a Swiss-style cheese, dotted with holes. But hey, you can use just about anything you want—regular Gruyère and Swiss do just fine. The De Soto is named after De Soto Parish (we have parishes instead of counties in Louisiana) and it's mild and melts very well, which makes it great for this dish.

The small, young peas jazz up the rather bland-looking chicken, and the Mornay sauce gives it an extra wallop.

This dish is featured on the lunch menu at Delmonico Restaurant and Bar, my new place on St. Charles Avenue in New Orleans.

- 4 skinless boneless chicken breasts (about 6 ounces each), cut in half and pounded into thin scallops
- Salt and freshly ground black pepper to taste
- 8 thin slices prosciutto
- 8 thin slices De Soto or Emmental-style cheese
- 1 cup bleached all-purpose flour
- Essence to taste (page 7)
- 2 large eggs, lightly beaten
- 2 tablespoons milk
- 1 cup fine dried bread crumbs
- 3 tablespoons olive oil
- 1 tablespoon unsalted butter
- 4 ounces sliced prosciutto, cut into thin strips
- 1 cup sweet young peas, fresh or frozen (defrost if frozen)
- 2 cups hot Mornay Sauce (page 12)

Season both sides of the chicken scallops with salt and pepper. Place 4 scallops on a clean work surface. Top each with 2 slices of the prosciutto, 2 slices of the cheese, and another chicken scallop. Press each gently but firmly together.

Put the flour in a shallow bowl and season with Essence. Combine the eggs and milk in another shallow bowl. Place the bread crumbs in another shallow bowl and season with Essence. Carefully dredge the chicken in the flour, tapping off any excess, then dip it in the egg wash, letting any excess drip off, then dredge it in the bread crumbs, coating evenly.

Heat the olive oil in a large sauté pan over medium-high heat. Add the chicken and cook until golden brown, about 4 minutes on each side. Remove carefully and drain on paper towels. Sprinkle with Essence.

In a small sauté pan, melt the butter over medium heat. Add the prosciutto strips and peas, season with salt and pepper, and cook for 2 minutes. Fold the prosciutto and peas into the Mornay sauce. Spoon the sauce into the center of each serving plate and top with the chicken.

Turbodog Chicken with Home Fries

Makes 4 servings

Turbodog beer is made by the people at Abita Brewing Company, which is located in Abita Springs, north of New Orleans across Lake Pontchartrain. They make several kinds of beer—all good. Turbodog, one of my *favorites, is a dark brown ale brewed with Willamette hops, from the north-western United States, and pale crystal and chocolate malts. Man, is it great, and it gives the batter a good kick! If you can't put your hands on Turbodog, you can substitute any dark beer that you like.*

I created this dish for Jay Leno when I appeared on The Tonight Show because he's a basic meat, or chicken, and potatoes man.

Put the potatoes in a large pot of salted water and bring to a boil. Reduce the heat to medium and cook until tender, about 10 minutes. Drain and set aside.

In a large sauté pan over medium-high heat, cook the bacon, stirring, until crispy. Add the potatoes and onions, season with salt and pepper, and cook, stirring, until the potatoes are lightly browned, 8 to 10 minutes. Set aside and keep warm.

Season the chicken with Essence and set aside. In a large mixing bowl, combine the flour and sugar. Add the beer, egg yolks, milk, and water and whisk until smooth. Season with salt and pepper, then cover and let stand for 30 minutes.

In a large, heavy pot or an electric fryer, heat 4 inches of oil to 360°F.

Uncover the batter and fold in the beaten egg whites. Dip the chicken strips a few at a time in the batter, letting the excess drip off. Carefully add the chicken to the hot oil without crowding and fry until golden brown, 4 to 6 minutes. Drain on paper towels, then season with Essence. Serve with the rémoulade and the home fries.

1½ pounds new or small red potatoes, quartered

Salt to taste

1 pound sliced bacon, chopped

2 cups thinly sliced yellow onions

Freshly ground black pepper to taste

4 skinless boneless chicken breast halves (about 6 ounces each), cut lengthwise into ½-inch-thick strips

Essence to taste (page 7)

1½ cups bleached all-purpose flour

1 tablespoon sugar

¼ cup Abita Turbodog beer

2 large egg yolks, beaten

6 tablespoons milk

6 tablespoons water

Vegetable oil for deep frying

2 large egg whites, beaten to stiff peaks

2 cups Rémoulade Sauce (page 166)

continued

Rémoulade Sauce

Makes about 2 cups

1 cup Emeril's Mayonnaise (page 14)

2 tablespoons Creole or whole-grain
  mustard

2 tablespoons ketchup

½ cup finely chopped green onions
  (green part only)

2 tablespoons finely chopped fresh parsley
  leaves

2 tablespoons finely chopped celery

1½ teaspoons chopped garlic

1 teaspoon sweet paprika

1 teaspoon Crystal Hot Sauce or the hot
  sauce of your choice

Salt and freshly ground black pepper to
  taste

In a medium-size mixing bowl, combine the mayonnaise, mustard, ketchup, green onions, parsley, celery, garlic, paprika, and hot sauce. Mix well, then season with salt and pepper.

Cover and chill for at least 2 hours before serving. It's best used within 24 hours.

Note: See salmonella warning on page 13 regarding raw eggs.

Chicken Pot Pie

Makes 6 servings

Chicken pot pie is a *New England thing and has been around since Rev-olutionary times. Nowadays you see pot pies made with lobster and corn, and sometimes clams and chorizo, but I still love a good basic one made with chicken.*

Preheat the oven to 400°F. Grease a 9 × 9 × 2-inch baking pan.

Heat the butter in a large sauté pan over medium-high heat. Add the onions and celery, season with salt and pepper, and cook, stirring, for 2 minutes. Stir in the flour and cook, stirring, for 3 to 4 minutes to make a blond roux. Stir in the chicken stock and bring the liquid to a boil. Reduce the heat to medium-low and simmer until the sauce begins to thicken, 4 to 6 minutes. Stir in the half-and-half and continue to cook for another 4 minutes. Season with salt and pepper. Stir in the potatoes, carrots, peas, chicken, and parsley, season with salt and pepper, and mix well.

Line the baking pan with one of the rolled-out piecrusts. Pour the filling into the prepared pan. Place the second crust on top of the filling. Carefully tuck the overlapping crusts into the pan, forming a thick edge. Crimp the edges, cut vents in the top crust, and place on a baking sheet. Bake until the crust is golden brown and crusty, 25 to 30 minutes. Let cool for 5 minutes before slicing to serve.

6 tablespoons (¾ stick) unsalted butter

1 cup chopped yellow onions

½ cup chopped celery

Salt and freshly ground black pepper to taste

6 tablespoons bleached all-purpose flour

2 cups Chicken Stock (page 8) or canned chicken broth

1 cup half-and-half

2 cups peeled and diced Idaho potatoes, cooked in boiling salted water until tender, 6 to 8 minutes

1 cup diced carrots, cooked in boiling salted water until tender, 4 to 5 minutes

1 cup sweet young peas, fresh or frozen (defrost if frozen)

2 cups shredded cooked chicken, white and dark meat

2 tablespoons finely chopped fresh parsley leaves

1 recipe Basic Savory Piecrust (page 168)

continued

167

Basic Savory Piecrust

Makes 2 piecrusts, enough for one 9-inch and one 10-inch crust

3¼ cups bleached all-purpose flour

1 teaspoon salt

1½ cups cold lard or solid vegetable
    shortening

4 to 5 tablespoons ice water, as needed

Combine the flour and salt in a large mixing bowl. Add the lard and work it in with your hands until the mixture resembles coarse crumbs. Add the water, 1 tablespoon at a time, working it in with your hands. Add only as much as you need to make a smooth ball of dough. Wrap it in plastic wrap and refrigerate for at least 30 minutes.

Remove the dough from the refrigerator and place it on a lightly floured work surface. For 2 crusts, cut the dough in 2 equal pieces and put the second half back in the refrigerator. For each crust, roll out the dough on the floured surface into a square about 14 inches across and ⅛ inch thick. Gently fold the square of dough in half and then in half again so that you can lift it without tearing it, and unfold it into a square baking pan. Fill and proceed as directed in the recipe.

Asparagus and Chicken Confit Rags

Makes 6 servings

Remember, we've already made confit of mushrooms, and now we're going to make chicken confit, and later we'll make one with duck. Simply use the recipe for duck confit, and substitute chicken for the duck. Got it?

I'm using fresh, young asparagus in this dish because I like the flavor of the confit and the texture and color of the bright green asparagus together.

Asparagus used to be available only in the springtime, but now it's found practically all year round. When shopping for asparagus, make sure it's not discolored and that the stalks are firm and not withered at all. If you buy large ones, you may have to peel the stalks with a vegetable peeler. Always snap off the woody bottoms.

Heat the olive oil in a large sauté pan over medium heat. Add the onions, season with salt and pepper, and cook, stirring, for 1 minute. Add the garlic and chicken confit and cook, stirring, for 2 minutes. Add the asparagus, season with salt and pepper, and cook, stirring for 1 minute.

Bring a large saucepan of salted water to a boil, add the pasta, and cook until tender, 4 to 5 minutes (longer if using the dried lasagna). Remove from the heat and drain.

In a large mixing bowl, toss the pasta with the chicken mixture. Season with salt and pepper, add the cheese, and drizzle with the truffle oil.

Serve warm garnished with the parsley.

1 tablespoon olive oil

1 cup minced yellow onions

Salt and freshly ground black pepper to taste

1 tablespoon chopped garlic

1 pound julienned chicken confit (follow directions for Duck Confit, page 175)

1 pound fresh green asparagus, trimmed, grilled until slightly tender, 2 to 3 minutes, and cut into 2-inch pieces

1/2 pound fresh pasta sheets or 1/2 pound dried lasagna, broken into pieces

1/2 pound smoked mozzarella cheese, diced

1 tablespoon white truffle oil (available in specialty food stores)

1 tablespoon chopped fresh parsley leaves

Whole Roasted Squabs Stuffed with Eggplant and Bacon Dressing

Makes 6 servings

Let's see, a squab chicken is called a poussin *in French. But then there is a true squab, which is very young, 4 to 6 weeks old, and very small, about 1¼ pounds. Sometimes they're called squab broilers. This is what you want to get at your local supermarket or specialty market.*

12 ounces sliced bacon, chopped

2 cups chopped yellow onions

½ cup chopped celery

½ cup chopped green bell peppers

Salt and cayenne to taste

1 medium-size eggplant, peeled and diced

3 tablespoons chopped garlic

1 tablespoon chopped fresh thyme leaves

1 tablespoon finely chopped fresh parsley leaves

½ cup chopped green onions (green part only)

4 cups crumbled Skillet Corn Bread (page 15)

2 cups Chicken Stock (page 8) or canned chicken broth

6 squabs (about 1¼ pounds each), dressed

3 tablespoons olive oil

12 shallots, peeled

1½ cups Veal Reduction (page 10)

1 tablespoon unsalted butter

1 pound haricots verts or thin green beans, trimmed and cooked in boiling salted water until just tender, about 2 minutes

Preheat the oven to 400°F. Line a large roasting pan with parchment paper.

In a large sauté pan over medium heat, fry the bacon, stirring, until crispy, 6 to 8 minutes. Add the onions, celery, and bell peppers, season with salt and cayenne, and cook, stirring, until soft, 3 to 4 minutes. Add the eggplant and cook, stirring, for 3 minutes. Season with salt and cayenne. Stir in 2 tablespoons of the garlic, the thyme, parsley, and green onions. Remove from the heat and pour into a large mixing bowl. Add the corn bread and stock, mix thoroughly, and season with salt and cayenne.

Rub the squabs with 2 tablespoons of the olive oil and season with salt and cayenne. Stuff the cavity of each with about ¾ cup of the dressing; don't pack the dressing in tightly. Toss the shallots with the remaining tablespoon olive oil and season with salt and cayenne.

Place the squabs and shallots in the prepared pan. Roast until the squabs are golden brown and the juices run clear from the cavities, 25 to 30 minutes (the internal temperature should read between 180° and 185°F on an instant-read meat thermometer). Remove from the oven. Place the shallots in a saucepan and cover with the veal reduction. Bring to a boil, then reduce the heat to a simmer and cook for 2 minutes. Season with salt and pepper.

Melt the butter in a large sauté pan over medium heat. Add the haricots verts and the remaining tablespoon garlic, season with salt and cayenne, and cook, stirring, to heat through, about 3 minutes.

Serve the squabs with the haricots verts and the shallot-veal reduction.

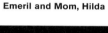

Emeril and Mom, Hilda

Duck Burritos with Chili Corn Sauce

Makes 6 servings

Thanks to former sous-chef Steve Howard, a native Texan who worked with Chef David McCelvey, this was the number one dish at NOLA for a long time. No kidding! I guess the idea of baked duck tucked into a burrito made just the right combination to satisfy our visitors from our neighboring state of Texas who had to get a little fix of Tex-Mex food. It really is a good dish and it takes a little time to get it all together, but, as they say, it's worth it!

1 whole duck breast (about 1 pound)

Salt and freshly ground black pepper to taste

1 teaspoon plus 1 tablespoon olive oil

½ cup minced yellow onions

1 cup fresh sweet corn kernels (from 1 medium-size ear)

1 tablespoon minced shallots

2 teaspoons chopped garlic

1 cup cooked black beans

1 cup cooked long-grain white rice

1 tablespoon chili powder

2 teaspoons ground cumin

1 cup Duck Stock (page 9)

1 tablespoon chopped fresh cilantro leaves

Vegetable oil for frying

6 large flour tortillas

12 toothpicks, if needed

Essence to taste (page 7)

1 recipe Chili Corn Sauce (page 173)

½ cup grated Cheddar cheese

½ cup grated Monterey Jack cheese

1 cup Cilantro Sour Cream (page 123)

Preheat the oven to 400°F.

Season the duck breast with salt and pepper. Heat 1 teaspoon of the olive oil in a large oven-proof sauté pan over medium heat. Place the duck breast, skin side down, in the pan and cook until the skin is crispy and brown, 10 minutes. Turn the duck breast over and cook for 10 minutes more. Transfer the pan to the oven. Roast for about 5 minutes for medium-rare; 8 minutes for medium; 10 minutes for well done. Remove from the oven and let the meat rest for about 2 minutes. Let cool and remove the skin. Shred the meat and set aside.

Heat the remaining 1 tablespoon olive oil in a large sauté pan over medium heat. Add the onions and cook, stirring, for 1 minute. Season with salt and pepper. Add the corn, shallots, and garlic, and cook, stirring, for another 2 minutes. Add the duck, black beans, and rice and season with the chili powder and cumin. Add the duck stock and bring to a boil. Reduce the heat to medium-low and simmer until the liquid has reduced by two thirds, 2 to 3 minutes.

Remove the pan from the heat and reseason with salt and pepper if necessary. Stir in the cilantro. Cool completely.

In a large, heavy, deep pot or an electric fryer, heat 4 inches of vegetable oil to 360°F. Spoon ¾ cup of the filling into the center of each tortilla. Lightly wet the edges of the tortilla with water, then fold in the sides of the tortilla and roll it up tightly, forming a burrito, making sure that the sides are completely sealed. If necessary, secure each end of the burrito with a toothpick. Place the burritos, a couple at a time, in the hot oil and fry until golden brown, 2 to 3 minutes on each side. Turn them with a spoon for even browning. Drain on paper towels. Season with Essence.

To serve, spoon equal amounts of the chili corn sauce into the center of each serving plate. Place the burrito on the sauce, then garnish with a sprinkle of the cheeses and a dollop of cilantro sour cream.

Chili Corn Sauce

Makes about 2½ cups

Heat the oil in a medium-size saucepan over medium heat. Add the onion, season with salt and pepper, and cook, stirring, for 1 minute. Add the corn, garlic, and jalapeño and season with salt and pepper. Cook, stirring, for 2 minutes. Add the heavy cream, bring to a gentle boil, and cook until the cream reduces by one fourth, 6 to 8 minutes. In a blender or using a handheld blender, puree the sauce until smooth. Season again with salt and pepper. Serve the sauce hot with the burritos.

1 teaspoon olive oil

¼ cup minced yellow onion

Salt and freshly ground black pepper to taste

3 cups fresh sweet corn kernels (from 3 medium-size ears)

1 teaspoon minced garlic

1 fresh jalapeño, seeded and minced

2 cups heavy cream

Duck Tacos

Makes 4 servings

I know you're saying duck tacos, yeah, yeah, yeah! But these are a hoot! I created them for the Cartoon Network for Space Ghost. What? You don't know about Space Ghost? Well, when I did them in the cartoon, Space Ghost said that these were not only out of this world, they were so good they were out of this planet! How about that? You better give them a try!

This tamarind sauce is made from the fruit of a shade tree native to Asia and northern Africa and India. And probably all you need to know is that tamarind sauce is used in East Indian and Middle Eastern cuisines much as we add lemon juice to flavor certain dishes, and it's used to make a sweet syrup to flavor soft drinks. You can get it at some Asian markets. Ask around, go on an adventure!

1 tablespoon olive oil

1 cup chopped yellow onions

Salt and freshly ground black pepper to taste

4 cups Duck Confit (page 175), shredded

½ cup tamarind sauce (available at Asian markets)

¼ cup chopped green onions (green part only)

Vegetable oil for deep frying

12 small flour tortillas

1 cup sour cream

3 tablespoons fresh lemon juice

2 tablespoons chopped fresh cilantro leaves

2 medium-size ripe Haas avocados, peeled, pitted, and diced

Heat the olive oil in a large sauté pan over medium heat. Add the onions, season with salt and pepper, and cook, stirring, for 1 minute. Add the duck confit and cook, stirring for 1 minute. Season with salt and pepper. Add the tamarind sauce and cook, stirring, for 2 minutes. Season again with salt and pepper. Stir in the green onions and remove from the heat.

In a large, heavy, deep pot or electric fryer, heat 4 inches of vegetable oil to 360°F. Fry the tortillas, a couple at a time, until golden brown, about 2 minutes. Drain on paper towels. Season with salt and pepper.

In a small mixing bowl, combine the sour cream, lemon juice, and cilantro and whisk to blend. Season with salt and pepper. In another small mixing bowl, combine the avocados, lime juice, garlic, and 2 tablespoons of the tomatoes. Season with salt and pepper. Stir to mix.

To assemble, lay 1 tortilla in the center of each plate. Place ½ cup of the duck mixture on top of each tortilla. Top the duck mixture with the shredded lettuce, the tomatoes, and cheese. Top with a second tortilla and repeat with the confit, lettuce, tomatoes, and cheese. Top with the remaining tortillas. Garnish with the cilantro sour cream and the avocado mixture.

3 tablespoons fresh lime juice

1 teaspoon minced garlic

1 cup plus 2 tablespoons peeled, seeded, and diced ripe tomatoes

2 cups shredded iceberg lettuce

1 cup grated Monterey Jack cheese

Duck Confit

Makes about 2 cups

Preheat the oven to 200°F.

Season the duck meat with salt and pepper and place in a large, shallow baking dish. Arrange the garlic evenly over the meat and tuck in the bouquets garnis. Add the oil and the reserved duck fat, cover with a sheet of aluminum foil, and bake until the meat pulls away from the bone, 12 to 14 hours.

4 duck leg portions with thighs attached (about 2 pounds), excess fat trimmed and reserved

Salt and freshly ground black pepper to taste

10 cloves garlic, peeled

2 recipes Bouquet Garni (page 7)

2 cups olive oil

Remove from the oven and cool completely. Strain and reserve the fat. Pick the meat from the bones. The meat can be used as is or it can be placed in a stoneware container, covered with some of the strained fat, making a ¼-inch layer over the meat, and stored in the refrigerator for up to 1 month.

Store the oil in an airtight container in the refrigerator for up to 1 month and use like butter.

Duck Rillette Risotto

Makes 8 to 10 servings

Arillette is meat—pork, rabbit, goose, poultry, or fish—that is slowly cooked in seasoned fat, then pounded or pulverized with some of the cooking fat into a mixture that resembles a smooth paste.

If you don't have the time to make your own rillette, there is a darn good product on the market (called Duck Rillette) that can be found in some meat shops and gourmet shops. See our Source Guide for more information.

1 tablespoon olive oil

1 cup chopped yellow onions

Salt and freshly ground white pepper to taste

½ pound Duck Rillette (page 177)

6 cups Duck Stock (page 9)

2 teaspoons chopped garlic

1 pound (2 cups) Arborio rice

1 tablespoon unsalted butter

¼ cup heavy cream

½ cup freshly grated Parmigiano-Reggiano cheese

3 tablespoons chopped green onions (green part only)

Heat the olive oil in a large sauté pan over medium heat. Add the onions and season with salt and pepper. Cook, stirring, until the onions are slightly soft, about 3 minutes. Add the duck rillette and cook, stirring, for 2 minutes. Add the stock and garlic, bring to a boil, reduce the heat to medium-low, and simmer for 6 minutes. Add the rice and cook, stirring constantly, until the mixture is creamy and bubbly, about 18 minutes. Add the butter, heavy cream, cheese, and green onions and reseason with salt and pepper. Simmer for 2 minutes and serve immediately.

Emeril with Erica Gruen, president of Food Network

Duck Rillette

Makes 2 ¼ cups

Combine all of the ingredients in a food processor and pulse once or twice to blend, but do not puree.

2 cups Duck Confit (page 175)

¼ cup minced shallots

1 tablespoon chopped garlic

1 tablespoon chopped fresh parsley leaves

1 tablespoon cognac

4 tablespoons (½ stick) unsalted butter

Salt and freshly ground black pepper to
taste

Left: Emeril on the set with *Emeril Live* executive chef Susan Stockton **Right:** *Emeril Live* associate producer Leigh Ann Ambrosi

Steen's Roasted Duck Club Sandwich

Makes 4 servings

I do like club sandwiches, but I get tired of the same old same old. On one occasion when I was hankering for a big, juicy sandwich, I spotted a roasted duck breast, smeared with my favorite cane syrup, made in Louisiana, coming out of the oven at Emeril's. Bing went the old lightbulb in my head! Why not a club sandwich with that! What a great sandwich!

I guess you should know this duck takes 3 days to prepare, so don't think you can whip this up tonight after you come home from work.

2 duck breasts (about 8 ounces each)

¼ cup kosher salt

¼ cup cracked black peppercorns

½ cup Steen's 100% Pure Cane Syrup

4 cloves garlic, peeled

8 dried juniper berries

8 black whole peppercorns

Salt and freshly ground black pepper to taste

1 tablespoon plus 1 teaspoon olive oil

½ cup thinly sliced red onions

1 cup shredded white cabbage

1 cup shredded red cabbage

1 cup well-washed shredded fresh spinach

½ cup finely chopped green onions
   (green part only)

¼ cup chopped fresh parsley leaves

1 tablespoon Creole or whole-grain mustard

¾ cup Aioli Mayonnaise (page 14)

8 slices brioche or French bread

12 thin slices Brie cheese

12 thin slices bacon, crisp fried

Rub the duck breasts with the kosher salt and cracked peppercorns, wrap them in plastic wrap, and refrigerate for 24 hours.

Remove the duck breasts from the refrigerator, rinse off the salt and pepper, dry them, then put them in a small glass dish and spread them with the syrup, garlic cloves, juniper berries, and whole peppercorns. Cover and refrigerate for 2 days.

Remove the breasts from the marinade.

Preheat the oven to 400°F.

Season the duck breasts with salt and pepper. Heat 1 teaspoon of the olive oil in a large oven-proof sauté pan over medium heat. Place the breasts, skin side down, in the pan and cook until the skin is crispy and brown, 10 minutes. Turn the breasts over and cook for 10 minutes more. Transfer the pan to the oven. Roast for about 5 minutes for medium-rare; 8 minutes for medium; 10 minutes for well done. Remove from the oven and let the meat rest for about 2 minutes, then cut diagonally into ¼-inch-thick slices. Set aside and keep warm.

In a large sauté pan, heat the remaining 1 tablespoon olive oil over medium heat. Add the red onions, season with salt and pepper, and cook, stirring, until slightly wilted, 1 to 2 minutes. Add the cabbages, spinach, green onions, and parsley and season with salt and pepper. Cook, stirring, for about 1 minute, just to warm the mixture slightly. Transfer the mixture to a large mixing bowl. Add the mustard and ¼ cup of the aioli mayonnaise and toss to mix thoroughly. Set aside.

Spread 1 side of all the slices of bread generously with the remaining ½ cup aioli mayonnaise. Arrange the duck equally on 4 slices of the bread. Top each with 3 slices of Brie, then 3 slices of bacon, and equal amounts of the slaw. Top with the remaining slices of bread.

To serve, cut the sandwiches in half diagonally.

In the control room at *Emeril Live*

Pork Fat Rules

Yeah, pork, you know, the other white meat! It's no secret

that I love pork and Dan Crutchfield

from Mississippi is the one to blame.

Really, this is a great story. You see, I

am a real stickler for fresh ingredients,

so I contacted Dan, who raises pigs, to

supply the restaurant with his best porkers. Well, Dan

makes a trip into the city once a week on Wednesdays

with a whole pig, dressed and ready for us. Everybody

waits in anticipation for his arrival, so we began calling

Wednesdays "pig day." Talk about hog heaven! Oh yeah,

babe!

We use everything except the squeal of that pig—pork belly, pork chops, ribs, shoulders, and butts, and all the trimmings. No waste here.

I love all the things that can be made with pork—bacon, sausages, pork patties, barbecue—full fat flavor! Wow! Yeah, yeah, yeah, the food police go crazy with all that, but take the advice of my good friend Julia Child and eat everything in moderation. There's no reason to exclude pork totally from your life. There are some cuts that are quite lean, and I really worry about people who don't have a little fat in their diet. Their skin and hair are dry, their eyes are sunken, they have no zing. Just teasing!

Pork fat rules! What's that cry the Arkansas Razorbacks have? Sooiiiieeeeee!

A line cook at NOLA Restaurant, during service

Homemade Bacon

Makes about 1 pound bacon

Why would anybody want to make his or her own bacon? Well, it's fun to do and I like to say I made my own. All you need is a smoker and some good charred wood, or lump charcoal, which burns cleaner and hotter, but charcoal briquettes can also be used in a pinch.

Pork belly is cut from the underside of the belly, and I suggest that you talk to your local butcher or call a slaughterhouse in your area to see if they'll part with a pound.

Combine the honey and salt in a medium-size mixing bowl and whisk to blend. Place the pork belly on a square of plastic wrap. Pour the honey mixture over the pork belly, then flip it so that the honey covers both sides, and wrap tightly in the plastic wrap. Place the pork in a plastic storage bag and seal tightly. Refrigerate for 36 hours.

1 cup honey

1 cup kosher salt

One 1-pound piece pork belly

2½ pounds lump charcoal or charcoal
   briquettes

3 cups hickory chips, soaked in water for
   30 minutes, then drained

Remove the plastic bag from the refrigerator. Unwrap the pork and rinse off the honey mixture. Pat dry with paper towels.

Mound the charcoal in the center of a grill. Ignite and let burn for 40 minutes. Add the hickory chips and allow them to smoke for about 10 minutes. The interior temperature of the grill should be 300°F. Place the pork near the outermost part of the grill rack. This is to avoid direct heat. You want the belly to absorb the maximum amount of smoke flavor before it is fully cooked. Smoke the belly, covered, for 30 minutes. There is no need to turn the belly during the smoking time. Spray the coals as often as necessary with a mist of water, but remember, smoke escapes each time the grill is uncovered.

Remove the pork belly and cool. Wrap it in plastic and refrigerate for 2 days before slicing.

Pork Dumplings

Makes 32 dumplings

Dumplings fascinate me and I'm always experimenting with different kinds of fillings. Here I've used pork, but you can use beef, or shrimp, or chicken. You need to experiment yourself to find what pleases your palate.

These were inspired when I enjoyed a selection of dim sum, which means "touch the heart" in Chinese. Dim sum refers to small snack dishes that the Chinese eat in great quantity in the middle of the day. I can see why, they're so tasty.

I want to give you a little trick about making certain that the filling is seasoned enough. What you do is make a little ball of the raw meat, poach it in hot water or fry it in a skillet, then taste it to be sure it's seasoned as you like it.

Oh, and you'll need a bamboo steamer, which is available at Asian markets, and while you're making your purchase, get some soy sauce, and maybe a couple of chili sauces to serve with these little dumplings.

These are great to serve as appetizers—just cook the dumplings in batches in the steamer and pass them around to guests. They're best served warm.

Put the pork, garlic, and green onions in a food processor and process until smooth. Add the sesame oil, soy sauce, and heavy cream and season with salt and pepper, then pulse once or twice to mix well.

With your fingers, lightly wet the edges of the wontons with water. Put about a tablespoon of the filling in the center, bring 1 corner up to another to form a triangle, and press to seal. Bring the bottom 2 corners of the triangle together to form a ring, press to seal, then fold the remaining tip over to resemble a bishop's hat.

½ pound ground pork

1 tablespoon chopped garlic

2 tablespoons chopped green onions (green part only)

2 tablespoons sesame oil

2 teaspoons soy sauce, plus more to serve

¼ cup heavy cream

Salt and freshly ground black pepper to taste

32 wonton wrappers

Asian chili sauce

Arrange the dumplings in the steamer, place it in a wok or large pan, and add enough water just to touch the bottom of the basket. Cover the steamer and steam until the dumplings are tender and translucent, 6 to 8 minutes.

Pass with the soy sauce and chili sauce on the side.

Andouille Stuffed Jalapeños

Makes 16 stuffed peppers

Now if you don't like hot stuff, stay away from these firecrackers! But if you can stand the heat, this is one heck of an appetizer.

1 teaspoon olive oil

2 ounces andouille or other smoked
  sausage, finely chopped

2 tablespoons finely chopped yellow onion

1 teaspoon minced garlic

1 tablespoon chopped fresh parsley leaves

½ cup softened cream cheese

Salt and freshly ground black pepper to
  taste

16 large fresh jalapeños

Vegetable oil for deep frying

3 cups bleached all-purpose flour

Pinch of baking powder

Essence to taste (page 7)

2 large egg yolks

¾ to 1 cup beer, as needed

Heat the olive oil in a small sauté pan over medium heat, and brown the andouille. Add the onion and cook, stirring, for 1 minute. Remove from the heat and let cool.

In a medium-size mixing bowl, combine the garlic, parsley, and cream cheese and mix well. Stir in the andouille mixture, mix thoroughly, and season with salt and pepper.

With a sharp knife, split the jalapeños in half lengthwise, leaving the stem intact. Remove the seeds. Stuff 1 heaping tablespoon of the filling in the center of each jalapeño, then press together to seal.

In a large, heavy, deep pot or an electric fryer, heat 4 inches of vegetable oil to 360°F.

Combine 1 cup of the flour and the baking powder in a shallow bowl and season with Essence. In a mixing bowl, whisk together the yolks and ¾ cup of the beer, then season with salt and pepper. Whisk in enough of the remaining flour to form a batter. The batter should be thick, like a pancake batter. If the batter is too thick, add the remaining ¼ cup beer to thin it. Dredge the stuffed peppers in the seasoned flour, tapping off any excess. Dip the jalapeños in the batter, coating completely. Let the excess drip off.

Gently lay the jalapeños in the hot oil, several at a time, and fry until golden brown, 3 to 4 minutes. Drain on paper towels. Season with Essence and serve.

Andouille and Potato Soup

Makes 6 to 8 servings

Andouille is a sausage favored by the Acadians in south Louisiana, but you can use any kind of sausage that's available in your area. The sausage infuses a terrific flavor and aroma to this potato soup, which is very simple to make.

Heat the oil in a large soup pot over medium heat. Add the onions, season with salt and pepper, and cook, stirring, for 2 minutes. Add the sausage and cook, stirring, for 2 minutes more. Stir in the garlic, thyme, and bay leaves. Add the potatoes and stock Bring to a boil, then reduce the heat to medium-low and simmer, uncovered, for 30 minutes. Season again if necessary. Add the parsley.

Remove the bay leaves and serve hot.

1 tablespoon olive oil

2 cups chopped yellow onions

Salt and freshly ground black pepper to taste

1 pound andouille or other smoked sausage, cut into ½-inch-thick slices

2 tablespoons chopped garlic

2 sprigs fresh thyme

2 bay leaves

2 pounds Idaho potatoes, peeled and diced

16 cups Chicken Stock (page 8) or canned chicken broth

¼ cup chopped fresh parsley leaves

Producer Emily Schwartz on the *Emeril Live* set during the Creole Christmas special

187

Pork Burgers in Gravy with French-Fried Sweet Potatoes

Makes 4 servings

I know, I know, burgers are usually made with beef, but in south Louisiana they're sometimes made with ground pork that's seasoned with garlic, then wrapped in caul to keep the juices locked in. Man, oh, man!

Caul is a thin, fatty membrane that lines the abdominal cavity of pigs and sheep, and resembles a lacy net. It is often used to wrap pâtés and forcemeats. Talk to your butcher and see if he has some to sell, or he might be able to order it through his meat supplier. You may have to soak it in warm water before using if it has dried out a bit.

1 pound ground lean pork

1 tablespoon chopped garlic

2 tablespoons chopped fresh parsley leaves

¼ cup chopped green onions
   (green part only)

1 teaspoon salt

¼ teaspoon cayenne

Dash of Worcestershire sauce

2 teaspoons prepared horseradish

½ teaspoon Tabasco sauce

Four 6-inch rounds pork caul fat

1 cup water

Vegetable oil for deep frying

2 medium-size sweet potatoes, peeled and
   cut into shoestrings

Essence to taste (page 7)

4 sandwich rolls, sliced in half

Combine the first nine ingredients in a large mixing bowl. Mix well. Shape into 4 equal patties. Wrap each patty with a piece of caul fat, covering it completely.

In a large sauté pan over medium-low heat, begin browning the patties, cooking for 2 minutes on each side. Add ½ cup of the water. Turn the patties over and cook for 2 minutes. Add the remaining ½ cup water and turn the patties over again. Cook until they are well browned and the juices run clear, about 8 minutes, flipping every 2 minutes. Remove from the heat and cover the pan with a sheet of aluminum foil to keep warm.

In a large, heavy, deep pot or an electric fryer, heat 4 inches of vegetable oil to 360°F. Fry the sweet potatoes in batches without crowding until golden brown, 3 to 4 minutes. Remove and drain on paper towels, then season with Essence.

Place each burger on half a roll, spoon "gravy" over it, and top with another half a roll. Serve with the fries.

Pork Roulades

Makes 4 servings

Roulade is simply a rolled stuffed meat, pork in this case. If you're Ital-ian, you know it better as braciola. This is a real kicked-up dish, full of flavor and absolutely delicious.

1½ pounds pork tenderloin, cut into
    4 pieces (6 ounces each), trimmed of fat

Salt and freshly ground black pepper to
    taste

12 slices bacon, plus 8 ounces sliced bacon,
    chopped

1 recipe Mushroom Duxelles (page 191)

1 large ripe Haas avocado, halved, peeled,
    pitted, and cut lengthwise into 16 slices

2 tablespoons chopped shallots

2 teaspoons chopped garlic

2 tablespoons Armagnac or cognac

1 cup Veal Reduction (page 10)

½ teaspoon sugar

1 teaspoon unsalted butter, at room
    temperature

1 recipe Creamy Polenta (page 207)

Preheat the oven to 400°F. Line a baking sheet with parchment paper.

Place each pork tenderloin between 2 pieces of plastic wrap. With a meat mallet, lightly pound out the pork tenderloin till about ⅛ inch thick. Unwrap and season both sides with salt and pepper. Lay 3 slices of the bacon on a flat sur-face. Place a pork tenderloin on top of the bacon along one end. Spread ¼ cup of the dux-elles over the top of each pork tenderloin. Lay 4 slices of the avocado on top of the duxelles. Gently roll up each tenderloin with the bacon.

Place the roulades, seam side down, on the prepared baking sheet, and roast until the bacon is brown and crisp and the pork meat is tender, about 30 minutes. Remove from the oven and let rest for 5 minutes before slicing. With a sharp knife, trim the ends of each roulade and cut each across into 4 slices. Cover with aluminum foil to keep warm.

Meanwhile, in a medium-size saucepan, fry the chopped bacon until crispy, about 8 minutes. Add the shallots, garlic, and Armagnac and cook for 1 minute. Stir in the reduction and sugar, season with salt and pepper, bring to a boil, and reduce the heat to a simmer. Cook, stirring, for 5 minutes. Whisk in the butter and remove from the heat. Serve the polenta with the roulades.

Mushroom Duxelles

Makes about 1 cup

Combine the mushrooms, onion, garlic, and walnuts in a food processor or blender and pulse until the mixture forms a coarse paste. Heat the oil in a medium-size skillet over medium heat, add the mushroom mixture, and season with salt and pepper. Cook, stirring, for 1 minute. Add the wine and cook, stirring, for 1 minute more. Remove from heat and let cool to room temperature before using.

¼ pound shiitake mushrooms, wiped clean and chopped (about 1½ cups)
2 tablespoons chopped yellow onion
2 teaspoons chopped garlic
½ cup walnut pieces
1 tablespoon olive oil
Salt and freshly ground black pepper to taste
Splash of dry white wine

Emeril Live musicians
Robert Landum and David
Hamburger, aka C. F. Steaks

Mixed Grill with Warm Potato and Chorizo Salad

Makes 6 servings

A *meal of sausage is a meal made in heaven as far as I'm concerned. You don't have to use the particular ones we have here. Go scout out a meat market or super-duper supermarket and see what it has to offer. I recommend using "fresh" pork sausages rather than smoked ones for this treatment, since they will take on an intense flavor while they are grilled. Just remember that it's best to blanch or poach the sausages for a few minutes in simmering water before putting them on the grill.*

2 pounds new potatoes, quartered

Salt

2½ pounds assorted sausages, such as fresh pork, venison, bratwurst, Italian, andouille, or kielbasa, cut into 2-inch links

5 tablespoons olive oil

¼ pound chorizo sausage, finely chopped

2 cups chopped yellow onions

Freshly ground black pepper to taste

2 tablespoons chopped garlic

2 tablespoons Creole or whole-grain mustard

2 tablespoons finely chopped fresh parsley leaves

Prepare the grill.

Put the potatoes in a large saucepan and add enough water to cover. Season with salt and bring to a boil over medium-high heat. Reduce the heat to medium and cook until the potatoes are fork tender, about 12 minutes. Remove from the heat, drain, then return the potatoes to the pot. Set aside and keep warm.

Bring a large pot of salted water to a boil. Add the sausages (except for the kielbasa and chorizo) and cook until they are plump, 3 to 5 minutes. Drain and place on a baking sheet. Brush the sausages, including the kielbasa, with 4 tablespoons of the olive oil. Place the sausages on the grill and cook for 3 to 4 minutes on each side.

Heat the remaining 1 tablespoon of the olive oil in a large sauté pan over medium heat. Add the chopped chorizo and cook, stirring, for 3 minutes. Add the onions. Season with salt and pepper, and cook, stirring, for 3 minutes. Stir in the garlic and mustard. Add the potatoes and cook until the potatoes are heated through, about 3 minutes. Season with salt and pepper. Stir in the parsley.

To serve, mound the potato salad in the center of the platter. Arrange the grilled sausages around the potato salad. Serve with crusty bread and a side of Creole mustard.

Emeril doing morning radio in New York City

Cuban Sandwich

Makes 4 servings

I have a good friend in Miami, Norman Van Aken, who says, when in Miami one has to have a Cuban sandwich. So he took me to this little sandwich shop where I had a sandwich that was my kind of sandwich. I mean, it was slathered with butter and loaded with shredded roasted pork, ham, pickles, and cheese. When I get a hankering for this stuff, I roast a little pork butt because I think it's full of flavor, but you can use a pork tenderloin if you prefer, and pig out.

It's important that the sandwiches be weighted down while they're being heated. You're going to have to be a little innovative here. Use a waffle iron, a brick wrapped in aluminum foil, or maybe a heavy iron skillet.

The sandwiches are big, but I have no trouble eating one by myself.

1 pork butt (about 1½ pounds), untrimmed

Salt and freshly ground black pepper to taste

4 Cuban or French bread loaves, each about 12 inches long

¼ pound (1 stick) unsalted butter, softened

8 slices Swiss cheese

1 pound sliced smoked ham

Hamburger dill chips (thin slices of pickles), 8 to 10 slices per sandwich

Preheat the oven to 250°F.

Season the pork generously with salt and pepper. Place in the center of a shallow roasting pan and roast until the meat is very tender, about 6 hours. Remove from the oven, let cool, then shred.

Cut the bread loaves in half lengthwise. Smear the butter on each half. Layer with the pork, cheese, ham, and the pickles on one half, then top with the second half of the loaf. Press together firmly. Heat a griddle or large skillet over medium heat. Place 1 or 2 sandwiches at a time on the griddle, put a weight on each, then heat them for 2 to 3 minutes on each side.

Slice each sandwich in half before serving hot.

Dirty Black-Eyed Peas

Makes 6 to 8 servings

Pork and beans are a natural together. Down in the Deep South, we cook our beans, flavored with pickled pork meat and ham hocks, long and slow until they're thick and creamy. They are a great accompaniment to any pork dish.

Pickled pork meat can be found at many meat markets and super-markets.

Fry the bacon in a large Dutch oven over medium heat until crispy. Add the onions, season with salt and pepper, and cook, stirring, for 2 to 3 minutes. Stir in the pickled pork meat and ham hocks and cook, stirring, for 2 minutes. Stir in the remaining ingredients, season with salt and pepper, bring to a boil, then reduce the heat to a simmer. Cook, uncovered, until the peas are tender, 1½ to 2 hours. Remove the pork meat and ham hocks and let cool. Thinly slice the pork meat and pull the meat from the ham hocks. Return the meat to the pot and let heat through again. Remove the bay leaves.

To serve, ladle into bowls.

½ pound sliced bacon, chopped

2 cups chopped yellow onions

Salt and freshly ground black pepper to taste

4 ounces pickled pork meat, cubed

2 smoked ham hocks (3 to 4 ounces each)

2 tablespoons chopped garlic

2 bay leaves

3 sprigs fresh thyme

1 pound dried black-eyed peas, rinsed, picked over, soaked in water to cover overnight, and drained

10 cups Chicken Stock (page 8) or canned chicken broth

Kicked-Up Pigs in a Blanket

Makes 18 rolls

I'm sure most of you have had, at one time or another, pigs in a blanket—you know, some kind of sausage (the pig) wrapped in some kind of dough (the blanket). There's all kinds of versions out there, but I especially like the one that's so common in south Louisiana, where they have this sausage called boudin in which ground pork is mixed together with cooked white rice, green onions, parsley, and lots of seasonings. Everyone from bankers to construction workers, from dainty ladies to small children, enjoys a link of hot boudin enclosed in a slice of bread either for breakfast or a snack. Talk about giving yourself a kick start!

If you don't have boudin, use whatever sausage is popular where you live. Hey, use some weenies if you want!

1 envelope (¼ ounce) dry yeast

2 tablespoons sugar

2 tablespoons plus 1 teaspoon vegetable oil

2 cups warm water (about 110°F)

6 cups bleached all-purpose flour

½ cup yellow cornmeal

2 teaspoons salt

1 cup Creole or whole-grain mustard

18 assorted smoked sausage pieces, each about 4 inches long

1 large egg beaten with 2 tablespoons water

1 recipe Onion Marmalade (page 197)

Combine the yeast, sugar, and 2 tablespoons of the vegetable oil in the bowl of an electric mixer fitted with a dough hook. Add the water. With the mixer on low speed, beat the mixture for about 4 minutes to dissolve the yeast. If the yeast doesn't begin to foam after a few minutes, it means it's not active and you'll have to start again with new yeast.

In a separate large mixing bowl, combine the flour, ¼ cup plus 2 tablespoons of the cornmeal, and the salt. Add this mixture to the yeast mixture. Mix on low speed until it lightly comes together, then increase the speed to medium and beat until the mixture pulls away from the sides of the bowl, forms a ball, and climbs slightly up the dough hook.

Remove the dough from the bowl. Coat the bowl with the remaining teaspoon vegetable oil, return the dough to the bowl, and turn it to oil all sides. Cover the bowl with plastic wrap, set in a warm, draft-free place, and let rise until doubled in size, about 2 hours.

Remove the dough from the bowl and turn it onto a lightly floured surface. Using your hands, gently roll it to form a narrow loaf about 24 inches long. Cut the dough into 18 equal portions (each about 2½ ounces). Using your hands, pat each portion out into rounds about 4 inches in diameter. Spread each with 1 teaspoon of the mustard, then place a sausage piece on the bottom of each round and roll the rounds up. Line 2 baking sheets with parchment or waxed paper and sprinkle them with the remaining 4 tablespoons cornmeal. Place the rolled-up sausages, seam side down, 9 on each baking sheet, about 2 inches apart on the paper. Cover with plastic wrap and let rise in a warm, draft-free place until doubled in size, about 30 minutes.

Preheat the oven to 425°F.

Brush the tops of the rolls with the egg wash, then bake until golden brown, 12 to 14 minutes.

Serve hot accompanied by the remaining mustard and the onion marmalade.

Onion Marmalade

Makes about 1½ cups

Heat the oil in a large sauté pan over medium-high heat. Add the onions, season with salt and pepper, and cook, stirring, until the onions are golden, 10 to 12 minutes. Add the sugar and cook, stirring, for 2 minutes. Add the vinegar and parsley and cook, stirring, for 1 minute. Remove from the heat, cool, and serve.

Can be stored in an airtight container in the refrigerator for up to 1 week.

2 tablespoons olive oil

4 cups finely chopped yellow onions

Salt and freshly ground black pepper to
    taste

¼ cup sugar

2 tablespoons white distilled vinegar

1 tablespoon finely chopped fresh parsley
    leaves

Where's the Meat? Vegetarians Beware!

I've never met a meat I didn't love. I'm particularly fond of

beef, but I'm pretty happy with

lamb, venison, veal, and rabbit.

When buying beef, don't

pinch pennies, and get the best

grade you can. If you're getting a

steak, have the butcher cut it nice

and thick, and have it trimmed of extra fat.

Do a little snooping around the meat department

and learn about cuts of lamb and veal. Walk on the wild

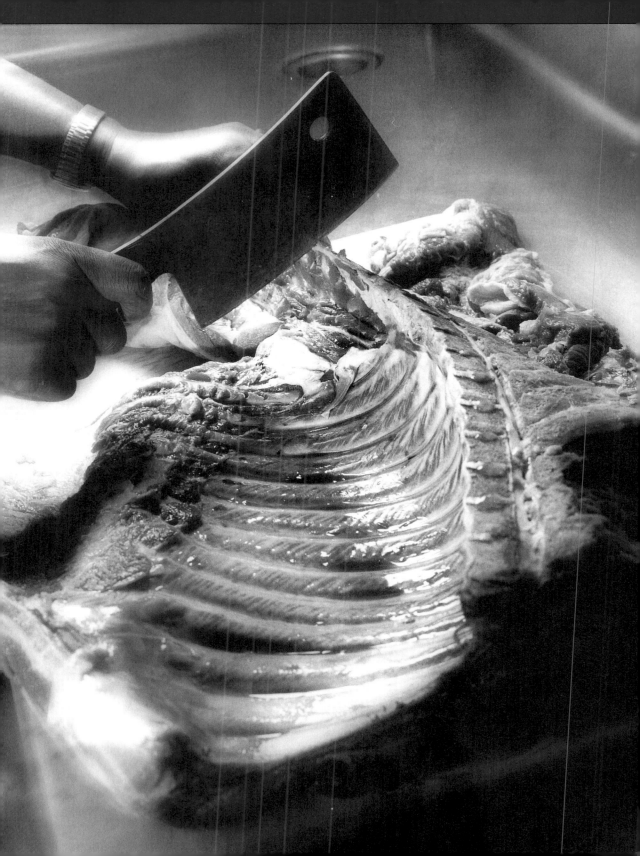

side and try some rabbit now and then. It has a nice texture and flavor.

Let's talk about cooking times, especially for beef. I prefer my beef medium-rare, but if you can't tolerate the blood and prefer meat well done, I can't guarantee it will be juicy and as tasty, but hey, that's your choice. It's your dollar, right? Eat it any way you like.

Funky Lamb Shanks

Makes 4 servings

Lamb shanks are not a fancy cut, but when properly prepared they are delicious, and they won't cost you your paycheck. Cooked long and slow with mushrooms and potatoes, the shanks make a terrific gravy.

Put the flour in a large mixing bowl and season with Essence. Season the shanks with Essence, add to the flour, and toss to coat evenly. Tap off any excess.

Heat the olive oil in a Dutch oven over medium heat. Add the shanks and sear for 4 minutes on each side. Add the onions and mushrooms, season with salt and pepper, and cook, stirring often, for 2 minutes. Add the wine, stock, garlic, and herbs and season with salt and pepper. Bring to a boil, cover, reduce the heat to medium-low, and simmer for 1 hour. Add the potatoes, season with more salt and pepper, and simmer until the meat begins to fall off the bones, 30 to 40 minutes. Remove the bay leaves.

Transfer the shanks and gravy to a large shallow bowl. Garnish with the green onions and serve hot.

1 cup bleached all-purpose flour

Essence to taste (page 7)

4 lamb shanks (about ½ pound each)

3 tablespoons olive oil

1½ cups chopped yellow onions

¼ pound assorted exotic mushrooms, such as shiitakes, chanterelles, black trumpets, and oysters, wiped clean and sliced (about 4 cups)

Salt and freshly ground black pepper to taste

2 cups dry red wine

3 quarts Veal Stock (page 10)

2 tablespoons minced garlic

2 bay leaves

4 sprigs fresh thyme

¼ cup finely chopped fresh parsley leaves

½ pound new or small red potatoes, quartered

1 tablespoon chopped green onions (green part only)

Lamb Roast Stuffed with Crawfish and Chèvre

Makes 10 to 12 servings

*T*he leg of lamb is probably the most popular cut of lamb, since it offers plenty of lean meat. It's ideal for stuffing when it's butterflied. Have your butcher do it for you. Then you've really got to pound this thing real good—hey, get out all your frustrations!

Sometimes I like to use goat cheese with spinach, the classic combination, but when crawfish are in season, roughly from January to June, they're great with spinach and goat cheese too. Have a party, invite some friends over—this serves a lot.

One more thing: in my opinion lamb should be served medium-rare to keep it moist and juicy; if you have a problem with that, go ahead and cook it longer, but I can't promise that it will be as tasty.

3 tablespoons olive oil

2 tablespoons minced shallots

½ cup chopped leeks (white part only, well washed)

Salt and freshly ground black pepper to taste

½ pound peeled crawfish tails

One 10-ounce bag fresh spinach, washed well, tough stems removed, and coarsely chopped (about 4 cups)

1 tablespoon minced garlic

1½ cups crumbled *chèvre* cheese

1 leg of lamb (9 to 10 pounds), trimmed of fat and butterflied with shank bone intact, pelvic bone removed

Preheat the oven to 400°F.

Heat 1 tablespoon of the olive oil in a large sauté pan over medium heat. Add the shallots and leeks, season with salt and pepper, and cook, stirring, for 1 minute. Add the crawfish tails, season with salt and pepper, and cook, stirring, for 1 minute. Add the spinach and garlic and cook, stirring, until the spinach wilts, about 2 minutes. Remove from the heat and pour into a large mixing bowl. Stir in the cheese and season with salt and pepper.

Place the lamb on a clean work surface. With a meat mallet, pound the lamb to about 1 inch thick. Rub with the remaining 2 tablespoons olive oil and the rosemary. Season with salt and pepper. Spread the crawfish-spinach filling evenly over the meat. Fold the bottom end of the meat inward, then fold both ends into the center. Tie crosswise with butcher's twine, at 3-inch intervals. Press the cracked peppercorns into the surface of the tied lamb. Put the roast in a large shallow roasting pan and cook until an instant-read meat thermometer reads 130° to 140°F for rare to medium-rare, about 1½ hours; 145° to 150°F for medium, about 2¼ hours; and 160°F for well done, about 2½ hours. Remove from the oven and let rest for 10 minutes before carving. Serve warm.

3 tablespoons chopped fresh rosemary leaves
Butcher's twine
½ cup cracked black peppercorns

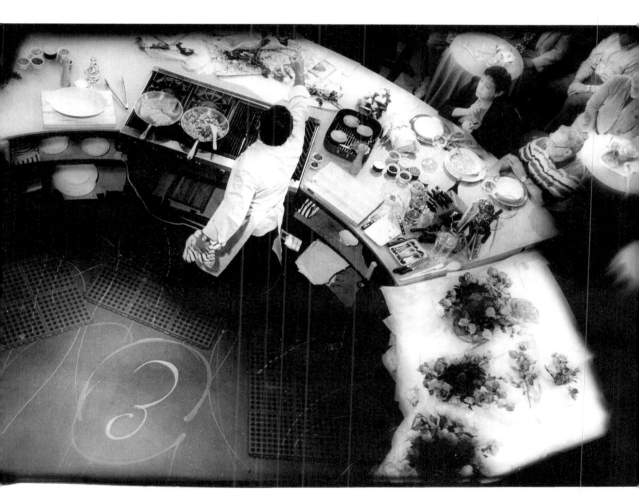

203

NOLA Rib-Eye Sandwich

Makes 4 sandwiches

This is a manly man dish, but that doesn't mean some of you ladies won't enjoy it. It's like a diner-type sandwich that usually has slices of roast beef, but since I love rib-eyes, I do this kicked-up version. It's a killer dish and that's all I have to say about that.

16 new or small red potatoes, quartered

Salt

1 cup heavy cream

¼ pound (1 stick) unsalted butter

½ cup Roasted Garlic Puree (page 121)

Freshly ground white pepper to taste

Vegetable oil for deep frying

1 medium-size red onion, thinly sliced and
    separated into rings

½ cup Crystal Hot Sauce or the hot sauce of
    your choice

1 cup bleached all-purpose flour

Essence to taste (page 7)

4 rib-eye steaks (about 10 ounces each)

2 tablespoons olive oil

¼ cup Worcestershire sauce

4 large hoagie buns (each about 6 inches
    long), toasted

Put the potatoes in a large saucepan and cover with salted water. Bring to a boil, reduce the heat to medium, and cook until fork tender, 8 to 10 minutes. Remove from the heat and drain. Put the potatoes back in the pot over low heat to dry them, then mash with a potato masher. Add the heavy cream, butter, and garlic puree and mix well, but remember the potatoes should be slightly lumpy. Season with salt and pepper. Set aside and keep warm.

In a large, heavy, deep pot or an electric fryer, heat 4 inches of vegetable oil to 360°F.

In a small mixing bowl, toss the onion with the hot sauce. Put the flour in a shallow bowl and season with Essence. Dredge the onion rings in the flour, shaking them to remove excess flour. Fry them in batches in the hot oil, turning them once, until golden brown, 2 to 3 minutes. Drain on paper towels, then season with Essence. Set aside and keep warm.

Rub the rib-eyes with the olive oil and season with Essence. Heat a large sauté pan over medium-high heat. Add the steaks and cook for 6 to 8 minutes on each side for medium-rare, 130° to 140°F; 10 minutes for medium, 145° to 150°F; 12 minutes for well done, 155° to 165°F. Remove the steaks from the sauté pan and add the Worcestershire, stirring to loosen any browned bits on the bottom of the pan.

To serve, spread equal amounts of the garlic potatoes on one half of each hoagie bun. Tuck in the steaks and drizzle with the pan drippings. Top with fried onion rings.

Stewed Eggplant with Panéed Steak

Makes 4 servings

Pane *is the Italian word for "bread." Panéed means "breaded." What we're doing is butterflying the filets, which means to split them down the center, cutting almost but not completely through. Go look at a butterfly—see what I mean? Then it's pounded to make it thinner, and because of this it takes a little less time to cook. Make sense? Trust me.*

The texture of the crunchy steak with the creamy polenta and stewed eggplant is what I like here.

2 tablespoons olive oil

2 cups chopped yellow onions

Salt and freshly ground black pepper to taste

1 large eggplant (about 1 pound), peeled and diced

3 cups peeled, seeded, and chopped fresh or canned tomatoes

3 bay leaves

2 tablespoons chopped garlic

Cayenne to taste

1 tablespoon chopped fresh parsley leaves

1 cup vegetable oil

1 cup bleached all-purpose flour

4 filet mignons (about 6 ounces each), butterflied and pounded to about ¼ inch thick

2 large eggs beaten with 2 tablespoons milk

1 recipe Creamy Polenta (page 207)

Heat the olive oil in a large, heavy skillet over medium heat. Add the onions, season with salt and black pepper, and cook, stirring, for 3 to 4 minutes. Add the eggplant, season with salt and black pepper, and cook, stirring, for 2 minutes. Add the tomatoes, bay leaves, and garlic and season with salt and cayenne. Cover the skillet, reduce the heat to low, and simmer until thick and mushy, about 45 minutes, stirring occasionally. Remove the bay leaves, stir in the parsley, and set aside.

Heat the vegetable oil in a large sauté pan over medium-high heat.

Put the flour in a shallow bowl and season with salt and cayenne. Season each filet with salt and cayenne. Dredge them in the seasoned flour, tapping off any excess flour, then dip each in the egg wash, letting the excess drip off. Dredge the filets in the flour for a second time, coating each side completely and tapping off any excess.

Gently lay the filets in the hot oil. Pan-fry until golden brown, 3 to 4 minutes on each side. Remove and drain on paper towels, then season with salt and cayenne.

To serve, spoon equal portions of the polenta into the center of each plate. Top each serving with a filet and spoon the eggplant mixture over each.

Creamy Polenta

Makes 3 cups

Put the milk and butter in a medium-size saucepan over medium heat and season with salt and pepper. Bring to a gentle boil, then add the cornmeal, a little at a time, whisking constantly. Cook until creamy and thick, about 4 minutes. Season generously with salt and pepper. Remove from the heat, add the cheese, and stir until it melts completely.

Serve hot.

3 cups milk

1 tablespoon unsalted butter

Salt and freshly ground white pepper to taste

¾ cup yellow cornmeal

¼ cup freshly grated Parmigiano-Reggiano cheese

Stage manager Rhoda Gilmore and Emeril

Pan-Roasted Filet Mignon Stuffed with English Stilton and Walnuts

Makes 4 servings

Give me some good blue cheese and I'm a happy, happy man! Stilton cheese is probably the king of English cheeses. Made with whole cow's milk and allowed to ripen for 4 to 6 months while being skewered numerous times to create the blue veins, it is rich and creamy, but slightly crumbly. When stuffed into a filet mignon that's cooked to a turn, it's a meal fit for, what else?, a king, and hey, we all want to be kings, right?

1 pound new or small red potatoes, quartered

1 tablespoon dried thyme

2 tablespoons olive oil

Salt and cracked black peppercorns to taste

1 cup Veal Reduction (page 10)

3 ounces sliced bacon, chopped

2 tablespoons chopped shallots

1 teaspoon chopped garlic

½ cup walnut pieces

4 filet mignons (about 8 ounces each)

Freshly ground black pepper to taste

1 cup crumbled Stilton cheese

½ cup port wine

1 cup vegetable oil

4 shallots, thinly sliced and separated into rings

¼ cup bleached all-purpose flour

1 tablespoon chopped fresh parsley leaves

Preheat the oven to 400°F.

In a medium-size mixing bowl, toss the potatoes with the thyme and 1 tablespoon of the olive oil. Season with salt and cracked peppercorns. Put the potatoes in a large ovenproof sauté pan. Roast until golden brown, about 20 minutes. Remove from the oven and transfer back to the mixing bowl.

Place the sauté pan over medium-high heat, add the veal reduction, and deglaze the pan, scraping the bottom to get any browned bits. Reduce the heat to medium and cook for 1 minute. Set aside and keep warm.

In a medium-size sauté pan over medium heat, fry the bacon until crispy, stirring occasionally, about 8 minutes. Add the chopped shallots, garlic, and walnuts and cook, stirring, for 2 minutes. Remove from the heat.

In the mixing bowl, toss the potatoes with the bacon mixture. Set aside and keep warm.

Using a sharp knife, cut a pocket about 2 inches long along the side of each filet. Season the inside of the pocket with salt and pepper. Stuff each pocket with 2 tablespoons of the cheese. Season the filets with salt and more cracked pepper.

Heat the remaining tablespoon olive oil in a large ovenproof sauté pan over medium-high heat. Sear the filets for 2 minutes on each side. Transfer the pan to the oven and roast for 6 to 8 minutes for medium-rare, 130° to 140°F; 10 minutes for medium, 145° to 150°F; and 12 minutes for well done, 155° to 165°F. Remove the filets from the pan, set aside and keep warm.

Return the sauté pan to the stove over medium-high heat. Add the port and deglaze the pan, scraping the browned bits off the bottom. Reduce the wine by half, cooking about 5 minutes.

Pour the vegetable oil into a deep, heavy saucepan and heat to 360°F. Season the shallot rings with salt and pepper. Put the flour in a shallow bowl and season with salt and pepper. Dredge the shallot rings in the flour and coat evenly, tapping off any excess. Fry them until golden brown, about 2 minutes. Drain on paper towels, then season with salt.

To serve, divide the potatoes into 4 equal portions and mound in the center of each plate. Lay a filet on top of the potatoes. Spoon the veal reduction over each filet. Drizzle each plate with the port wine reduction. Garnish with the remaining ½ cup Stilton cheese, the fried shallots, and the parsley.

Emeril Live executive producer Karen Katz

Rock Shrimp Stuffed Filet

Makes 4 servings

This is my version of surf and turf—rock shrimp stuffed into a filet mignon. These firm small shrimp with their lobsterlike flavor can stand up well to the beef. If you can't get rock shrimp, you can use regular shrimp, crabmeat, crawfish—heck, whatever you can find.

Go to the Vegetable World chapter, find the recipe for Emeril's Potato Truffle Charlotte (page 132), and serve that with this. Outstanding!

3 tablespoons olive oil

1 teaspoon finely minced yellow onion

1 teaspoon finely minced green onion
   (green part only)

1 teaspoon finely minced celery

1 teaspoon finely minced red bell pepper

2 teaspoons minced shallots

1 teaspoon minced garlic

Salt and freshly ground black pepper to
   taste

¼ pound rock shrimp, peeled

2 tablespoons water

2 tablespoons fine dried bread crumbs

Essence to taste (page 7)

4 filet mignons (about 6 ounces each)

Heat 1 tablespoon of the olive oil in a medium-size sauté pan over medium heat. Add the yellow onion, green onion, celery, red pepper, shallots, and garlic and season with salt and pepper. Cook, stirring, until slightly limp, about 1 minute. Add the shrimp, water, and bread crumbs, season with Essence, and cook, stirring, for 2 minutes. Remove from the heat and allow to cool for at least 15 minutes.

Preheat the oven to 400°F.

Using a sharp knife, cut a pocket into the side of the filets about 2 inches long and 2 inches deep. Season with Essence inside and out of the pocket. Fill each with about ¼ cup of the stuffing.

Heat the remaining 2 tablespoons olive oil in a large ovenproof sauté pan over medium heat. Add the filets and sear for 2 to 3 minutes on each side. Remove from the heat and place in the oven. Cook for 6 to 8 minutes for medium-rare, 130° to 140°F; 10 minutes for medium, 145° to 150°F; and 12 minutes for well done, 155° to 165°F.

Beef and Baby Root Vegetable Fricassee

Makes 4 servings

I like the sound of the word fricassee *(FRIHK-uh-see) and I love the dish itself, which is usually made with meat or chicken and vegetables cooked in butter, ending up like a rich, thick stew. The baby root vegetables are popping up in a lot of markets; you can use regular root vegetables, but you'll have to cut them into small dice.*

Combine the oil and flour in a large, heavy saucepan over medium heat. Stir slowly and constantly until the roux is the color of chocolate, 15 to 20 minutes.

Season the meat with Essence. Add to the roux and cook for 3 minutes, stirring constantly to coat the meat with the roux. Add the onions and celery, season with salt and cayenne, and cook for 2 minutes, stirring constantly. Add the bay leaves and wine. Stir for 1 minute, until a paste forms. Add the water and stir to blend. Add the pearl onions, carrots, turnips, potatoes, garlic, and thyme, season with salt and black pepper, bring to a boil, and reduce the heat to medium-low. Cover and simmer for 30 minutes. Remove the lid and continue to cook until the meat is very tender, 30 to 40 minutes. Remove the bay leaves and adjust the seasoning if needed.

Serve over the grits.

¾ cup vegetable oil

¾ cup bleached all-purpose flour

1 pound beef stew meat, such as top round
or bottom round, trimmed of fat and cut
into 2-inch chunks

Essence to taste (page 7)

1 cup chopped yellow onions

1 cup chopped celery

Salt and cayenne to taste

2 bay leaves

1 cup dry red wine

5 cups water

½ pound pearl onions, peeled

¼ pound baby carrots, peeled

¼ pound baby turnips, peeled

¼ pound new or small red potatoes,
quartered

1 tablespoon chopped garlic

½ teaspoon dried thyme

½ teaspoon freshly ground black pepper

1 recipe Cheesy Bacon Grits (page 51)

'Sixty-one Panéed
Veal Chops with Fettuccine

Makes 4 servings

I have a standing joke with my staff. Whenever I refer to a dish that I made during the time I was at Commander's Palace, I tell them, "Yeah, back in the good old days, in 'sixty-one . . . " Needless to say, I wasn't there in 1961 because I was a small child, but it's just to say it was way back when. Get it?

Anyway, this was one super dish that was very popular there and the panéed, or breaded, veal was a dish that found its way from the country kitchens to the fashionable New Orleans restaurants. I kicked it up a notch by using whopper big double-cut veal chops. Served with fettuccine tossed with cream and freshly grated cheese, it's still an all-time favorite with me.

4 double-cut veal loin chops (14 ounces each), butterflied
Essence to taste (page 7)
2 cups bleached all-purpose flour
2 large eggs lightly beaten with 2 tablespoons milk
1 cup vegetable oil
1 cup heavy cream
1 tablespoon chopped garlic
Salt and freshly ground white pepper to taste
6 cups salted water
½ pound fresh fettuccine
½ cup freshly grated Parmigiano-Reggiano cheese, plus extra for garnish

Preheat the oven to 400°F.

Wrap each veal chop in plastic wrap and pound with a meat mallet until very thin, then season with Essence. Put the flour in a large shallow bowl and season with Essence. Put the egg mixture in another large shallow bowl and season with Essence.

Dredge the chops in the flour, coating each side evenly, tapping off any excess. Dip in the egg mixture, letting any excess drip off, then dredge again in the flour, tapping off any excess.

Heat ¼ cup of the oil in a medium-size sauté pan over medium-high heat. Add 1 of the veal chops and fry until golden brown, 2 to 3 minutes on each side. Drain on paper towels. Season with Essence. Repeat with the remaining oil and chops. Put the cooked chops on a baking sheet and put in the oven for 4 to 5 minutes.

Meanwhile, put the heavy cream and garlic in a large sauté pan over medium heat and season with salt and pepper. Cook, stirring often, until the cream is bubbly and thick, about 4 minutes.

Heat the water in a large saucepan over medium-high heat and bring to a boil. Add the pasta and cook until tender, 2 to 3 minutes. Drain and add the pasta to the reduced cream. Add the cheese and season again with salt and pepper.

To serve, remove the pasta from the sauté pan with tongs and make several nests with it in the center of a large platter. Spoon any sauce remaining in the pan over the pasta. Place the veal on top of the pasta and sprinkle with cheese.

Smothered Oxtails over Spinach and Sweet Corn Mash

Makes 4 servings

The oxtail was once really from an ox, but these days the term generally refers to beef or veal tail. Although it's bony, and sometimes tough, the tail has quite a lot of flavor, which makes it ideal for braising. This is a great one-pot dish that can be simmered all afternoon.

The butcher will have to cut the tails for you. The very skinny tips can be put into the pot to extract the flavor, but only the larger pieces will have enough meat to serve for the meal.

2 oxtails (about 4 pounds), cut into 1-inch pieces

Salt and freshly ground black pepper to taste

1 cup bleached all-purpose flour

Essence to taste (page 7)

½ cup plus 1 tablespoon olive oil

2 cups chopped yellow onions

1 cup chopped carrots

1 cup chopped celery

3 tablespoons chopped garlic

3 bay leaves

2 tablespoons chopped fresh thyme leaves

1 cup dry red wine

2 quarts Veal Stock (page 10)

¼ cup chopped fresh parsley leaves

1½ pounds new or small red potatoes, quartered

¼ pound (1 stick) unsalted butter, cubed

½ to ¾ cup heavy cream, to your taste

Season the oxtails with salt and pepper. Put the flour in a shallow bowl and season with Essence. Dredge the oxtails in the flour, coating each side evenly and tapping off the excess.

Heat ½ cup of the olive oil in a large Dutch oven over medium heat. Add the oxtails and cook until very brown, 2 to 3 minutes on each side. Transfer the oxtails to a platter and set aside.

Add the onions to the pot, season with salt and pepper, and cook, stirring, for 2 minutes. Add the carrots and celery, season with salt and pepper, and cook, stirring, for 1 minute. Add 2 tablespoons of the garlic, the bay leaves, and thyme and cook for 1 minute. Add the wine and deglaze, scraping the bottom and sides to loosen any browned particles. Add the stock, bring to a boil, and reduce the heat to medium-low. Return the oxtails to the pot and cook, covered, until the sauce is stewlike and the meat starts to fall off the bone, about 2 hours. Baste the oxtails often during the cooking time. Check the seasoning and add salt and pepper if needed. Stir in the parsley.

Meanwhile, put the potatoes in a large saucepan and cover with water. Season the water with salt. Bring to a boil, then reduce the heat to medium and simmer until the potatoes are fork tender, about 10 minutes. Drain. Return the potatoes to the pan over low heat and stir the potatoes for 1 minute to dry them. Add the butter and heavy cream, season with salt and pepper, and mash the potatoes until slightly smooth. Set aside and keep warm.

Heat the remaining 1 tablespoon olive oil in a medium-size sauté pan over medium heat. Add the corn, season with salt and pepper, and cook, stirring, for 2 to 3 minutes. Add the spinach and the remaining 1 tablespoon garlic, season with salt and pepper, and cook for another minute. Fold into the mashed potatoes and keep warm.

To serve, mound the mashed potato mixture in the center of each serving plate. Lay a few of the oxtails on top of the potatoes and spoon some of the gravy over the top. Garnish with the fried parsnips.

continued

2 cups fresh sweet corn kernels
    (from 2 medium-size ears)
One 10-ounce bag fresh spinach, well
    washed, and tough stems removed
1 recipe Fried Parsnips (page 216)

Stuart Foreman and cameraman Al Ligouri on *Emeril Live*

215

W h e r e ' s   t h e   M e a t ?   V e g e t a r i a n s   B e w a r e !

Fried Parsnips

Makes 4 servings

1 large parsnip (4 to 5 ounces), peeled

Vegetable oil for deep frying

Salt and freshly ground black pepper to
taste

Using a vegetable peeler, cut paper-thin strips lengthwise from top to bottom of the parsnip, turning it as you work, making about 40 strips, about 10 strips per serving.

In a large pot or an electric fryer, heat 4 inches of oil to 360°F. Drop the strips, all at one time, into the hot oil. Be very careful, as the hot oil may splatter. Using a slotted spoon, gently stir the strips around in the oil until golden brown, about 1 minute. Remove and drain on paper towels, then season with salt and pepper.

Venison Chili Cheese Fries

Makes 6 to 8 servings

I know that a lot of you guys out there probably are deer hunters, so here's your chance to use that meat you have in the freezer.

This is one of those real he-man dishes, hearty and hardy with lotsa pow and bam! But hey, I've seen quite a few ladies dig into this who don't come up for air until they've eaten the whole thing!

Heat the vegetable oil in a large sauté pan over medium heat. Add the onions, season with salt and cayenne, and cook, stirring, until they begin to wilt, about 2 minutes. Add the venison, chili powder, cumin, crushed red pepper, and oregano, season with salt and cayenne, and cook until all the pink in the meat disappears, 5 to 6

2 tablespoons vegetable oil

2 cups chopped yellow onions

Salt and cayenne to taste

2 pounds ground venison

1 tablespoon chili powder

2 teaspoons ground cumin

Crushed red pepper to taste

2 teaspoons dried oregano leaves

2 tablespoons chopped garlic

minutes. Add the garlic, tomatoes, tomato paste, and 2½ cups veal stock, bring to a boil, and reduce the heat to medium-low. Simmer, uncovered, until the meat is tender, about 1 hour, stirring occasionally. Skim off any fat that rises to the surface.

Combine the masa harina flour with the remaining ½ cup stock and mix to blend. Slowly add to the pot, stirring to blend. The mixture will thicken. Cook for 30 minutes, then season again with salt and cayenne. It should be thick enough to coat the back of a spoon.

In a heavy, deep pot or an electric fryer, heat 4 inches of vegetable oil to 360°F. Fry the shoestring potatoes in batches until golden brown, 3 to 4 minutes per batch. Drain on paper towels, then season with salt and cayenne.

Preheat the oven to 400°F.

Cover the bottom of a large, glass rectangular baking pan with the shoestring potatoes. Combine the Cheddar and Jack cheeses. Sprinkle the cheese over the fries. Bake just until the cheese melts, 3 to 4 minutes. Remove the pan from the oven and spoon the chili over the top of the fries. Garnish with the sour cream and jalapeños. Serve immediately.

3 cups peeled, seeded, and chopped fresh or canned tomatoes

2 tablespoons tomato paste

3 cups Veal Stock (page 10) or canned veal broth

2 tablespoons masa harina flour (found in some large supermarkets and specialty food shops)

Vegetable oil for deep frying

2 large Idaho potatoes, peeled and cut into shoestrings, rinsed in cool water and patted dry

½ pound grated Cheddar cheese

½ pound grated Monterey Jack cheese

1 cup sour cream

½ cup sliced pickled jalapeños

Signing *Emeril's Creole Christmas* in New York City

Country-Style Rabbit Ragout with Maytag White Cheddar Grits

Makes 4 servings

The word ragout comes from the French verb ragoûter, which means "to stimulate the appetite," and that perfectly describes this wonderful, thick, rich, well-seasoned stew of rabbit. Yes, sirree, babe!

Oh, and by the way, I like to use Iowa's Maytag white Cheddar cheese simply because it's American made and has a superb flavor to boot. See the Source Guide for information.

¾ cup bleached all-purpose flour

Essence to taste (page 7)

1½ pounds uncooked rabbit loin, cubed

Salt and freshly ground black pepper to taste

2 tablespoons olive oil

½ cup chopped yellow onions

½ cup diced carrot

½ cup peeled and diced Idaho potato

½ cup peeled, seeded, and chopped fresh or canned tomatoes, undrained

2 tablespoons chopped shallots

¼ cup plus 2 tablespoons chopped green onions (green part only)

1 tablespoon chopped garlic

4 cups Veal Stock (page 10)

3½ tablespoons unsalted butter

2½ cups milk

½ cup quick-cooking white grits

2 tablespoons heavy cream

¼ cup plus 2 tablespoons grated Maytag or other white Cheddar cheese

Put the flour in a medium-size mixing bowl and season with Essence. Season the rabbit with salt and pepper, and add to the flour. Toss, lightly coating each piece, shaking off any excess.

Heat the olive oil in a medium-size sauté pan over medium heat. Add the rabbit, and cook, stirring often, until lightly golden, 1 to 2 minutes. Add the onions, carrot, potato, tomatoes, shallots, green onions, and ¼ cup of the garlic, season with salt and pepper, and cook, stirring, for 2 to 3 minutes. Add the veal stock and reduce by half, 3 to 4 minutes. Add 2 tablespoons of the butter and season with salt and pepper.

Bring the milk, seasoned with salt, to a boil in a medium-size saucepan over medium heat. Add the remaining butter. While stirring, slowly add the grits, breaking up any lumps. Cook over medium heat, stirring occasionally, until the grits are tender and slightly thick, 15 to 20 minutes. Add the heavy cream and ¼ cup of the cheese, stirring until the cheese is completely melted. Season with salt and pepper.

To serve, mound the grits in the center of a serving bowl. Spoon the ragout over the top. Place the fried parsnips in the center of the ragout, pushing them down into the grits. Sprinkle with the remaining 2 tablespoons cheese and green onions.

1 recipe Fried Parsnips (page 216)

Emeril Live **musicians David Hamburger, aka C. F. Steaks, and Matt Weiner, aka Bouillabaisse**

Emeril's **TV** Dinners

Creole

Jazz Brunch

When I took over the reins as executive chef at

Commander's Palace in New

Orleans, I was introduced to a

tradition begun by the Brennans

–what is now known all over the

world as Jazz Brunch.

On Saturdays and Sundays,

colorful helium balloons festooned all of the dining

rooms and not one but two jazz bands circulated

throughout the restaurant creating a festive, party

atmosphere.

Nowhere else had I experienced such exuberance over brunch! It incorporated all that is great and good about New Orleans—kicked-up cocktails, haute Creole cuisine, and the best jazz around. Working during the brunch, I was as happy as the guests who sometimes had to be swept out before dinner service began!

To be sure, Ella, Dick, John, and Dottie of the Brennan clan were great teachers, mentors, and friends, who inspired me always to make a dining experience fun. If it's not fun, they often commented, then it's not worth doing.

So began my love affair and downright respect for this wonderful celebration of brunch, a cross between breakfast and lunch, that New Orleanians practically venerate.

If you come down to the Crescent City, be sure and visit Delmonico Restaurant and Bar, my newest restaurant; join us for brunch, and you'll see what I mean about a bash at brunch.

Yeah, I hear the musicians warming up. It's time to fire up the stoves and get ready for a real party!

Emeril Live **food producer Felicia Willett and Hilda Lagasse talking during a commercial on the Mother's Day show**

Stan's Mint Julep

Makes 1 quart

In New Orleans, we like to begin our brunches with what my friend Ella Brennan calls "eye-openers." This, and the Pimm's Cup, should get your engine running and your gastric juices flowing. The first is a mint julep, one of the South's most popular alcoholic drinks, said to have been created in Kentucky. It's usually made with bourbon, but every southern state has its own recipe. In Georgia, the locals use cognac and—what else?—peach brandy.

One summer evening I found myself in the company of a dear gentleman, Stan Dry, at his home not far from Vermilion Bay off Louisiana's coast. He snipped fragrant mint from his garden, and before I knew it, he was mixing up mint juleps to enjoy while we listened to the sounds of frogs, cicadas, and herons as the sun sank in the western sky. When I took my leave, he poured some of the mint-flavored syrup into a bottle and added some bourbon for me to take home. Now that's what I call a southern gentleman. Here's to you, Stan! Oh, and please use only crushed ice, not cubed. Trust me, it's better.

Combine the water and sugar in a large nonreactive saucepan over medium heat and stir to dissolve the sugar. Add the mint and bring to a boil. Remove from the heat, cover, and steep for 30 minutes.

Strain the mint syrup through a strainer lined with several thicknesses of cheesecloth. Let cool.

2 cups bottled spring water

¾ cup sugar

3 cups loosely packed fresh mint leaves

2 cups bourbon

Fresh mint sprigs for garnish

Combine the cooled mint syrup with the bourbon and pour into a sterilized bottle. Wait at least 1 month before drinking. To serve, fill a julep cup or collins glass with clear, crushed ice and fill with the mint julep mixture. Garnish with a sprig of fresh mint.

223

Pimm's Cup

Makes 1 serving

Once I got settled in New Orleans, I would, on occasion, wander around the French Market acquainting myself with some of the local pubs on my day off. One sultry afternoon I stumbled into the Napoleon House, a local favorite, on the corner of Chartres and St. Louis. It was there I made friends

with the bartenders, who introduced me to one of their more popular drinks, a Pimm's Cup, which is a bottled concoction containing liquor that's available at most liquor stores. According to lore, back in 1840, James Pimm had an oyster bar in the heart of the city of London and his clientele was flocking to sample a new drink he blended on the premises. (Sounds like my kind of man.) By 1859, Mr. Pimm was bottling his famous drink and distributing it to bars and restaurants throughout England. Well, I guess it somehow came over the ocean, and New

Orleanians, most of whom like to drink anything at any time of day, added this to their repertoire. From what I can gather, there are Pimm's Cups in several versions, numbered from 1 to 7, with No. 1 Cup, which is gin-based, being the most common.

Sweet-and-sour mix can be found in most liquor stores and super-markets. It's a mix that's added to various drinks, such as daiquiris and whiskey sours. Ask around, I'm sure you'll find it.

Fill a tall glass with crushed ice. Add the Pimm's and sweet-and-sour mix. Stir to blend thoroughly. Splash with the lemon-lime soda and garnish with the cucumber.

Crushed ice

1½ ounces Pimm's Cup No. 1

1½ ounces sweet-and-sour mix

Splash of lemon-lime soda, like 7-Up or Sprite

1 slice cucumber, 5 to 6 inches long, cut lengthwise

Mini Grilled Truffle Cheese Sandwiches

Makes about 10 servings

While you're sipping on those eye-openers, you can munch on these little grilled cheese sandwiches. If you don't have truffle oil, use butter. De Soto cheese, similar to Swiss, is produced by a favorite purveyor of mine in Louisiana, but you can use baby Swiss or any kind of Swiss you can find in your market area. I tend to use a brioche-type bread, but you can use French bread, just don't use any of that plain old sliced sandwich bread.

Brush both sides of each slice of bread with the truffle oil or butter. Place a slice of cheese on top of each of 4 slices of bread, then top with the remaining slices of bread. Grill the sandwiches on a hot griddle or in a nonstick skillet over medium heat until golden and the cheese has melted, 2 to 3 minutes on each side.

Cut each sandwich into 5 finger-size slices to serve.

8 slices brioche or French bread (each about ¼ inch thick)

¼ cup white truffle oil (available in specialty food stores) or softened unsalted butter

4 slices De Soto (or Swiss-style) cheese (each about ¼ inch thick)

Potato Gaufrettes with Lobster Rémoulade

Makes 4 servings

Gaufrette *is a fancy term to describe waffle-looking wafers. Here we're making potato gaufrettes and the potatoes are cut with a mandoline using a crisscross blade. If you don't have one of those fancy gadgets, just cut the potatoes very thin, like potato chips. In New Orleans we usually have shrimp rémoulade, but, you know me, I like to kick things up, so I used lobster here. But don't be afraid to use shrimp, crabmeat, or bay scallops.*

Vegetable oil for deep frying

1 large Idaho potato, peeled

Salt and freshly ground black pepper to taste

1 large egg

½ cup chopped yellow onions

¼ cup chopped green onions (green part only)

¼ cup chopped celery

2 tablespoons chopped garlic

2 tablespoons prepared horseradish

¼ cup Creole or whole-grain mustard

3 tablespoons ketchup

2 tablespoons chopped fresh parsley leaves

3 tablespoons fresh lemon juice

¾ cup olive oil

1 pound cooked lobster meat, cut into small dice

4 cups assorted baby greens, such as romaine, frisée, red oak leaf, and/or radicchio

2 tablespoons extra virgin olive oil

4 ounces goat cheese, crumbled

In a large, heavy pot or an electric fryer, heat the vegetable oil (about 4 inches) to 360°F.

Using a mandoline fitted with the crisscross blade, cut the potatoes lengthwise into thin wafflelike chips. Fry the potatoes in batches until golden brown, about 2 minutes, then drain on paper towels, and season with salt and pepper. Set aside and keep warm.

In a food processor or blender, combine the egg, both onions, celery, garlic, horseradish, mustard, ketchup, parsley, and lemon juice. Season with salt and pepper and process until smooth. With the machine running, pour the olive oil in a steady stream through the feed tube. The mixture will thicken. Season again with salt and pepper. Toss one-half of the mixture with the lobster meat in a medium-size mixing bowl.

In another medium-size mixing bowl, toss the greens with the extra virgin olive oil and season with salt and pepper.

To serve, mound the greens in the center of 4 serving plates. Arrange the potatoes around the greens, then top with a spoonful or two of the lobster rémoulade. Garnish with the goat cheese.

The remaining half of the pre-lobster rémoulade can be reserved (refrigerated) and used as a dipping sauce for fried or boiled seafood, or tossed with lump crabmeat.

Blueberry Beignets

Makes 20 beignets

If you've ever visited New Orleans, you probably visited the French Quarter and indulged in those wonderful fried doughnuts known as beignets. When blueberries are in season during the summer months, why not add them to the beignet batter to dress them up a bit?

¼ cup warm water (about 110°F)

1 envelope (¼ ounce) active dry yeast

¼ cup granulated sugar

2 tablespoons vegetable shortening

½ teaspoon salt

1 pint fresh blueberries, rinsed, picked over, and stemmed

½ cup boiling water

½ cup heavy cream

1 large egg, beaten

4 to 4½ cups bleached all-purpose flour, as needed

Vegetable oil for deep frying

Confectioners' sugar

Combine the water and yeast in a small mixing bowl and whisk to dissolve the yeast. Put the bowl in a warm draft-free place until the yeast bubbles and the mixture almost doubles in bulk, about 10 minutes. If it doesn't do this, the yeast is dead and you'll have to start again with new yeast.

In a large mixing bowl, combine the granulated sugar, shortening, salt, and blueberries. Stir in the boiling water. Using a fork, lightly mash the blueberries against the side of the bowl. Cool the mixture to lukewarm. Add the heavy cream, the yeast mixture, and egg. Add 2 cups of the flour and blend well. Stir in the remaining flour, ¼ cup at a time, until the dough is smooth and not sticky. If the dough becomes too stiff to stir easily with a spoon, work in the flour with your fingers. Turn the dough out onto a floured work surface and pat the dough into a rectangle about 1 inch thick. Lightly dust the surface of the dough with flour. Roll out the rectangle to at least 12½ inches long by 10 inches wide and about ¼ inch thick. With a sharp knife, cut the dough into twenty 2½-inch-square beignets.

In a large, heavy pot or an electric fryer, heat the oil (about 4 inches) to 360°F. Fry the beignets, 2 to 3 at a time, until golden brown and crispy on all sides, 3 to 5 minutes. Drain on paper towels. Sprinkle with confectioners' sugar and serve warm.

Pecan Waffles with
Pecan and Banana Syrup

Makes 4 to 8 servings

I f you're a waffle lover, this is the one for you, babe. The pecan and banana syrup is out-a-sight and you can use it on lots of other things, like vanilla ice cream, pain perdu, or, heck, biscuits and corn bread.

If your waffle iron isn't nonstick, you will have to lightly oil it. Read the instructions that came with it.

Heat 2 tablespoons of the butter in a medium-size sauté pan over medium heat. Add the pecan pieces and cook, stirring, until golden, 2 to 3 minutes. Add the banana slices and syrup and bring to a simmer. Set aside and keep warm.

Combine the flour, ground pecans, sugar, baking powder, and salt in a medium-size mixing bowl. In a large mixing bowl, beat the egg yolks and vanilla together slightly. Beat the milk and the 1 stick of melted butter into the egg mixture. Fold the flour mixture into the egg mixture. Stir until combined yet still slightly lumpy. In a small mixing bowl beat the egg whites until stiff peaks form. Gently fold into the batter, leaving little fluffs.

¼ **pound (1 stick) plus 2 tablespoons**
unsalted butter, melted
1 **cup pecan pieces**
2 **medium-size ripe bananas, peeled and cut**
crosswise into ½-inch-thick slices
2 **cups pure maple syrup**
1½ **cups bleached all-purpose flour**
⅓ **cup ground pecans**
⅓ **cup sugar**
1 **tablespoon baking powder**
¼ **teaspoon salt**
2 **large egg yolks**
1 **teaspoon pure vanilla extract**
1¾ **cups milk**
2 **large egg whites**

If using a Belgian waffle iron, pour 1 cup of the batter onto the grids of a pre-heated and lightly greased waffle iron. (Regular waffle irons will take only about ½ cup.) Close the lid. Do not open during cooking time. For the Belgian waffle iron, cook until golden and crisp, 3 to 4 minutes. Smaller waffle irons will take 1½ to 2 minutes.

Serve hot with the pecan and banana syrup.

Smoked Trout Hash with Choron Sauce

Makes 4 servings

From the city that brought you Brennan's and all its specialty egg dishes comes my version of an egg dish. Two perfectly poached eggs sit atop a great hash made with smoked trout, then drizzled with a choron sauce, which is made by combining tomatoes and tarragon with hollandaise.

½ cup peeled, seeded, and chopped fresh or canned tomatoes, drained

2 tablespoons chopped fresh tarragon leaves

1 tablespoon plus 2 teaspoons chopped garlic

Salt and cayenne to taste

3 tablespoons plus 1 teaspoon white distilled vinegar

1 cup dry red wine

1 tablespoon chopped fresh parsley leaves

2 large egg yolks

1 teaspoon fresh lemon juice

2 teaspoons water

¼ pound (1 stick) unsalted butter, melted and kept warm

Vegetable oil for deep frying

2 medium-size Idaho potatoes, peeled and cut into small dice

Freshly ground black pepper to taste

1 tablespoon olive oil

½ cup minced yellow onions

8 ounces smoked trout, flaked

4 large eggs

1 tablespoon snipped fresh chives

Combine the tomatoes, tarragon, and 1 tablespoon of the garlic in a medium-size nonreactive saucepan over medium heat. Season with salt and cayenne. Stir in 3 tablespoons of the vinegar and the wine, and bring to a boil. Reduce the heat to medium-low and simmer until the mixture is dark brown and thick, 20 to 25 minutes. Remove from the heat and stir in the parsley.

Set a stainless steel bowl over a pot of simmering water. Add the egg yolks with the lemon juice and water, and season with salt and cayenne. Whisk until the eggs are pale yellow in color and slightly thick. Remove the bowl from the pot and whisk in the butter, 1 tablespoon at a time, until all the butter is incorporated. Fold the tomato mixture into the egg mixture, set aside, and keep warm.

In a large, heavy pot or an electric fryer, heat the vegetable oil (about 4 inches) to 360°F. Fry the potatoes until golden brown, 3 to 4 minutes. Drain on paper towels. Season with salt and black pepper.

Heat the olive oil in a large sauté pan over medium heat. Add the onions, season with salt and cayenne, and cook, stirring, for 2 minutes. Add the remaining 2 teaspoons garlic and the trout. Season with salt and cayenne and cook, stirring, for 1 minute. Add the potatoes, season with salt and cayenne, and cook for 2 to 3 minutes, stirring gently.

Pour cold water into a 10-inch sauté pan to a depth of about 2 inches. Bring to a simmer, then reduce the heat so that the surface of the water barely shimmers. Add the remaining teaspoon vinegar. Break the eggs into individual saucers, gently slide them, one at a time, into the water, and with a large spoon, lift the white over the yolk. Repeat once or twice to enclose the yolk completely in the white. Poach until the whites are set and the yolks feel soft when touched gently, 3 to 4 minutes.

When ready to serve, spoon the trout hash into the center of 4 plates. With a slotted spatula, gently lift the eggs out of the water and let them drain a few seconds, season with salt and cayenne, then transfer the eggs to the top of the hash. Drizzle with the sauce and garnish with chives.

Crabmeat Omelets with Tasso Hollandaise

Makes 4 servings

I can't say enough about how lavish brunch dishes are in New Orleans. I was intrigued by the many dishes prepared with eggs, all served with luxurious sauces. I soon realized that I had better get on the bandwagon and develop some egg dishes. Here's an omelet that will knock your socks off. Just be sure to get the best crabmeat you can find or, if that's not an option, try shrimp or chunks of lobster. Oh, man!

FOR THE CRABMEAT MIXTURE

1 pound lump crabmeat, picked over for shells and cartilage

¼ cup minced shallots

¼ cup chopped green onions (green part only)

Salt and freshly ground black pepper to taste

FOR THE TASSO HOLLANDAISE

2 large egg yolks

1 teaspoon fresh lemon juice

Dash of Tabasco sauce

2 teaspoons water

Salt and freshly ground black pepper to taste

¼ pound (1 stick) unsalted butter, melted

2 ounces tasso, smoked sausage, or ham, chopped

Combine the crabmeat, shallots, and green onions in a small mixing bowl. Season with salt and pepper.

In a stainless steel bowl set over a pot of simmering water (be careful not to let the bowl touch the water), whisk the egg yolks with the lemon juice, Tabasco, and water until pale yellow in color. Season with salt and pepper. Remove the bowl from the pot and, whisking vigorously, add the melted butter, 1 tablespoon at a time, until all the butter is incorporated. Add the tasso and continue whisking for 30 seconds. Keep warm.

In a large mixing bowl, whisk the eggs and heavy cream together and season with salt and pepper.

In a 6-inch nonstick sauté pan over medium heat, heat 2 tablespoons of the butter until it foams. Pour in one-fourth of the egg-cream mixture and cook, shaking the pan and stirring rapidly with a fork, holding the tines parallel to the bottom of the pan. The omelet should remain runny in the center but firm on the bottom.

Lift the handle of the skillet and gently knock the pan on the surface of the stove so the omelet slides to the bottom curve of the pan. Add ¼ cup of the crab mixture and ¼ cup of the grated cheese in the center of the omelet, then, with a fork, quickly fold the omelet from the top down. Let it stand for a few moments, then slide it onto a serving plate. Repeat the process until all the egg mixture and butter are used.

To serve, spoon the sauce over each omelet and garnish with green onions.

FOR THE OMELETS

8 large eggs

¼ cup heavy cream

Salt and freshly ground black pepper

¼ pound (1 stick) unsalted butter

1 cup grated smoked Gouda cheese

FOR THE GARNISH

2 tablespoons finely chopped green onions
   (green part only)

Shrimp Quiche

Makes 8 servings

Who says real men don't eat quiche? I love it and so do a lot of my buddies who come over to watch football games. It's an all-time favorite for brunches, too, full of cheese and shrimp and all kinds of good stuff.

FOR THE PASTRY SHELL

2½ cups bleached all-purpose flour

2 teaspoons salt

¼ teaspoon cayenne

1 cup solid vegetable shortening

2 to 3 tablespoons water, as needed

FOR THE FILLING

2 tablespoons unsalted butter

¼ cup small-diced yellow onion

3 tablespoons small-diced red bell pepper

2 teaspoons chopped garlic

1¾ teaspoons salt

¼ teaspoon plus ⅛ teaspoon cayenne

½ pound medium-size shrimp, peeled and
    deveined (about 1 cup)

2 cups heavy cream

4 large eggs

¼ teaspoon Tabasco sauce

½ teaspoon Worcestershire sauce

2 tablespoons snipped fresh chives

3 tablespoons freshly grated Parmigiano-
    Reggiano cheese

½ cup grated white Cheddar cheese

For the dough, combine the flour, salt, and cayenne in a large mixing bowl. Add the shortening and, using your hands, work it into the flour until the mixture resembles coarse crumbs. Add enough water to make a smooth ball of dough and mix until the dough comes away from the sides of the bowl. Form the dough into a ball. Cover the ball with plastic wrap and refrigerate for at least 1 hour.

Remove the dough from the refrigerator and let it sit for about 5 minutes. Lightly dust your work surface with flour. Roll the dough out to a 12-inch circle about ¼ inch thick. Fold the dough into fourths and place in a 10-inch fluted quiche pan. Unfold the dough and press it, using your fingers, firmly onto the bottom and sides of the pan. Roll a wooden rolling pin over the pan to cut off the excess dough. Prick the bottom of the crust all over with a fork.

Preheat oven to 350°F.

To make the filling, melt the butter in a medium-size sauté pan over medium heat. Add the onion, bell pepper, garlic, 1 teaspoon of the salt, and ¼ teaspoon of the cayenne, and cook, stirring, for 4 minutes. Add the shrimp and cook, stirring, for 2 minutes. Remove from the heat and let cool.

In a medium-size mixing bowl, whisk together the heavy cream, eggs, the remaining ¾ teaspoon salt, the remaining ⅛ teaspoon cayenne, the Tabasco, Worcestershire, chives, and Parmigiano-Reggiano cheese. Spoon the shrimp mixture into the pastry shell. Sprinkle the white Cheddar cheese over the shrimp. Pour the cream mixture over the cheese. Place in the oven and bake until the center sets and the top is golden brown, about 55 minutes. Remove from the oven and cool for 5 minutes on a wire rack before slicing to serve.

Ice Cream Bombe

Makes 12 servings

If you really want to impress your friends, this is a dessert that will do the trick. It just takes a little time to assemble, but hey, they're worth it, right? And, if you're really tight on time, you can always buy regular old ice cream at the grocery store to substitute for what we have here. Now, I don't guarantee it'll be as great, but at least you've made an effort.

¼ cup milk

2 tablespoons plus 2 teaspoons unsalted butter

8 large eggs

1 cup plus 2 tablespoons granulated sugar

1 cup bleached all-purpose flour

1 teaspoon baking powder

⅓ cup unsweetened cocoa powder

⅛ teaspoon salt

1 teaspoon pure vanilla extract

1 pint Chicory Coffee Ice Cream (page 239), softened

1 pint Creole Cream Cheese and Praline Ice Cream (page 240), softened

1 pint Chocolate Ice Cream (page 241), softened

2 cups Sweetened Whipped Cream (page 37)

2 cups Chocolate Sauce (page 73)

Confectioners' sugar

Preheat the oven to 350°F.

In a small saucepan, warm the milk and 2 teaspoons of the butter over medium-low heat. With an electric mixer fitted with a wire whip, beat the eggs and 1 cup of the sugar on medium-high speed in a large mixing bowl until the mixture is pale yellow and thick and has tripled in volume, about 8 minutes. With the mixer on low, beat in the warm milk mixture.

Sift the flour, baking powder, cocoa, and salt together in a medium-size mixing bowl. Fold into the egg mixture and blend thoroughly until smooth. Add the vanilla and mix gently.

Grease a 17 × 12-inch baking pan (or jelly-roll pan) with 2 tablespoons butter. Sprinkle with the remaining 2 tablespoons sugar.

Pour the cake batter into the prepared pan, spreading it evenly. Bake until the cake springs back when touched, about 15 minutes. Cool for about 2 minutes, then gently flip it out onto a large wire rack or a large piece of parchment paper. Let cool completely.

Place a 1½-quart mixing bowl upside down on the sponge cake. Using a knife, cut out the shape of the bowl, discarding the trimmings. Line the mixing bowl with plastic wrap. Spoon and spread the bottom and sides of the mixing bowl evenly, about 3 inches deep, with the coffee ice cream. Place the bowl in the freezer and freeze until firm, about 30 minutes. Spread the Creole cream cheese ice cream evenly over the bottom and the sides, about 3 inches deep. Place the bowl in the freezer and freeze until firm, about 30 minutes. Fill the center of the bowl with the chocolate ice cream. Place the circle of sponge cake on top of the filled bowl. Cover the bowl tightly with plastic wrap, place in the freezer, and freeze until firm, about 2 hours.

Remove from the freezer and remove the plastic wrap. Unmold onto a large serving platter. Garnish the mold with the whipped cream. Slice into serving pieces, drizzle with the chocolate sauce, sprinkle with confectioners' sugar, and serve.

Berries Romanoff

Makes 6 servings

In the classic Romanoff, the only berry used is strawberries, but you can use any combination of fresh berries—whatever is available in your area—for this easy but delicious dessert that's fit for royals like you and me.

To make the chocolate shavings, get a chunk of chocolate, semi-sweet or milk chocolate, and, with a vegetable peeler, shave the chocolate. Easy, huh?

½ cup Grand Marnier

1 cup sour cream

½ pint vanilla ice cream, softened

2 cups Sweetened Whipped Cream
(page 37)

1 pint fresh raspberries, rinsed and
picked over

1 pint fresh blueberries, rinsed, picked
over, and stemmed

1 pint fresh blackberries, rinsed and
picked over

1 pint fresh strawberries, rinsed, picked
over, hulled, and halved

2 ounces chocolate shavings

2 tablespoons shredded fresh mint leaves

Confectioners' sugar

Combine the Grand Marnier and sour cream in a large mixing bowl and whisk to blend. Stir in the ice cream. Fold in the whipped cream. Arrange the berries on a serving platter, then pour the cream mixture over the top of the berries. Garnish with the chocolate curls, mint, and confectioners' sugar and serve.

Coauthor Marcelle
Bienvenu's husband,
Rock Daddy, aka
Rock Lasserre

Chicory Coffee Ice Cream

Makes about ½ gallon

In New Orleans we drink coffee that has chicory blended into the coffee grinds. If you can't get your hands on some of this stuff, I recommend substituting either an espresso blend or whatever suits your fancy. It's important to use instant coffee granules. No big deal!

You'll need an ice cream machine to make this ice cream.

In a large nonreactive saucepan over medium heat, combine the instant coffee, milk, heavy cream, sugar, and pepper together and whisk until the sugar is dissolved. Heat the mixture to the scalding point (when bubbles form around the edge of the pan). Remove from the heat.

2 tablespoons Community New Orleans Blend instant coffee granules or granules of any instant coffee

1 quart milk

2 cups heavy cream

2 cups sugar

Pinch of freshly ground black pepper

8 large egg yolks

Beat the egg yolks in a large mixing bowl. Add the cream mixture, about ¼ cup at a time, to the beaten egg, whisking well between each addition, until it is all used. Pour the mixture back into the saucepan and cook, stirring, over medium heat until the mixture becomes thick enough to lightly coat the back of a spoon, 2 to 3 minutes.

Remove from the heat and strain through a fine-mesh sieve into a glass bowl. Cover the top of the mixture with plastic wrap (this will keep a skin from forming) and let cool completely.

Place the mixture in the refrigerator and chill completely. Pour the mixture into an ice cream machine and follow the manufacturer's directions for the churning time.

Creole Cream Cheese and Praline Ice Cream

Makes about ½ gallon

reole cream cheese is a New Orleans thing, but I understand it can be found now and then around the country. Check with your supermarket. You can always substitute drained ricotta or small curd cottage cheese in a pinch.

You will need to use an ice cream machine to make the ice cream.

1 vanilla bean

2 cups heavy cream

½ cup sugar

Pinch of salt

5 large egg yolks

2¾ cups Creole cream cheese

1 cup crumbled Pralines (page 241)

Using a sharp knife, split the vanilla bean in half, scrape out the insides, and reserve the bean. In a large nonreactive saucepan over medium heat, combine the heavy cream, sugar, vanilla pulp, the scraped bean, and salt. Heat the cream to the scalding point (when bubbles form around the edges of the pan). Remove from the heat.

Beat the egg yolks in a large mixing bowl. Add the cream mixture, about ¼ cup at a time, to the beaten eggs, whisking well between each addition, until it is all used. Pour the mixture back into the saucepan and cook, stirring, over medium heat until the mixture becomes thick enough to coat the back of a spoon, 2 to 3 minutes.

Remove from the heat. Stir in the cream cheese and blend thoroughly. Cover the top of the mixture with plastic wrap (this will keep a skin from forming) and let cool. Place in the refrigerator and chill completely. Remove from the refrigerator and fold in the pralines. Pour the mixture into an ice cream machine and follow the manufacturer's instructions for churning time.

Pralines

Makes about 2 dozen

This is more than you'll need for the ice cream, but now you have some sweet things to munch on while watching television. Hey, it beats those Oreo cookies!

Combine the sugar, butter, and water in a large, heavy saucepan over medium heat. Stir to dissolve the sugar. Continue to stir for 3 to 4 minutes. The mixture will begin to boil. Add the pecans and continue to stir for about 5 minutes.

> 1 pound light brown sugar
>   (about 2½ packed cups)
> 2 tablespoons unsalted butter
> ¼ cup water
> 1 cup pecan pieces

Remove from the heat and drop by the spoonful onto waxed paper. Cool completely. Remove from the paper with a thin knife. The pralines can be stored in an airtight container at room temperature for about 2 weeks.

Chocolate Ice Cream

Makes about ½ gallon

In a large nonreactive saucepan over medium heat, combine the milk, heavy cream, sugar, and chocolate chips. Whisk until the sugar is dissolved and the chocolate melts completely. Heat the mixture to the scalding point (when bubbles form around the edges of the pan). Remove from the heat.

> 1 quart milk
> 2 cups heavy cream
> 1 cup sugar
> ½ pound semisweet chocolate chips
> 8 large egg yolks, beaten

Beat the egg yolks in a large mixing bowl. Add the cream mixture, about ¼ cup at a time, to the beaten eggs, whisking well between each addition, until it is all used. Pour the mixture back into the saucepan, and cook, stirring, over medium heat until the mixture becomes thick enough to lightly coat the back of a spoon, 2 to 3 minutes.

Remove from the heat and strain through a fine-mesh strainer into a glass bowl. Cover the top of the mixture with plastic wrap (this keeps a skin from forming) and let cool. Place the mixture in the refrigerator and chill completely.

Pour the mixture into the ice cream machine and follow the manufacturer's instructions for the churning time.

Swingin' Sweets

I began working in a Portuguese bakery in Fall River

when I was ten years old, not so much to make extra money, but because I was curious about what went on in the back, behind the swinging doors. It always smelled good and everybody was always busy. I started out as a pot washer, but I moved up quickly because I probably pestered the heck out of those guys. I especially remember Mr. Amarillo, who always took the time to show me some of the tricks of the trade.

Other than my mother, these were the people who instilled in me a fascination and love of food.

While at Commander's Palace, I became quick buddies with Lou Lynch, the pastry chef, who I'm happy to say is with me now at Emeril's and who is continually showing me new ideas and creating knockout desserts in keeping with our philosophy that everything be made from scratch and with the freshest, top-of-the-line ingredients.

I encourage you to use fine chocolate, seasonal fruits, and homemade ice cream whenever possible. Dress up desserts with drizzles of chocolate sauce, fresh mint, bams of granulated and confectioners' sugar, cocoa powder, dollops of whipped cream—all simple stuff, but all good.

Don't be intimidated by desserts, they're not to be struggled over, but to be enjoyed.

**Bernard Carmouche, chef de cuisine at
Emeril's Restaurant, sampling some sweets**

Praline Bread Pudding

Makes 12 servings

Bread puddings of all kinds are served throughout the state of Louisiana and I'll tell you why they're so popular. People around here can be very frugal and they dislike waste of any kind, so this is a great way to use day-old or slightly stale bread. I'm always looking for ways to dress up my bread puddings and adding pralines is one that's well received whenever I fix it.

In a large mixing bowl, combine the eggs, brown sugar, cinnamon, nutmeg, and vanilla and whisk to blend. Whisk in the heavy cream and milk. Fold in the bread and pralines. Cover with plastic wrap and refrigerate for 2 hours.

Preheat the oven to 350°F. Grease 12 muffin tins with the butter.

Spoon the mixture evenly into the muffin tins, then place the tins on a baking sheet. Bake until the centers spring back when touched, 30 to 35 minutes. Remove from the oven and let cool for about 5 minutes.

Serve warm with the crème anglaise.

4 large eggs

1 cup firmly packed light brown sugar

½ teaspoon ground cinnamon

Pinch of freshly grated nutmeg

1 teaspoon pure vanilla extract

3 cups heavy cream

1 cup milk

6 thick slices day-old bread, cut into 1-inch cubes (about 6 cups)

2 cups crumbled Pralines (page 241)

1 tablespoon unsalted butter, softened

2 cups Crème Anglaise (page 246)

continued

Crème Anglaise

Makes 2½ cups

Crème anglaise is a rich custard sauce that can be served hot or cold.

5 large egg yolks

½ cup sugar

2 cups heavy cream

1 teaspoon pure vanilla extract

Put the yolks in a saucepan and add the sugar. Beat with a wire whisk until thick and lemon-colored.

Put the heavy cream in a nonreactive saucepan and heat to the scalding point (when bubbles form around the edge of the pan). Gradually add the cream to the yolk mixture, beating constantly. Cook until the mixture thickens slightly. Do not overcook or boil, as the sauce will curdle. Remove from the heat and stir in the vanilla.

Strain through a fine-mesh sieve into a cold bowl. Cover with plastic wrap, pressing it down on the surface to prevent a skin from forming if not using immediately.

Will keep refrigerated for 24 hours.

Anne's Apple Fer

Makes 16 servings

My friend Annie-Girl, aka Anne Kearney, who helped me with one of my cookbooks as well as with my first television shows, opened up her own restaurant, Peristyle, in New Orleans a couple of years ago. She's one fine lady and one great chef.

This fer (French for iron) is French-inspired and was once made in a cast-iron skillet, but here we make it in a springform pan. It's a beauty of a *dessert that she features at her restaurant and that I know you'll love, and you can have it right at your home!*

Line the bottom and over the sides of a 10-inch springform pan with parchment paper.

In a medium-size heavy skillet, combine ½ cup of the granulated sugar, the brown sugar, water, and 2 tablespoons of the Armagnac. Season with salt and pepper. Bring to a boil, reduce the heat to medium, and cook, stirring occasionally, until it reduces by half and caramelizes, 10 to 15 minutes. Remove from the heat.

Melt the butter in a medium-size sauté pan over medium heat. Add the apples and cook until golden, about 5 minutes. Stir in the raisins and the remaining 2 tablespoons Armagnac and cook, stirring gently, for 2 minutes. Season with salt.

Spoon the apples and raisins into the springform pan and pour the caramel over the apples. Refrigerate for 30 minutes.

Preheat the oven to 350°F. In a large mixing bowl, whisk the milk, eggs, the remaining ¾ cup granulated sugar, the flour, and vanilla together until smooth. Strain the batter through a fine-mesh sieve over the apple-and-caramel mixture. Bake until the center sets, about 1½ hours.

Remove from the oven and cool for 30 minutes. Then remove the sides from the pan, turn it over on a serving plate, and serve warm, garnished with the whipped cream, confectioners' sugar, and mint sprigs.

1¼ cups granulated sugar

1 cup firmly packed light brown sugar

½ cup water

¼ cup Armagnac

Salt and freshly ground white pepper to taste

1 tablespoon unsalted butter

4 apples, such as Granny Smith or McIntosh, cored, peeled, and quartered

¼ cup golden raisins

3 cups milk

5 large eggs

1¼ cups plus 2 tablespoons bleached all-purpose flour

4½ teaspoons pure vanilla extract

2 cups Sweetened Whipped Cream (page 37)

Confectioners' sugar

Sprigs of fresh mint

Emeril's Profiteroles with Fresh Coconut Ice Cream

Makes about 2 dozen profiteroles; 6 to 8 servings

You gotta hear this story. Years ago, my friend Marcelle needed to do a piece on profiteroles for her weekly column in the **Times-Picayune**, *so she asked me to show her how to make them. A hurricane was approaching New Orleans when she met me in the kitchen at Commander's Palace. Ella Brennan was evacuating the restaurant and tying down the patio furniture, but Marcelle and I were determined to do our thing. With the wind and rain crashing around us, we made ourselves a batch of these beauties just as the electricity went out. But we were happy, sitting in the darkened kitchen munching on these sweet things. I think that was when we really bonded!*

¼ pound (1 stick) unsalted butter

1 cup milk

2 tablespoons granulated sugar

1 cup bleached all-purpose flour

½ teaspoon baking powder

Pinch of salt

5 large eggs

1 pint Fresh Coconut Ice Cream (page 249), softened

1 recipe Chocolate Sauce (page 73)

Confectioners' sugar

Preheat the oven to 400°F. Line a baking sheet with parchment paper.

Combine the butter, milk, and granulated sugar in a large nonreactive saucepan over medium heat and cook until the butter melts completely.

Combine the flour, baking powder, and salt in a medium-size mixing bowl, then add it to the milk mixture. Cook, stirring with a wooden spoon, until it forms a ball and pulls away from the sides of the pan. Remove from the heat and turn into a mixing bowl. With an electric mixer set on medium speed, beat the dough, adding the eggs one at a time until well blended. Continue beating until the dough is shiny and soft enough to fall from the spoon. Cool slightly, then put the dough in a pastry bag fitted with a plain tube, and pipe about 2 dozen golf-ball-size rounds onto the baking sheet, 2 inches apart. (Or use a large spoon and spoon them onto the baking sheet.) Bake for 10 minutes, then reduce the oven temperature to 350°F, and continue to bake until firm and golden brown, 20 to 25 minutes. Transfer the profiteroles to a wire rack to cool completely. With a serrated knife, cut the profiteroles in half lengthwise.

To serve, fill each half with a spoonful of the coconut ice cream, then drizzle with the chocolate sauce, and sprinkle with the confectioners' sugar.

Fresh Coconut Ice Cream

Makes about ½ gallon

In a large nonreactive saucepan, combine the milk, heavy cream, coconut cream, sugar, and pepper together over medium heat and whisk until the sugar is dissolved. Heat the mixture to the scalding point (when bubbles form around the edge of the pan).

Beat the egg yolks in a large mixing bowl. Add the cream mixture, about ¼ cup at a time, to the beaten eggs, whisking well between each addition, until all is used. Pour the mixture back into the saucepan and cook over medium heat until the mixture becomes thick enough to lightly coat the back of a spoon, 2 to 3 minutes.

1 quart milk

2 cups heavy cream

1 cup Coco Lopez coconut cream

1 cup sugar

Pinch of freshly ground black pepper

8 large egg yolks

6 ounces frozen grated unsweetened coconut, defrosted

Remove from the heat and strain through a fine-mesh sieve into a glass bowl. Fold in the coconut. Cover the top of the mixture with plastic wrap (this will keep a skin from forming) and let cool completely.

Place the mixture in the refrigerator and chill completely. Pour the mixture into an ice cream machine and follow the manufacturer's directions for the churning time.

Milk Chocolate Cheesecake

Makes one 10-inch cheesecake; 12 servings

Felicia learned how to make this cheesecake when she was a teenager to sell to her mother's friends when she needed some extra cash. She had a great business going for a few years!

This is a good basic recipe, so you might want to be creative. Delete the chocolate, add pecans to the crust, use different kinds of cookie crumbs—whatever floats your boat.

Traditionally a cheesecake is baked in a water bath to prevent it from cracking down the center, but you can bake this one without the water bath— just let it cool for a few minutes once it's removed from the oven and run a thin knife around the edges to loosen it slightly. Let it cool completely in the pan, then refrigerate. You may want to bring it to room temperature before slicing it to serve. Oh, and Felicia says to dip your cutting knife in a pitcher of warm water, then wipe it dry, before cutting the cheesecake, or any cake or pie for that matter.

2 cups chocolate cookie crumbs, such as
    Oreos or chocolate wafers
¼ pound (1 stick) unsalted butter, melted
3 pounds cream cheese, softened
2 cups sugar
6 large eggs
1 cup heavy cream
½ cup bleached all-purpose flour
Pinch of salt
1 teaspoon pure vanilla extract
8 ounces milk chocolate, melted

Preheat the oven to 350°F.

Combine the cookie crumbs and melted butter in a medium-size mixing bowl. Thoroughly mix together, then press into the bottom of a 10-inch springform pan.

Beat the cream cheese in a food processor until smooth. Add the sugar and process. Add the eggs 1 at a time, running the processor in between each addition. Add the heavy cream, flour, salt, and vanilla and process until smooth, scraping down the sides of the bowl as needed. With the motor running, add the chocolate in a steady stream. Pour the mixture into the prepared pan. Bake until the center of the cake sets, about 1 hour and 15 minutes.

Remove from the oven and loosen the sides of the cake with a thin knife. Cool completely. If you like it slightly chilled, refrigerate for about 1 hour.

¼ cup Grand Marnier

2 pints assorted fresh berries, such as raspberries, strawberries, and blackberries, rinsed and hulled if needed

2 cups Sweetened Whipped Cream (page 37)

Sprigs of fresh mint

In a medium-size mixing bowl, combine the Grand Marnier and berries, cover, and refrigerate for at least 2 hours.

To serve, slice the cheesecake, spoon the berries on the slices, and top with the whipped cream and mint sprigs.

Emeril and Elmo doing desserts

251

Old-Fashioned Chocolate Pudding

Makes 4 servings

Mr. Lou is the master of this chocolate pudding, which has been served with assorted house-made cookies at Emeril's for years. It's one of those down-home desserts that never loses its popularity.

2 cups plus 2 tablespoons milk

¾ cup sugar

4 ounces milk chocolate, chopped

3 large egg yolks

2 tablespoons cornstarch

½ teaspoon pure vanilla extract

1 tablespoon unsalted butter

1 cup Sweetened Whipped Cream
   (page 37)

2 ounces semisweet chocolate shavings

In a medium-size nonreactive saucepan, combine 2 cups of the milk and the sugar over medium-high heat. Bring to a boil and stir to dissolve the sugar, then reduce the heat to medium. Add the chopped chocolate and whisk until it completely melts. Remove from the heat.

Combine the egg yolks, cornstarch, and the remaining 2 tablespoons milk in a small mixing bowl and whisk until smooth. Slowly add the chocolate mixture, whisking constantly, until it is all used. Pour the mixture back into the saucepan and cook over medium heat until the mixture thickens, 3 to 4 minutes. Remove from the heat. Add the vanilla and butter and stir until the butter melts.

Pour the mixture into a glass bowl. Press a piece of plastic wrap down over the surface to prevent a skin from forming. Let cool completely. Refrigerate for 4 hours. Remove the plastic wrap and beat with a wire whisk until smooth.

To serve, spoon into dessert bowls and garnish with the whipped cream and chocolate shavings.

Lemon Pound Cake

Makes 8 servings

Joe, the pastry chef at NOLA, has an Aunt Polly in North Carolina who makes a great lemon pound cake that he serves at the restaurant. But because Joe cannot divulge the recipe, I've created this one that is pretty darn close. Don't worry, Aunt Polly, your recipe is still safe.

Preheat the oven to 325°F. Grease a 9 × 5 × 3-inch loaf pan with 1 tablespoon of the butter. Dust the pan with the tablespoon of flour.

Combine 1 cup of the granulated sugar and the lemon juice in a medium-size nonreactive saucepan over medium-high heat. Bring to a boil, stirring to dissolve the sugar, and cook until the mixture reduces by half, about 3 minutes. Remove from the heat and let cool.

With an electric mixer fitted with a wire whip, cream the remaining 2 sticks butter with the remaining 1 cup of sugar in a large mixing bowl until light, fluffy, and smooth. Add the eggs, one at a time, beating well after each addition.

In a medium-size mixing bowl, combine the remaining 2 cups flour, the baking powder, and salt. Add to the butter mixture, about ½ cup at a time, beating until all is well blended. Fold in the lemon zest. Pour the mixture into the prepared pan. Bake until the center springs back when touched, about 50 minutes.

Remove from the oven and cool on a wire rack for 10 minutes. Remove the cake from the pan and place it on the wire rack. With a toothpick or wooden skewer, make tiny holes randomly on the top of the cake. Pour half of the sugar-lemon syrup over the cake. Brush the sides of the cake with the remaining syrup.

½ pound (2 sticks) plus 1 tablespoon
  unsalted butter, cubed and softened

2 cups plus 1 tablespoon unbleached
  all-purpose flour

2 cups granulated sugar

1 cup fresh lemon juice

6 large eggs, at room temperature

1 teaspoon baking powder

Pinch of salt

2 tablespoons finely grated lemon zest

1 cup confectioners' sugar

¼ cup water

1 recipe Lemon Pastry Cream (page 254)

1½ cups Sweetened Whipped Cream
  (page 37)

1 cup fresh blueberries, rinsed, picked over,
  and stemmed

continued

In a small mixing bowl, combine the confectioners' sugar and water and whisk until smooth. Pour over the top of the cake and spread evenly, letting it drip down the sides. Let stand for about 15 minutes.

Slice the cake into ½-inch-thick slices. Spread the lemon pastry cream evenly on half of the slices. Place the remaining slices over the lemon pastry cream to form sandwiches. Slice each sandwich in half diagonally and top each with the whipped cream and blueberries.

Lemon Pastry Cream

Makes about 3½ cups

5 large egg yolks

¾ cup cornstarch

3 cups heavy cream, plus ½ cup more,

   if needed

½ cup fresh lemon juice

1½ cups sugar

In a medium-size mixing bowl, combine the egg yolks, cornstarch, and 1 cup of the heavy cream. Whisk to blend well. Set aside.

Combine 2 cups of the heavy cream, the lemon juice, and sugar in a large heavy nonreactive saucepan over medium heat. Whisk to dissolve the sugar and bring to a gentle boil. Slowly add the egg mixture, whisking constantly as it thickens, about 5 minutes. Be forewarned, the mixture will break. Don't be alarmed. Pour it into a glass bowl and press a piece of plastic wrap down over the surface to prevent a skin from forming. Let cool completely to room temperature. When cooled, pour the mixture into a medium-size mixing bowl. With an electric mixer fitted with a wire whip, beat at medium speed to recombine. If it doesn't, warm another ½ cup of heavy cream and slowly add it to the mixture. Whip until you have a thick and creamy custard.

Sweet Potato and Pecan Pie

Makes one 10-inch pie; 8 servings

I think sweet potatoes are way underrated. They're creamy, have a rich color, and are good for you to boot. Combining them with pecans is a natural in Louisiana, and these pies are very popular during the holiday season.

If you don't have Steen's syrup, use any cane syrup you can find.

Preheat the oven to 375°F. Place the sweet potatoes on a baking sheet and drizzle with the olive oil. Season with salt and pepper. Bake until they are fork tender, 1 to 1½ hours. Cool, peel, and mash.

In a large mixing bowl, combine the potatoes, the Steen's syrup, the spices, 1 of the eggs, and ½ teaspoon of the vanilla. Mix well. Line a 10-inch deep-dish pie pan with the rolled-out pie dough, then pour the filling into the pastry shell. Spread the pecan pieces evenly over the filling.

In another large mixing bowl, combine the remaining 4 eggs, remaining 1 teaspoon vanilla, granulated sugar, brown sugar, corn syrup, and salt and stir to blend. Pour over the pecans. Bake until the filling sets and the pastry is nicely browned, about 1 hour.

Remove from the oven and cool for 10 minutes before slicing to serve. Garnish with chocolate sauce, whipped cream, and confectioners' sugar.

1 pound sweet potatoes, scrubbed

1 tablespoon olive oil

Salt and freshly ground black pepper to taste

½ cup Steen's 100% Pure Cane Syrup

1 teaspoon ground cinnamon

½ teaspoon ground ginger

½ teaspoon freshly grated nutmeg

5 large eggs

1½ teaspoons pure vanilla extract

1 unbaked 10-inch Basic Savory Piecrust (page 168)

1½ cups pecan pieces

½ cup granulated sugar

½ cup firmly packed light brown sugar

¼ cup light corn syrup

Pinch of salt

½ cup Chocolate Sauce (page 73), warmed slightly

1 cup Sweetened Whipped Cream (page 37)

Confectioners' sugar

Suzanne's Pumpkin Chiffon Pie

Makes one 10-inch pie; 8 servings

Suzanne Gibbard (Felicia's mom) gave me a taste of her pumpkin chiffon pie at a Thanksgiving dinner, which was so good, I've come up with this version to say thank you.

Oh, to toast the pecans, all you have to do is preheat the oven to 375°F. Place the pecans on a baking sheet in the oven and toast until golden and fragrant, 5 to 6 minutes. Watch carefully so they don't burn. After they are cooled, they can be stored in an airtight container at room temperature for 2 weeks.

One 12-ounce box vanilla wafers
½ cup finely chopped pecans
¼ pound (1 stick) unsalted butter, melted
1½ cups eggnog
2 cups mashed cooked fresh pumpkin
¾ cup firmly packed light brown sugar
3 large egg yolks
½ teaspoon ground cinnamon
Pinch of freshly grated nutmeg
Pinch of salt
Pinch of ground ginger
1 envelope unflavored gelatin
1 teaspoon pure vanilla extract
3 large egg whites
¾ cup granulated sugar
1 cup heavy cream
2 tablespoons bourbon
½ pound pecan halves, toasted

Preheat the oven to 400°F.

In a food processor, combine the vanilla wafers and chopped pecans. Process until the mixture resembles coarse crumbs. With the machine running, add the butter and process until blended. Press the mixture into the bottom and up the sides of a 10-inch deep-dish pie pan and bake until golden, 10 to 12 minutes.

In a large saucepan, combine the eggnog, pumpkin, brown sugar, egg yolks, cinnamon, nutmeg, salt, and ginger and mix well. Place over medium heat and cook for 10 minutes, stirring constantly. Remove from the heat and sprinkle the gelatin over the mixture. Whisk until the gelatin dissolves, then stir in the vanilla extract. Cover and refrigerate for 1 hour.

Beat the egg whites with an electric mixer in a medium-size mixing bowl until soft peaks form. Gradually add ¼ cup of the granulated sugar and continue to beat until the peaks are stiff. Fold the egg whites into the pumpkin mixture. Spread evenly over the crust and refrigerate for about 2 hours.

With an electric mixer, beat the heavy cream with the remaining ½ cup sugar until medium peaks form. Stir in the bourbon. Spread the whipped cream evenly over the top of the pie. Garnish with the pecan halves.

Lemon Chess Pie

Makes one 10-inch pie; 8 servings

Chess pie is one of the South's favorites and it's really very simple to make. I tweaked it with lots of lemon juice just because I like the way lemons perk up the mouth.

Preheat the oven to 350°F.

In a large mixing bowl, combine the sugar, cornstarch, and lemon zest. Whisk in the eggs, 1 at a time. Stir in the lemon juice and butter and blend thoroughly.

Fit the rolled-out dough into a 10-inch pie pan, trimming the edges.

Pour the egg mixture into the pie shell and bake until the top is lightly browned and the center sets, 20 to 25 minutes. Remove from the oven and let cool to room temperature.

Slice and serve.

1½ cups sugar

1 tablespoon cornstarch

1 tablespoon grated lemon zest

4 large eggs

½ cup fresh lemon juice

¼ pound (1 stick) unsalted butter, melted
   and cooled

1 unbaked 10-inch Basic Savory Piecrust
   (page 168)

Brandied Peach Custard Pie

Makes one 9-inch pie; 8 servings

During the summer I enjoy peach desserts because we have fabulous Louisiana peaches from the northern part of the state. If you're lucky enough to have local peaches in your area, you might want to experiment with this. I like it warm, but there are some who prefer it chilled. Take your pick.

Be very careful when igniting the brandy to flambé. Use long matches, be sure to roll up your sleeves, and keep your hair away from the flame.

3 tablespoons unsalted butter

½ cup granulated sugar

4 medium-size fresh peaches, peeled, pitted, and cut into ¼-inch wedges

¼ cup brandy

2 cups heavy cream

4 large eggs

½ cup firmly packed light brown sugar

½ teaspoon ground cinnamon

¼ teaspoon freshly grated nutmeg

1 unbaked 9-inch Basic Savory Piecrust (page 168)

Confectioners' sugar

Sprigs of fresh mint

1 cup Sweetened Whipped Cream (page 37)

Preheat the oven to 450°F.

Heat the butter in a large sauté pan over high heat. Add the granulated sugar and stir until it dissolves. Add the peaches and cook, stirring, until the sugar starts to turn dark amber in color, 5 to 6 minutes. Add the brandy, carefully ignite it, and flambé the peaches. Remove from the heat and allow to cool for about 10 minutes.

In a large mixing bowl, combine the heavy cream, eggs, brown sugar, cinnamon, and nutmeg and whisk until smooth.

Fit the rolled-out dough into a 9-inch pie pan, trimming and crimping the edges. Spoon the peach mixture into the piecrust. Place aluminum foil around the crust to prevent it from browning too much, then bake for 30 minutes. Remove the foil, then pour the cream mixture over the peaches. Bake until the custard sets, about 1 hour. Remove from the oven and let cool for about 20 minutes.

To serve, place a slice of the pie on each plate and garnish with the confectioners' sugar, mint sprigs, and whipped cream.

Deep-Dish Apple Cobbler with Wisconsin Cheddar Cheese

Makes one 10-inch cobbler; 8 servings

Cobblers are an American favorite and I kicked this one up a notch by using 2 kinds of apples splashed with Calvados, the apple brandy from northern France. I know, cobblers usually have a top crust, but my version is more like a pie. When adding the Calvados to flambé, use long matches, roll up your sleeves, and keep the flame away from your hair.

Preheat the oven to 350°F.

In a large sauté pan, melt 3 tablespoons of the butter. Add the granulated sugar, ½ cup of the brown sugar, the lemon juice, and 1 tablespoon of the flour. Stir the mixture for 1 minute to dissolve the sugars. Add the apples and cook, stirring, for 3 minutes. Stir in the pecans and cook for 1 minute. Add the Calvados and carefully flambé the apples. Cook, stirring, for 1 minute. Sprinkle with the nutmeg, cinnamon, and a pinch of the salt. Mix thoroughly, then remove from the heat. Set aside and let cool.

In a large mixing bowl, combine the remaining 4 tablespoons butter, the remaining ½ cup brown sugar, the remaining 1 cup flour, and the remaining pinch salt. Using your hands, blend well, until the mixture resembles coarse crumbs.

Fit the rolled-out dough into a 10-inch pie pan, trimming the edges. Pour the apple filling into the pie shell. Sprinkle the crumb mixture evenly over the top, then bake until the top is lightly browned, about 45 minutes. Remove from the oven and sprinkle the cheese over the top. Return the pie to the oven and bake until the cheese is melted and bubbly, about 8 minutes. Serve warm with vanilla ice cream.

---

7 tablespoons unsalted butter

½ cup granulated sugar

1 cup firmly packed light brown sugar

3 tablespoons fresh lemon juice

1 cup plus 1 tablespoon bleached
    all-purpose flour

2 pounds Granny Smith apples, cored,
    peeled, and sliced ¼ inch thick

2 pounds McIntosh apples, cored, peeled,
    and sliced ¼ inch thick

1 cup pecan pieces

2 ounces Calvados

Pinch of freshly grated nutmeg

1 teaspoon ground cinnamon

2 pinches of salt

1 unbaked 10-inch Basic Savory Piecrust
    (page 168)

4 ounces Wisconsin sharp Cheddar cheese,
    grated

8 scoops vanilla ice cream

Emerilisms

Bam! / **Wake up out there**

I'm not makin' this up / **I went to school for this**

Happy, Happy, Happy / **This tastes great and I cooked it, you can, too**

Here, make some friends / **Pass this food around**

Trinity / **This combo of onions, green peppers, and celery will make every recipe taste good**

Pasta rags / **What you make when you can't use the pasta machine correctly**

Pork fat rules / **This ain't no diet food**

Kick it up a notch! / **Add some Essence**

Take it to notches unknown to mankind / **No one else cooks like this on their show**

We're not building a rocket ship here / **Don't be intimidated by cooking**

We won't go there / **Keep my PG rating, there're kids in the audience**

Hi, Hilda! / **Love ya, Ma!!**

Steer it! / **Stir it! I haven't lost my Massachusetts accent**

OK, Rhoda, yeah, yeah, yeah / **I'm takin' too long to cook, go to commercial, we got to pay for this show**

Got to have a little wine / **When in doubt . . . add liquor to the recipe**

We're not like those other late-night shows / **You gain weight when you watch this show**

Hello, Houston / **Hello, camera control**

Who makes up these rules? / **I'm here to break the rules**

Gaaahlic, it's a beautiful thing / **My momma taught me that**

Go get a frozen Oreo / **Don't change that dial, I'll be right back**

Whatever it takes / **Go the extra mile**

Oh yeah, babe! / **Love it, love it, love it!**

Smell-a-Vision / **Culinary Television**

Source Guide

The C. S. Steen Syrup Mill, Inc.
P.O. Box 339
Abbeville, LA 70510
(318) 893-1654 or (800) 725-1654
www.steensyrup.com
Steen's 100% Pure Cane Syrup

Maytag Cheese Company
(800) 247-2458
Blue cheese, white Cheddar cheese

Chicory Farm
3401 Tolmas Drive
Metairie, LA 70002
(504) 877-4550
Exotic mushrooms and locally
produced cheeses

Baumer Foods, Inc.
4301 Tulane Avenue
New Orleans, LA 70119
(504) 561-0392
Crystal Hot Sauce

Zapp's
307 East Airline Highway (U.S. 61)
P.O. Box 1533
Gramercy, LA 70052
(800) HOT-CHIP
Assorted flavored potato chips

Abita Brewing Company
(800) 737-2311, ext. 23
www.abita.com
Turbodog beer and other beers

Community© Coffee Company, LLC
4000 South Sherwood Forest
   Boulevard
Baton Rouge, LA 70821
(800) 525-5583
www.communitycoffee.com
Chicory coffee

Carriage Foods, Inc.
2437 Delaware Avenue
Kenner, LA 70063
(504) 466-9391
Duck rillette, also duck confit and
duck breast

Hudson Valley Foie Gras
(914) 292-2500
Foie gras

New Orleans Fish House
921 South Dupre Street
New Orleans, LA 70125
(800) 839-3474
Seaweed salad, crawfish, shrimp,
mussels, oysters, and whole fish

Specialty Game
8121 Ogden Avenue
Lyons, IL 60534
(800) 998-GAME
www.specialtygame.com
Venison

LA Organic Resource, Inc.
2628 Missouri
Metairie, LA 70003
(504) 441-7707
(504) 538-2376 (pager)
Exotic mushrooms

Zatarain's
(504) 367-2950
www.zatarain.com
Spices, crab and shrimp boil mixes,
Creole mustard

Lil' Fisherman
3301 Magazine Street
New Orleans, LA 70115
(504) 897-9907
and
7420 West Judge Perez
Arabi, LA 70032
(504) 271-9907
(888) 271-9907
Andouille, boudin, soft-shell crabs,
and other seafood

Cook's Help
"potato thredder" $44.99
Available through Kitchen &
Company
(800) 747-7224 to place an order

When you're not watching Emeril, try
checking him out really live at one of
his restaurants:

Emeril's Restaurant
800 Tchoupitoulas
New Orleans, LA 70130
(504) 528-9393

NOLA Restaurant
534 Rue St. Louis
New Orleans, LA 70130
(504) 522-6652

Delmonico Restaurant and Bar
1300 St. Charles Avenue
New Orleans, LA 70130
(504) 525-4937

Emeril's New Orleans Fish House
3799 Las Vegas Boulevard South
Las Vegas, NV 89109
(702) 891-7374

And for a taste of Emeril in your own
kitchen, you can order the Essence of
Emeril Spice Pack
Emeril's New New Orleans Cooking
cookbook
Louisiana Real & Rustic cookbook
Emeril's Creole Christmas cookbook

All other merchandise from:

Emeril's Homebase
638 Camp Street
New Orleans, LA 70130
(504) 524-4241
or visit us on our Website at
http:\\www.emerils.com

Index